What Can This Book Do for You?

Within a few years, your high school experience will lead you into the adult world of work. This book is designed to give you guidance, ideas, and answers about the many options life offers and the steps you will need to take for each.

What First?

Take a few minutes to claim ownership of this book. Write in your name. Lay out your career and life goals as you see them today. Consider the obstacles you may have to overcome in order to achieve them. If you don't have a formal plan, that's OK. Answering these questions will help you make one. The first steps might not be easy, but there are no right or wrong answers.

What Next?

Your needs, goals, ideas, and talents are unique to you; what is right for you will not be right for others. But the steps in the process of choosing a career direction (and understanding what education you might need to get there) are the same whether you aspire to repair car engines or to design the next generation of space shuttles.

Think of This Book As a Road Map

Knowing where you want to go and what roads will lead you there is the first step in the process. You can always change your destination and chart a new course. Here's the map . . . the rest is up to you!

Students: Get a Ju Road to Success

CW01390493

My Name	Age	Grade	Date started

My current goal after I graduate from high school is to: _____

_____

_____

Steps at school to reach my goal:

❏ **Curriculum planning:** _____

_____

_____

❏ **Clubs, teams, associations:** _____

_____

_____

❏ **Career research:** _____

_____

_____

Steps outside of school to reach my goal:

❏ **Volunteer work:** _____

_____

_____

❏ **Shadowing/mentor program:** _____

_____

_____

❏ **Job experience:** _____

_____

_____

❏ **Extracurricular activities:** _____

_____

Challenges my goal presents:

_____

_____

Ideas to overcome these challenges:

_____

_____

Table of CONTENTS

Dear High School Student,

Whether graduation seems light years away or alarmingly close, it's never too early—or too late—to think about what comes after high school. Do you know what your next step will be?

Enter *Get a Jump*. This magazine is designed to help you launch your career, whether this means first going on for more schooling or directly entering the work force. You have a multitude of options and some crucial choices to make. In the pages that follow, we have tried to give you a jump start on planning the future that's right for you.

Get a Jump was created by Thomson Central Ohio. After three successful editions in that state, *Get a Jump 2000* is being introduced to five new states: Pennsylvania, Illinois, Michigan, Texas, and Florida. One thing all these states have in common is that a large percentage of students choose to remain in state after high school to take advantage of the wealth of postsecondary opportunities available to them close to home.

This year, *Get a Jump* is being produced by Peterson's, another Thomson Learning Company. Peterson's is the country's largest educational information/communications company, providing the academic, consumer, and professional communities with books, software, and online services in support of lifelong education access and career choice. Peterson's Web site at petersons.com is the only comprehensive—and most heavily traveled—education resource on the Internet.

We are grateful to our colleagues at Thomson Central Ohio for their assistance and for making this such a smooth transition. We look forward to helping you make a smooth transition as you move through and beyond high school.

Peterson's Editorial Staff

Let Us Hear from You

If you have questions or feedback on *Get a Jump*, please e-mail us at:

getajump@petersons.com

If you are a teacher and are interested in information on how to use *Get a Jump* in your classroom, please send us a message.

We know what trying to get into college feels like.

Personal Organizer

Don't lose your head. We've got a whole new way to get you into college.

Introducing CollegeQuest.com. It's the only place where you can get everything you need. For

The Universal Application

starters, it helps prepare you for SATs* and ACTs* with full-length practice tests. It also gives

you accurate information to help you select the right college, with personalized searches, virtual campuses

and comparison charts. Not to mention one of the largest scholarship and award searches available.

Virtual Campus

You even get the option to complete applications online or on paper with our comprehensive

eApply service. Best of all, The Universal Application™ is accepted at over 1,000 colleges, trade

schools and universities. Imagine the time and aggravation you'll save.

Preparation

It's all brought to you by Peterson's, the company that's been helping students get into college

since Mom and Dad were driving that little van with flowers all over it.

Financing

So visit CollegeQuest.com. And stop running around like a, well, you know.

collegequest.com/run ⓅPETERSON'S
GUIDANCE YOU CAN TRUST

*SAT is a registered trademark of The College Board. ACT is a registered trademark of American College Testing, Inc. College Quest is a registered trademark. The Universal Application and the College Quest logo are trademarks of Peterson's, a division of Thomson Information, Inc.

CHAPTER 1

Explore YOUR OPTIONS

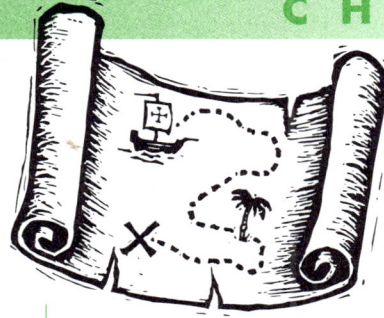

Your Future Is Here

Every year, thousands of students ask themselves, "What do I want to do after I graduate from high school?"

Will you continue your education beyond high school by attending a two-year or four-year college or vocational or technical school or by joining the armed forces? Or will you start your career by entering the workforce? These are questions you will have to think about and plan for well before you receive your high school diploma.

A high school diploma by itself is not sufficient preparation for many occupations. But neither is a college degree. Different fields of work require specific types of training. Just as there are occupations that require college or advanced degrees, so too are there occupations for which technical training, work experience, or training in a particular skill is the most important entry requirement.

Employers always want to hire the best-qualified people available, but this does not mean that they always choose those applicants who have the most education. The type of education and training an individual has had is as important as the amount. For this reason, a vital part of the career planning process is deciding what types as well as how much education and training to pursue.

People who have definite career goals may not find this decision difficult. Many occupations have specific education requirements. Physicians, for example, must generally complete at least three years of college, four years of medical school, and, in most states, one year of residency. Cosmetologists generally complete a state-approved program that ranges from eight to eighteen months.

But for most people, the decision is more difficult. Either they have yet to choose a field of work or the field they have selected may be entered in a variety of ways. Some may know only that they want jobs that provide status and a large income. Or an individual may wish to be an auto mechanic but cannot decide whether to learn on the job, attend a vocational school, seek an apprenticeship, or pursue a combination of these options.

Making this type of decision requires specific information about the types of education and training preferred for various occupations and a knowledge of one's own abilities and aspirations.

Devising a strategy

Of the roughly 60 percent of high school students who head to college, about 20 percent actually graduate with a degree. What will the other 80 percent do? What about the 40 percent who enter the workforce right after high school? One thing is certain—all of these individuals will need to develop a career.

According to Webster's dictionary, a career is "a profession or other calling demanding special preparation and undertaken as a life's work." A job is a stepping-stone along the career path.

Career planning should begin early. Some students have known since they were children what they want to do; others will need to determine their interests. However, all students should plan for a career in the following ways:

- Take the proper courses in order to gain the academic knowledge you will need.
- Investigate careers both in and out of school. Participate in mentoring, job shadowing, and career-day opportunities whenever possible.
- Get some on-the-job experience in a field that interests you.
- Research two-year and four-year colleges, vocational and technical schools, and apprenticeship programs.
- Prepare for and take aptitude and college entrance tests.
- Participate in school and state career development activities.

Educational Attainment– 1997

Only 16 percent of Americans earn a bachelor's degree or higher. It is important for all high school students to prepare for a career.

Source: U.S. Census Bureau, March 1997 Current Population Survey.

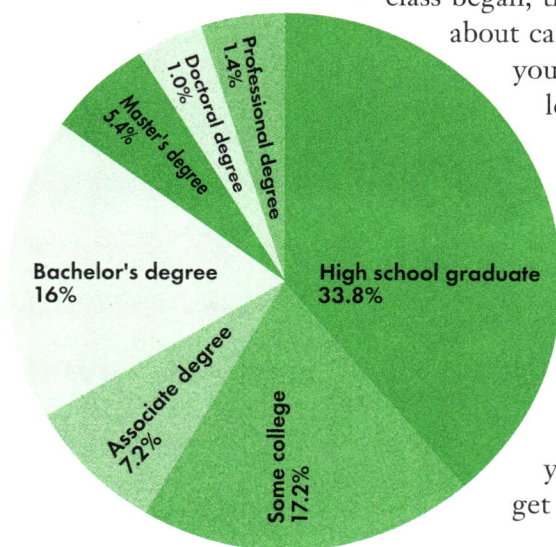

Professional degree 1.4%

Doctoral degree 1.0%

Master's degree 5.4%

Bachelor's degree 16%

Associate degree 7.2%

Some college 17.2%

High school graduate 33.8%

A teacher once asked a classroom of students to bring something to class that flies. Students brought kites, balloons, and models of airplanes, blimps, hot-air balloons, helicopters, spaceships, gliders, and seaplanes. When the class began, the teacher explained that the lesson would be about career planning: "Deciding what to do with your life is a lot like learning to fly. There are lots of ways to do it. Some people take direct flights. Others stop at points of interest along the way. The pace of the journey is an individual matter, as well. That's why it is important to know who you are and what you want."

You may not choose your life's career by reading *Get a Jump*, but you will participate in decision-making processes and identify resources available to you as you make plans for the future. Now let's get started.

Real-life skills

To succeed at any career, students will need to keep learning. This means that life after high school will require that you continue to build skills, develop relationships, tap into internal resources and talents, and recognize opportunities. Other critical skills include:

- Planning/Organizing
- Creativity/Innovation
- Continuous Improvement
- People Management
- Common Sense
- Flexibility
- Paperwork
- Stress Tolerance
- Problem Solving/Analytical Skills
- Drive/Energy
- Teamwork
- Leadership
- Independence/Tenacity
- Networking
- Interpersonal Skills
- Goal Orientation

Success is a combination of the appropriate education or training, hard work, and good luck. Employees who work very hard for managers with high standards, learn transferable skills, and get a chance to show their worth are already on the path to success. But most important, your career should be of interest to you, make use of your abilities, and help you meet your life's goals.

Reasons to Continue Your Education

There are many good reasons to continue your education. Often it is not one single reason that motivates someone, but rather a combination of several reasons. It is a good idea, however, to keep your options open for as long as possible, even if you are not completely sure. That way, you'll have a head start and be ready when and if you decide to pursue further education.

Prepare for a career

Postsecondary education offers endless possibilities for career development. In the next decade, you will need to be prepared to change jobs and continually learn new skills in order to keep up with changes in industry, communications, and technology. Education and training will give you a solid background.

Learn critical-thinking and analytical skills

An English teacher said it best: "Writing a complex sentence requires a complex thought." More than any other skill, education teaches you to think. Furthering your learning will help you to think critically, organize and analyze information, and write clearly.

Earn a higher income

Your generation may be the first in history not to surpass its parents' material wealth. Though money isn't everything, it is necessary for survival. A good education prepares you to become a solid member of society. Someone once said: "I have never been hired by a poor man."

Increase opportunities for growth and challenges

Just as you exercise your body, education exercises your mind. You will be fascinated by all there is to know. No matter what your area of interest, education holds the key to the most interesting and challenging information you can imagine—and more. Explore your outer limits and become a lifelong learner!

Prepare for a more fulfilling work life

There is a philosophy called "flow" that combines optimal levels of intellectual challenge with the appropriate ability to do a job. You may experience this feeling when you are taking a test and "everything clicks" or when you play a video game and your concentration level is at its peak. This is what happens when you combine education and training with the right job. Work becomes more like play, which is far more satisfying and rewarding than just going through the motions.

Meet new people

Make new friends, but keep the old . . . so the song goes. By furthering your education, you will widen your circle of friends and, chances are, form meaningful lifelong relationships.

Gain exposure to a variety of cultures and values

As you have probably already figured out, not everyone is like you. Nor should they be. Furthering your education is a good way to expose yourself to many types of people from various backgrounds and geographic locations, with different viewpoints and opinions. Become a part of this "cultural stew" and you may discover you like people and things you never knew existed.

Make important contacts

The friends, professors, supervisors, and classmates you meet after high school are potential contacts for life.

These personal and professional contacts will provide valuable ties for future jobs, committees, and associations within the community.

Have fun and participate in extracurricular activities

Academics are an important part of continued education, but there are plenty of opportunities for fun. There are hundreds of sports, clubs, groups, activities, and associations just waiting for you to join. Many people claim that their college years were the best years of their lives.

Fulfill a dream

Beginning in childhood, some people dream of being a teacher or a scientist. For many, continuing their education provides the opportunity to fulfill a dream for one's self or family. Picture yourself learning the skills that will prepare you for an exciting and rewarding career.

Make your parents proud

While making your parents proud is not a good reason by itself, it is a good reason if further education is one of your goals and expectations. Just think of the bragging rights that your parents will have when you are enrolled in the program of your choice. Of course, they will thank their lucky stars when you complete that education and are no longer on the family payroll!

Interest in a particular school

Have you been a fan of a particular school for as long as you can remember? Was your bedroom decorated with colorful pennants or did you wear a certain team jacket? Well, here is your chance to be a student at your favorite institution. It is fun and rewarding to become a student of a school that you have admired.

Employment Growth

Relative to education and training levels

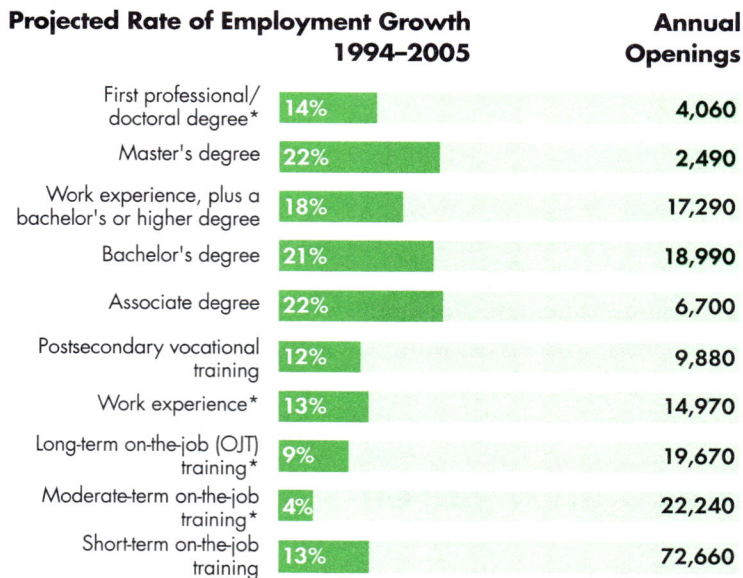

Projected Rate of Employment Growth 1994–2005		Annual Openings
First professional/ doctoral degree*	14%	4,060
Master's degree	22%	2,490
Work experience, plus a bachelor's or higher degree	18%	17,290
Bachelor's degree	21%	18,990
Associate degree	22%	6,700
Postsecondary vocational training	12%	9,880
Work experience*	13%	14,970
Long-term on-the-job (OJT) training*	9%	19,670
Moderate-term on-the-job training*	4%	22,240
Short-term on-the-job training	13%	72,660

* **First professional degree** (e.g., doctor, lawyer)/**doctoral degree** (e.g., Ph.D.)—requires three to four years of full-time study beyond the bachelor's degree.

Work experience—job requirement for skills obtained by having worked in the same or in a related occupation.

Long-term OJT—on-the-job training provided by an employer that consists of twelve months or more of combined work experience and formal classroom instruction.

Moderate-term OJT—one to twelve months of combined experience and informal training.

Short-term OJT—usually develops the skills needed after a short demonstration of up to one month of experience and instruction.

Source: Ohio Job Outlook.

Barriers to Continuing Your Education

Nobody in my family has ever done it

You can be the first! It's a little scary and not always easy, but you can begin a family tradition of continuing your education after high school. Just think how great you'll feel being the first person in your family to receive a degree, diploma, or certificate. And remember, if you do it, someone else in your family may follow your lead. It's never too late to go back to school.

My grades are not good enough

Don't let less-than-perfect grades stand in your way. Different institutions have different requirements, including what grades they accept. Schools also evaluate you for admission as a whole person, including your participation in extracurricular activities; your talents, such as academics and athletics; and your employment and volunteer history. There are also classes that you can take to improve your skills in various subject areas. Get a tutor now or form a study group in high school to improve your grades as much as possible. Take the appropriate high school curriculum so that you'll have more options when making decisions about continuing your education.

I can't afford it

Many families cannot afford to pay education costs completely out of pocket. That's why there are so many opportunities for financial aid—scholarships, grants, and work-study programs. Federal, state, school-sponsored, private, and career-specific financial aid resources are available to students who take the time to look. Talk to a guidance counselor, go to the library, and read the Dollars and Cents section of *Get a Jump* for more information about how to finance your continued education. Be creative and persistent. It can happen for you.

I don't know how to apply or where I want to go

This is one of the most important decisions you will make. Fortunately, there are resources to help you decide which institution to select. Talk to friends, family members, neighbors, and your guidance counselor, pastor, coach, and/or librarian. *Get a Jump* includes a guide to two-year and four-year colleges as well as vocational and technical schools in your state. Think of it as an elaborate buffet—a nice change from your high school cafeteria.

I think it may be too difficult for me

You can continue your education if you are willing to work hard. Human beings are able to do almost anything if they set their minds to it. Think back to something you have done in your life that seemed too difficult in the beginning. Didn't you find that once you began, put your mind to it, and stuck with it that you succeeded? It's the same with education and training. Thousands of high school graduates do it each year, and you can, too.

I'm not sure I'll "fit in"

One of the best things about furthering your education is the chance to meet new people and engage in new experiences in new surroundings. Schools attract a wide variety of students from many different backgrounds. Chances are you won't have any problem finding someone else with interests that are similar to yours. Schools also differ in size, location, student body, and lifestyle, so there should be one that meets your needs. Advance visits and interviews can help you determine which school is right for you.

I don't even know what I want to do with my life

It is common for students not to know this information about themselves until they get to experience some of the choices. *Get a Jump* offers a self-assessment test to help you determine what your interests and talents are. *Get a Jump* also offers a list of the most popular majors and the fastest-growing careers. Continued education opens doors for you that are exciting and rewarding.

There is no way I can pursue my education full-time

Part-time students are becoming the norm. In fact, a recent study determined that 43 percent of undergraduate students attend part-time. Most schools offer evening and weekend classes, and many offer work-study opportunities to help students pay for their education. Also, some employers will pay or reimburse you if you are working and want to further your education. If you are enrolled part-time, it takes longer to graduate. But if full-time enrollment is not an option for you, don't give up the opportunity to continue your education. There are many nontraditional ways to achieve your goals.

Choosing a Career

Of the estimated 15 million people searching for employment in the American job market, approximately 12 million are individuals who are looking for a new occupation or a different employer. With that many unsatisfied workers, it's best to take some time to consider what it is you really want to do. When you begin to think about an occupation that you'll enjoy, consider your interests and abilities as well as your fantasies or ambitions. Is there a particular type of job you've always dreamed of doing?

A good way to gather information about potential occupations is by talking with people who have achieved goals similar to yours. "Informational interviews" take place when you talk to teachers, neighbors, and adult friends about their experiences. If you don't have any contacts in a field that sparks your interest, don't hesitate to call someone and ask permission to visit his or her work environment. For instance, if you're interested in a career in nursing, you could visit a hospital, doctor's office, or nursing home. Offering to volunteer your services, whether by candy striping or reading to elderly patients, can be the best way to find out if it's the type of work you'll be happy doing.

If you're not sure what kind of work you'd like to do, contact a career counselor, who can help you explore your options and possibly administer some interest and/or aptitude tests. You might also think about contacting a college career planning and placement office, a vocational school placement office, the counseling services of community agencies, or a private counseling service, which may charge you a fee. Many high schools offer job-shadowing programs, where students actually shadow someone in a particular occupation for an entire day or more. Don't forget that as a high school student, your best resource is your high school guidance counselor.

Whatever avenue you decide to take, make sure you don't settle for "second best." The work should be interesting and challenging enough to motivate you and keep you happy at the same time. There should be plenty of opportunities for personal growth, and you'll want to be comfortable living on the wages you will earn.

• •

Increase Your Earning Power

People with more education tend to earn more money. Look at the average yearly earnings of workers by educational level.

Professional degree	**$67,246**
Doctoral degree	**$52,558**
Master's degree	**$41,092**
Bachelor's degree	**$34,498**
Associate degree	**$27,209**
Some college	**$25,407**
High school diploma	**$21,585**
Less than high school diploma	**$16,267**

Source: 1992 Current Population Report, U.S. Bureau of Census.

• •

Fastest-Growing Occupations

This chart shows the percent of employment growth by occupation and number of annual openings, projected from 1996 to 2006.

118%	249,000	Database administrators, computer support specialists, and computer scientists
109%	235,000	Computer engineers
103%	520,000	Systems analysts
85%	171,000	Personal and home-care aides
79%	66,000	Physical and corrective therapy
76%	378,000	Home health aides
74%	166,000	Medical assistants
74%	22,000	Desktop publishing
71%	81,000	Physical therapists
69%	11,000	Occupational therapy assistants and aides
68%	76,000	Paralegals
66%	38,000	Occupational therapists
59%	241,000	Teachers, special education
55%	98,000	Human services workers
52%	42,000	Data processing equipment repairers
51%	44,000	Medical records technicians
48%	64,000	Dental hygienists
48%	138,000	Amusement and recreation attendants
47%	30,000	Physician assistants
46%	37,000	Respiratory therapists
46%	183,000	Adjustment clerks
45%	155,000	Engineering, science, and computer systems managers
45%	67,000	Emergency medical technicians
45%	19,000	Manicurists
42%	112,000	Bill and account collectors
41%	74,000	Residential counselors
41%	123,000	Instructors and coaches, sports and physical training
38%	77,000	Dental assistants
38%	100,000	Securities and financial services sales workers

Source: Employment Projections, Occupational Outlook Program, U.S. Bureau of Labor Statistics.

Occupations with the Largest Job Growth

This chart shows the numerical changes in employment by occupation, projected from 1996 to 2006.

530,000	Cashiers
520,000	Systems analysts
467,000	General managers and top executives
411,000	Registered nurses
408,000	Salespersons, retail
404,000	Truck drivers, light and heavy
378,000	Home health aides
370,000	Teacher aides and educational assistants
333,000	Nursing aides, orderlies, and attendants
318,000	Receptionists and information clerks
312,000	Teachers, secondary school
299,000	Child-care workers
262,000	Clerical supervisors and managers
249,000	Database administrators, computer support specialists, and computer scientists
246,000	Marketing and sales worker supervisors
246,000	Maintenance repairers, general utility
243,000	Food counter, fountain, and related workers
241,000	Teachers, special education
235,000	Computer engineers
234,000	Food preparation workers
222,000	Hand packers and packagers
221,000	Guards
215,000	General office clerks
206,000	Waiters and waitresses
188,000	Social workers
183,000	Adjustment clerks
174,000	Cooks, short order and fast food
171,000	Personal-care and home-care aides
168,000	Food service and lodging managers
166,000	Medical assistants

Source: Employment Projections, Occupational Outlook Program, U.S. Bureau of Labor Statistics.

Self-Assessment Inventory

If you take time out now to think about your future, it will help you clarify what lies ahead. That's because the better you understand your own wants and needs, the better you will be able to make decisions. Fill out this inventory when you have uninterrupted time to think and to explore your thoughts, feelings, and values. There are no right or wrong answers. You may wish to share the inventory with your parents or your guidance counselor. Or you can use it as a personal discovery tool for your eyes only.

Who do you admire most and why? _____

_____

What is your greatest strength? _____

What is your greatest talent? _____

What skills do you have that are unique? Describe how you currently use these skills in your life.

Athletic ability _____

Mechanical ability _____

Ability to work with numbers _____

Leadership skills _____

Teaching skills _____

Artistic skills _____

Analytical skills _____

Check the three areas that most interest you.

❏ Providing a practical service for people
❏ Self-expression in music, art, literature, or nature
❏ Organizing and record keeping
❏ Meeting people and supervising others
❏ Helping others in need, either mentally, spiritually, or physically
❏ Solving practical problems

❏ Working in forestry, farming, or fishing
❏ Working with machines and tools
❏ Taking care of animals
❏ Physical work out of doors
❏ Protecting the public via law enforcement or fire fighting
❏ Medical, scientific, or mathematical work
❏ Selling, advertising, or promoting

Answer the following questions True (T) or False (F).

T F I get satisfaction not from personal accomplishment, but from helping others.

T F I'd like to have a job in which I can use my imagination and be inventive.

T F In my life, money will be placed ahead of job security and personal interests.

T F It is my ambition to have a direct impact on other people's lives.

T F I am not a risk-taker and would prefer a career that offers little risk.

T F I enjoy working with people rather than by myself.

T F I would not be happy doing the same thing all the time.

What matters most to you? Rate the items on the list below from 1 to 10, with 10 being "extremely important," 5 being "somewhat important," and 1 being "not at all important."

_____ Good health	_____ Seeing the world
_____ Justice	_____ Love
_____ Marriage/Family	_____ Fun
_____ Faith	_____ Power
_____ Fame	_____ Individualism
_____ Beauty	_____ Charity
_____ Safety	_____ Honor
_____ Friendship	_____ Intelligence
_____ Respect	_____ Wealth
_____ Accomplishment	

If you were in a blizzard survival situation, check that which would be your most likely role.

❏ The leader
❏ The one who explains the situation to the others
❏ The one who keeps morale up
❏ The one who invents a way to keep warm and melt snow for water

❏ The one who listens to instructions and keeps the supplies organized

❏ The one who positions sticks and rocks to signal SOS

What are your goals for the next five years? _____

_____

Where would you like to be in ten years? _____

_____

What has been your favorite course and why? _____

_____

What was your least favorite course and why? _____

_____

Who was your favorite teacher and why? _____

_____

What are your hobbies? _____

_____

What are your extracurricular activities? _____

_____

What jobs have you held? _____

_____

What volunteer work, if any, have you performed? _____

_____

Have you ever "shadowed" a professional for a day? If so, what did you learn? _____

_____

Do you have a mentor? If so, who? What have you learned from this person? _____

_____

Do you want to stay close to home, or would you prefer to travel to another city after high school? _____

_____

My career goals are to: _____

_____

My interests, skills, and knowledge supporting my career goals are: _____

_____

To fulfill my career goals, I will need additional skills and knowledge in: _____

_____

I will obtain the additional skills and knowledge by taking part in the following educational activities: _____

_____

I will need a degree, certification, and/or specialized training in: _____

When I look in the classified ads of the newspaper, the following job descriptions sound attractive to me: _____

_____

The information I have given indicates that I will be selecting courses that are primarily:

❏ College path (Four-year or two-year education that offers liberal arts courses combined with courses in your area of interest.)

❏ Vocational path (One or more years of education that includes "hands-on" training for a specific job.)

❏ Combination

After high school, I plan to:

❏ work full-time.

❏ work part-time and attend school.

❏ attend college full-time.

❏ attend technical college.

❏ enter the military as a career.

Look over your responses. Are there patterns or recurring themes? If you still can't decide where your interests lie, contact your guidance counselor for advice. Take the Campbell™ Interest and Skills Inventory, the Strong Interest Inventory, the Self-Directed Search, or other assessment tests that your guidance counselor recommends.

Interest and Skill Surveys on the Web

Still not sure if you're on the right career path? Truth is, most adults will change fields at least once during their working years. Here are a few Web sites where you can receive valuable direction by completing a career interest questionnaire or by reading about various occupations *before* submitting your first admission application.

The College Board—Career Search
http://www.collegeboard.org/career/bin/career

This site shows you what to expect from a job by providing information on training and qualifications, what earnings to expect, and what the future promises for each occupation. Find out more about a career you're already

Peterson's © 1999

thinking about, or complete an online questionnaire to determine which fields match your interests and abilities.

Occupational Outlook Handbook
http://stats.bls.gov/ocohome.htm

This information is available through the Bureau of Labor Statistics, an agency within the U.S. Department of Labor. More information than you'll ever need, including help with writing your resume, interviewing, and knowing which jobs are hot and which are not.

Mapping Your Future
http://mapping-your-future.org/

This site is sponsored by a group of guaranty agencies that participate in the Federal Family Education Loan Program (FFELP) and are committed to providing information about higher education and career opportunities. This site also provides a ten-step plan for determining and achieving your career goal.

Career Services—University of Waterloo
http://www.adm.uwaterloo.ca/infocecs/CRC/manual-home.html

A great online career interest survey and the strategies to get the job that's right for you.

Bowling Green University—Career Services
http://www.bgsu.edu/offices/careers/process/step1.html

A thorough self-assessment, followed by the tools to translate what you learn about yourself into a career plan.

Personality Tests on the WWW
http://www.2h.com/Tests/personality.phtml

A wealth of quick and fun tests to determine your interests and aptitude levels, including your IQ.

CareerWeb
http://www.cweb.com

Check out this giant database of employers and career-related companies if you're interested in professional, managerial, or technical positions. Includes an employment search readiness assessment.

CareerMosaic
http://www.careermosaic.com

The best single location for information about jobs, internships, and career assessment. Go directly to their College Connection page. Be sure to browse some of the college career centers that are in hypertext.

Online Career Center
http://www.occ.com

One of the first and most comprehensive sites; includes information about thousands of job and career fairs, advice on resumes, and much more.

FutureScan
http://www.futurescan.com

Allows you to take a close look at different occupations by reading the profiles of real people in the field and by submitting e-mail questions to working professionals.

The World of Work

Before making a list of majors and careers to investigate, think about your preferences in the following areas to make sure you are making selections that have a high probability of success for you.

Work conditions: What hours are you willing to work? Do you feel most satisfied in an environment that is indoors/outdoors, varied/regular, noisy/quiet, or casual/traditional?

Duties: What duties do you feel comfortable carrying out? Do you want to be a leader, or do you perform best as a team player?

People: Do you want to work with other people or more independently? How much people contact do you want/need?

Education: How much special training or education is required? How much education are you willing to seek? Can you build upon the education or experience you have to date? Will you need to gain new education or experience?

Benefits: What salary and benefits do you expect? Are you willing to travel?

Disadvantages: There are disadvantages with almost any job. Can you imagine what the disadvantages may be? Can you confirm or disprove these beliefs by talking to someone or researching the industry or job further? If these disadvantages really exist, can you live with them?

Personal qualities: What qualities do you want in the employer you ultimately choose? What are the most important qualities that you want in a supervisor? In your coworkers?

Once you've narrowed your interests and checked them against your personal style and needs, you will be ready to find out which education or training path will offer the skills you need to make it happen.

We've got *your* number:

100 — Among the nation's 100 "most wired" universities (*Yahoo/ Internet Life* magazine)

14 — Among the top 14 universities in the enrollment of National Merit Scholars

9 — 9th in *Money* magazine's "Best Buys" among universities of science and technology

5 — 5th in the nation for number of U.S. patents awarded

2 — 2nd among universities in the nation for the number of top technologies honored by *R&D Magazine*

1 — 800 262-3810 (call for an application, for more information, or to arrange a campus visit)

It all adds up to your best bet!

IOWA STATE UNIVERSITY
Helping you become your best.

Toll-free: 800 262-3810 Web: www.iastate.edu

Career Planning Checklist

This checklist can be used to help you make sure you have the skills to develop educational plans and career goals. When you demonstrate specific skills, check them off. This will allow you to assess your skills over time.

- ☐ Y ☐ N I can identify attitudes/skills that employers look for in job applicants.
- ☐ Y ☐ N I know how to use career information resources.
- ☐ Y ☐ N I know my work traits and interests.
- ☐ Y ☐ N I know my academic strengths.
- ☐ Y ☐ N I can describe the educational programs available to me.
- ☐ Y ☐ N I can describe the entrance requirements for these programs (including vocational and technical schools and colleges).
- ☐ Y ☐ N I know the high school graduation requirements.
- ☐ Y ☐ N I can identify local job opportunities.
- ☐ Y ☐ N I can identify job-seeking and application skills.
- ☐ Y ☐ N I can use at least four sources to find educational and career information.
- ☐ Y ☐ N I know how to plan for long-range goals.
- ☐ Y ☐ N I am in a course of study that leads to my career goals.
- ☐ Y ☐ N I can demonstrate positive job interviewing skills.
- ☐ Y ☐ N I have discussed my educational plans/career goals with my parents.
- ☐ Y ☐ N I have discussed my educational plans/career goals with my counselor.
- ☐ Y ☐ N I have discussed my educational plans/career goals with my teacher(s).
- ☐ Y ☐ N I have had one or more work, leisure, and/or educational experience(s) outside of school that relate(s) to my career goals.
- ☐ Y ☐ N I have taken action on my post–high school plan.

Source: Vocational Instructional Materials Laboratory, The Ohio State University.

Planning in HIGH SCHOOL

College Planning Time Line

Whether you decide to attend a two-year community or technical college or a four-year college or university, to pursue a vocational education, or to join the military, it is in your best interest to begin planning as early as possible. The following time line will help keep you on track.

Ninth grade

- In the fall, meet with your counselor to begin discussing colleges and careers and to update your academic planning.
- Make sure you are enrolled in college-preparatory or tech-prep courses.
- Work to your academic potential. The grades you earn in ninth grade will be included in your final high school GPA and class rank. This is important for college admission and scholarships.
- Explore your interests and possible careers. Take advantage of career day opportunities.
- Participate in extracurricular activities (school and nonschool sponsored).
- Talk to your parents about planning for college expenses. Continue or begin a savings plan for college.
- Look at college information available in your counselor's office. Use the Internet to check out college Web sites. Make a preliminary list of colleges that might interest you.
- Tour a nearby college if possible. Visit relatives or friends who live on or near a college campus. Check out the dorms. Go to the library or student center. Get a feel for college life.
- Investigate summer enrichment programs.

Tenth grade

Fall

- In October take the PSAT/NMSQT (Preliminary SAT/National Merit Scholarship Qualifying Test) for practice. Participate in Student Search Service to start receiving mail from colleges.
- Ask your guidance counselor about the American College Testing program's PLAN (Pre-ACT) assessment program, which helps determine study habits and academic progress and interests. This test will help to prepare you for the ACT next year.
- Take geometry if you have not already done so. Take biology and a second year of foreign language.
- Become familiar with general college entrance requirements.
- Participate in your school's or state's career development activities.

Winter

- Remember the importance of being a well-rounded individual. Work toward leadership positions in the activities that you like best. Become involved in community service and/or other volunteer activities.
- Read, read, read. Read as many books as possible from a comprehensive reading list, like the one that follows on page 22. Learn about current affairs.
- Work on your writing skills. Locate a teacher or another adult who will advise and encourage your abilities as a writer.

Spring

- Keep your grades up so you can have the highest GPA and class rank possible.
- Ask your counselor about postsecondary enrollment options and Advanced Placement courses.
- Continue to assess your strengths, weaknesses, goals, and favorite subjects. Explore careers relative to your interests/abilities.
- Begin thinking about the type of college you would prefer (two-year or four-year, small or large, rural or urban).

- If you are interested in attending a military academy, now is the time to start planning and getting information.
- Write to colleges and obtain their academic requirements for admission.
- Visit a few more college campuses. Read all the mail you receive from colleges. You may see something you like.
- Attend college fairs.
- Keep putting money away for college. Try to get a summer job.
- Investigate summer enrichment programs.
- Consider taking SAT II Subject Tests in the courses you took this year while the material is still fresh in your mind. These tests are offered in May and June.

Eleventh grade

Fall

- Meet in the fall with your counselor to review college-preparatory course selection.
- Check class rank based on grade point averages for freshman and sophomore years. It is never too late to improve your grades. Colleges look for an upward trend.
- Sign up for and take the PSAT/NMSQT. In addition to National Merit Scholarships, this is the qualifying test for the National Scholarship Service and Fund for Negro Students and the National Hispanic Scholar Recognition Program.
- Work through sample questions provided with the explanatory materials in the PSAT/NMSQT Student Bulletin.
- Be sure you have a social security number.
- Examine the reasons you want to continue your education. Focus on your goals for life and the career training you need.
- Make a list of colleges that meet your most important criteria (size, location, distance from home, majors, academic rigor, housing, and cost). Weigh each of the factors according to their importance to you.
- Continue visiting college fairs. You may be able to narrow your choices or add a college to your list.
- Speak to college representatives who visit your high school.
- Begin building your college application online at http://www.collegequest.com.
- If you are interested in one of the military academies, start the application process now. See your guidance counselor.

Winter

- Collect information about college application procedures, entrance requirements, tuition and fees, room and board costs, student activities, course offerings,

faculty composition, accreditation, and financial aid. The Internet is a good way to visit colleges and obtain this information. Begin comparing the schools by the factors that you consider to be most important.
- Discuss your PSAT score with your counselor.
- Begin narrowing down your college choices. Find out if the colleges you are interested in require the SAT, ACT, or Subject Tests for admission.
- Register for the SAT I and additional SAT II Subject Tests, which are offered several times during the winter and spring of your junior year. You can also take them again in the fall of your senior year if you are unhappy with your scores.
- Register for the ACT, which is usually taken in April or June and then again very late in the junior year or in the fall of the senior year, if necessary.
- Begin preparing for the tests you've decided to take.
- Have a discussion with your parents about the colleges you are interested in. Examine financial resources and gather information about financial aid.
- Set up a filing system, with individual folders for each college's correspondence and printed materials. You can also track your colleges on line via CollegeQuest.

Spring

- Meet with your counselor to review senior year course selection and graduation requirements.
- Discuss ACT/SAT scores with your counselor. Register to take the ACT and/or SAT again, if you'd like to try to increase your score.
- Discuss the college essay with your guidance counselor and/or English teacher.
- Stay involved with your extracurricular activities. Colleges look for consistency and depth in activities.
- Consider who you will ask to write your recommendations.
- Inquire about personal interviews at your favorite colleges. Call or write for early summer appointments. Make necessary travel arrangements.
- See your counselor to apply for on-campus summer programs for high school students. Apply for a summer job. Be prepared to pay for college application, financial aid, and testing fees in the fall.
- Request applications from schools you're interested in by mail or via the Internet.

Summer

- Visit the campuses of your top five college choices.
- After each college interview, send a thank-you letter to the interviewer.
- Talk to people you know who have attended colleges that you are interested in.

- Continue to read books, magazines, and newspapers.
- Practice filling out college applications and then type the final application forms or apply on line through CollegeQuest.
- Take some time to volunteer in the community.
- Compose rough drafts of your college essays. Have a teacher read and discuss them with you. Polish them and prepare final drafts. Proofread your final essays three times.
- Develop a financial aid application plan, including a list of the aid sources, requirements for each application, and a timetable for meeting filing deadlines.

Twelfth Grade

Fall
- Continue to take a full course load of college-prep courses.
- Continue to work on your grades. Make sure you have the courses necessary for high school graduation.
- Continue to participate in extracurricular and volunteer activities. Demonstrate initiative, creativity, commitment, and leadership.
- All male students must register for selective service on their eighteenth birthday to be eligible for federal and state financial aid.
- Talk to counselors, teachers, and parents about your final college choices.
- Make a calendar showing application deadlines for admission, financial aid, and scholarships. If you apply on line via College Quest, this information will be tracked for you.
- Check resource books, computer programs, and guidance office information for scholarships and grants. Ask colleges about scholarships for which you may qualify.
- Give recommendation forms to the teachers you have chosen, along with stamped, self-addressed envelopes for returning them to colleges. Be sure to fill out your name, address, and school name on the top of the form. Ask teachers who know you well and who will write positive letters about you. Letters from a coach, activity leader, or an adult who knows you well outside of school (i.e., volunteer work contact) are also valuable. Talk to them about your goals and ambitions.
- Give School Report forms to the proper school office. Fill in your name, address, and any other required information on top. Verify with your guidance counselor the schools to which transcripts, test scores, and letters are to be sent. Give your counselor any necessary forms at least two weeks before they are due or whenever your counselor's deadline is, whichever is earlier.

- Register for and take the ACT, SAT I, or SAT II Subject Tests as necessary.
- Be sure you have requested (either by mail or on line) that your test scores be sent to the colleges of your choice.
- Mail or send electronically any college applications for early decision admission by November 1.
- Visit colleges while classes are in session, if possible.
- ROTC scholarship applications are usually due by December 1.
- Print extra copies or make photocopies of everything you send.

Winter
- Attend whatever college-preparatory nights are held at your school or by local organizations.
- Send midyear grade reports to colleges. Continue to focus on your schoolwork!
- Fill out the Free Application for Federal Student Aid (FAFSA) and, if necessary, the Financial Aid Profile (FAP). These forms can be obtained from your guidance counselor. You can also go http://www.ed.gov/offices/OPE/express.html to download the forms and/or file electronically. These forms may not be processed prior to January 1.
- Mail or send electronically remaining applications and financial aid forms before winter break. Know the deadlines. Each school is different. Make sure you apply to at least one college you know you can afford and where you will be accepted.
- Follow up and check to make sure that all application information, including recommendations and test scores, is received by colleges.
- Meet with your counselor to verify that all applicable forms are in order and have been sent out to colleges.

Spring
- Notification of decision by colleges usually occurs between March 15 and April 15.
- Notification of financial aid awards usually occurs between April 1 and May 1.
- Compare financial aid packages from colleges and universities to which you have been accepted.
- Make your choice and notify all schools of your intent by May 1. Send a deposit to your chosen school by May 1 as well. Request that your guidance counselor send a final transcript to the college in June. If possible, do not make your selection without making a campus visit.
- Nonrefundable deposits on freshman tuition are due. Inform other colleges of your decision not to attend.
- Be sure that you have received a FAFSA acknowledgement.
- If you applied for a Pell Grant (on the FAFSA), you will receive a Student Aid Report (SAR) statement. Review

this Pell notice and forward it to the college you plan to attend. Make a copy for your records.

- Complete follow-up paperwork for the college of your choice (scheduling, orientation session, housing arrangements, and other necessary forms).

Summer

- If applicable, apply for a Stafford Loan (formerly Guaranteed Student Loan) through a lender. Allow eight weeks for processing.
- Receive orientation schedule from your college.
- Receive residence hall assignment from your college.
- Receive course scheduling and cost information from your college.
- Congratulations! You are about to begin the greatest adventure of your life. Good luck.

Suggested Courses for Grades 9–12

You can begin preparing for college and a career as early as the ninth grade by taking an active role in planning your high school curriculum. If you plan to attend college, you should know that there are minimum high school curriculum requirements for unconditional college admission. Even if you don't plan to immediately enter college, it is recommended that you take the most demanding courses you are able to handle.

Examples of suggested classes are listed on this page. Some courses, categories, and names might vary from state to state, but the following may be used as a guideline. Talk with your guidance counselor to select the curriculum that best meets your needs and skills.

Of course, learning also occurs outside of school. While outside activities will not make up for poor academic performance, skills learned from jobs, extracurricular activities, and volunteer opportunities will help you become a well-rounded student and will strengthen your college or job application.

Recommended college-preparatory curriculum

English	Four units with emphasis on composition (English 9, 10, 11, 12)
Mathematics	Three units (algebra I, algebra II, geometry) are essential. Trigonometry, precalculus, calculus, and computer science are recommended for some fields of study.
Social Science	Three units (American history, world history, government/economics)
Science	Four units (earth science, biology, chemistry, physics)
Foreign Language	Three units (at least 2 years in the same language)
Fine Arts	One to 2 units
Other	Keyboarding, computer applications, computer science I, computer science II, physical education, health

College-preparatory curriculum combined with a vocational program

English	Four units
Mathematics	Three units (algebra I, algebra II, geometry)
Social Science	Three units (American history, world history, government/economics)
Science	Two units (earth science, biology)
Foreign Language	Three units (at least 2 years in the same language)
Fine Arts	One to 2 units
Other	Keyboarding, computer applications, physical education, health, and half-days at the Career Center during the junior and senior years.

Postsecondary Enrollment Options

One way to get a head start on college is to take college courses while you are still in high school. Postsecondary enrollment options allow some students to do this and receive both high school and college credit for the courses taken.

Postsecondary enrollment is designed to provide an opportunity for qualified high school students to experience more advanced academic work. Participation in a postsecondary enrollment program is not intended to replace courses available at the high school but, rather, to enhance the educational opportunities available to students while in high school.

High School Courses Completed

Chart the high school curriculum that you, your parents, and your counselor decide is best for you.

Fill in the name of the course and the grade you receive as you complete each year.	Tenth-Grade Course	Letter Grade	Eleventh-Grade Course	Letter Grade	Twelfth-Grade Course	Letter Grade
English						
Mathematics						
Social Science						
Science						
Foreign Language						
Fine Arts						
Other						
Other						

There are two options for postsecondary enrollment:

- Option A—qualified high school juniors and seniors take courses for college credit. Students enrolled under Option A must pay for all books, supplies, tuition, and associated fees.
- Option B—qualified high school juniors and seniors take courses for high school and college credit. For students enrolled under Option B, the local school district covers the related costs, provided the student completes the selected courses. Otherwise, the student and parent will be assessed the costs.

Certain preestablished conditions must be met for enrollment, so check with your high school counselor for more information.

What Is the SCANS Report?

SCANS stands for the Secretary's Commission on Achieving Necessary Skills, a part of the U.S. Department of Labor. SCANS published a report called "What Work Requires of Schools," which identifies the employability skills that employers look for in prospective employees. Schools are using the five competencies identified in the report to prepare students for the workforce. The five competencies are listed, and each has subgoals that are not listed:

- Resources: Identifies, organizes, plans, and allocates resources
- Interpersonal: Works with others
- Information: Acquires and uses information
- Systems: Understands complex interrelationships
- Technology: Works with a variety of technologies

According to the report, in order to be proficient in these competencies, a student must have a three-part foundation:

- Basic skills: Reads, writes, performs arithmetic and mathematical operations, listens, and speaks
- Thinking skills: Thinks creatively, makes decisions, solves problems, visualizes, and knows how to learn and reason
- Personal qualities: Displays responsibility, self-esteem, sociability, self-management, and integrity and honesty

SCANS serves a dual purpose:

- To help young people identify skills or experiences that will be helpful to them in gaining employment (i.e., responding to interview questions, etc.).
- To help young people adjust their thinking to the workplace (i.e., "How do I make that transition? What skills do I need to be employable?").

Potential employers look for experience, but many individuals cannot identify their applicable experience to an employer.

Vocational Education

Nearly 11 million youths and adults gain instruction, skills training, and support services through vocational education. Vocational education is designed to help students develop competency in occupational, academic, and employability skills. The strength of vocational education is its "real world" orientation, both work-based and school-based. Learning is offered through a practical combination of applied academics, "hands-on" instruction, and skills training. Job shadowing, mentorship programs, and job placement assistance are key components of vocational education.

Vocational education programs are available and accessible to most high school students and adults through local public school systems. Students' vocational interests and talents are often measured using Work Keys, the ACT's workplace skills assessment tool. Vocational education students can then choose from a variety of traditional, high-tech, and service industry training programs. In Ohio, for example, vocational programs are clustered in five broad categories.

Agricultural education

These programs prepare students for careers in agricultural production, animal production and care, agribusiness, agricultural and industrial mechanics, environmental management, farming, horticulture and landscaping, food processing, and natural resource management.

Business education

These programs prepare students for careers in accounting and finance and computer and data processing, as well as administrative/secretarial and management/supervisory positions in professional environments (banking, insurance, law, public service).

Family and consumer sciences

These programs prepare students for careers in child care, food management and production, clothing and interiors, and hospitality and facility care. Core elements include personal development, family life and planning, resource management, and nutrition and wellness.

Trade and industrial and health occupations

These programs prepare individuals for careers in such fields as auto mechanics, construction trades, cosmetology, electronics, graphics, public safety, and welding. Health occupations programs offer vocational training for careers in dental and medical assisting, practical nursing, home health care, and medical office assisting.

Marketing education

These programs prepare individuals for careers in sales, retailing, advertising, food and restaurant marketing, and hotel management.

For more information about secondary vocational education programs, call 202-205-5451 or e-mail the U.S. Department of Education, Office of Vocational and Adult Education, at ovae@inet.ed.gov.

Tech Prep

Tech prep is an educational path that parallels college-prep and vocational/technical courses of study. During the two-year course, the focus is on blending academic and vocational/technical competencies. Students who wish to follow this more specific course of study must plan to start the program's curriculum by the ninth grade. Upon completion, students will be able to make a smooth transition into advanced training in the workforce and/or attend college to earn an associate degree. This course will also enable students to finance their college experience by working in their chosen field while they increase their expertise and knowledge in it.

For more information about the tech-prep course of study, contact a teacher and/or guidance counselor, who can get in touch with one of the tech-prep contacts in your state.

School to Work

Today's workplaces, and those of the twenty-first century, require a new kind of worker—one who excels at solving problems, thinking critically, working in teams, and constantly learning on the job.

The School-to-Work approach to learning is based on the fact that individuals learn best by doing and by relating what they learn in school to their experiences as workers. This approach has come to be accepted as a better way to educate all young people. Instead of traditional general track and vocational education programs that were based on the theory that students who didn't go to college needed to be taught a skill they could use to

Labor market patterns that support the need for vocational education

- Vocational education prepares students for 80 percent of the occupations that the U.S. Bureau of Labor Statistics predicts will account for the largest number of new jobs during the next decade.
- The fastest-growing occupations include technicians, health-care workers, skilled trades workers, retail workers, paralegals, and secretaries.
- Eighty percent of all U.S. jobs don't require a college diploma but do demand skills attainable through vocational education.

Source: Ohio Department of Education.

make a living for the rest of their lives, the school-to-careers approach is based on the concept that education for all should be made more relevant and useful to multiple future careers and lifelong learning.

Developed with the input of business, education, labor, and community-based organizations that have a strong interest in how students prepare for careers, the School-to-Work system contains three fundamental elements: school-based learning, work-based learning, and activities connecting the two.

School-based learning

School-to-Work programs restructure the educational experience so that students learn how academic subjects relate to the world of work. Teachers work together with employers to develop broad-based curricula that help students understand the skills needed in the workplace. Students actively develop projects and work in teams, much like the modern workplace. Teachers work in teams to integrate their usually separate disciplines and create projects that are relevant to work and life in the real world.

Work-based learning

Employers provide experiences for students that develop broad, transferable skills. Work-based learning provides students with opportunities to study complex subject matter as well as vital workplace skills in a hands-on, "real life" environment. Working in teams, solving problems, and meeting employers' expectations are workplace skills that students learn best through doing and master under the tutelage of adult mentors.

Connecting activities

Connecting activities provide program coordination and administration; integrate the worlds of school and work through school and business staff exchanges, for example; and provide student support, such as career counseling and college placement.

Students in School-to-Work programs:

- Learn about their job possibilities by "shadowing" existing workers in different departments and discussing work and life with adult mentors
- Experience the workplace environment firsthand through volunteer work, internships, and paid work experiences
- Apply academics to real tasks performed in the workplace and participate as productive employees

- Acquire the skills necessary for successful careers
- Formulate goals and plans for a future previously unimagined

Today's high-skill job market demands that all high school graduates have both advanced academic knowledge and workplace skills and training. The School-to-Work movement aims to improve the way students are prepared for college, careers, and citizenship.

For more information about the School-to-Work program, ask a teacher and/or guidance counselor, who can contact a state School-to-Work Regional Coordinator, or contact the STW Learning and Information Center at 800-251-7236.

Other volunteer opportunities

- Do you like kids? Volunteer at your local parks and recreation department, or for a Little League team, or to be a "big brother" or "big sister."
- Planning a career in health care? Volunteer at a local blood bank, clinic, hospital, retirement home, or hospice. There are also several organizations that raise money for disease research.
- Interested in the environment? Volunteer to assist in a recycling program. Create a beautification program for your school or community. Plant trees or flowers or design a community garden.
- Just Say No. Help others stay off drugs and alcohol by volunteering at a crisis center, hot line, or prevention program. Help educate younger kids about the dangers of drug abuse.
- Lend a hand. Collect money, food, or clothing for the homeless. Food banks, homeless shelters, and charitable organizations need your help.
- Is art your talent? Share your knowledge and skills with youngsters, the elderly, or local arts organizations that require volunteer help to present their plays, recitals, and exhibitions.
- Help fight crime by forming a neighborhood watch, or organize a team to clean up graffiti.

Your church or synagogue may also have projects that need youth volunteers. The United Way, your local politician's office, civic groups, and special interest organizations also provide exceptional opportunities to serve your community. Ask your principal, teachers, or counselors for additional ideas.

For more information on joining in the spirit of youth volunteerism, write to the Consumer Information Center, Dept. 588C, Pueblo, CO 81009, and request the *Catch the Spirit* booklet.

Suggested Reading List Grades 9–12

Adams, Richard
Watership Down

Aesop
Aesop Fables

Agee, James
A Death in the Family

Anderson, Sherwood
Winesburg, Ohio

Anonymous
Go Ask Alice

Asimov, Isaac
Short Stories

Austen, Jane
Emma
Northanger Abbey
Pride and Prejudice
Sense and Sensibility

Baldwin, James
Go Tell It on the Mountain

Balzac, Honore de
Pere Goriot

Beckett, Samuel
Waiting for Godot

Bolt, Robert
A Man For All Seasons

Brontë, Charlotte
Jane Eyre

Brontë, Emily
Wuthering Heights

Brooks, Gwendolyn
In the Mecca
Riot

Browning, Robert
Poems

Buck, Pearl
The Good Earth

Butler, Samuel
The Way of All Flesh

Camus, Albert
The Plague
The Stranger

Cather, Willa
*Death Comes for the
   Archbishop*
My Antonia

Cervantes, Miguel
Don Quixote

Chaucer, Geoffrey
The Canterbury Tales

Chekhov, Anton
The Cherry Orchard

Chopin, Kate
The Awakening

Collins, Wilkie
The Moonstone

Conrad, Joseph
Heart of Darkness
Lord Jim
The Secret Sharer
Victory

Crane, Stephen
The Red Badge of Courage

Dante
The Divine Comedy

Defoe, Daniel
Moll Flanders

Dickens, Charles
Bleak House
David Copperfield
Great Expectations
Hard Times
Oliver Twist
A Tale of Two Cities

Dickinson, Emily
Poems

Dinesen, Isak
Out of Africa

Dostoevski, Fyodor
The Brothers Karamazov
Crime and Punishment

Douglass, Fredrick
The Life of Fredrick Douglass

Dreiser, Theodore
An American Tragedy
Sister Carrie

Early, Gerald
Tuxedo Junction

Eliot, George
Adam Bede
Middlemarch
Mill on the Floss
Silas Marner

Eliot, T. S.
Murder in the Cathedral

Ellison, Ralph
Invisible Man

Emerson, Ralph Waldo
Essays

Faulkner, William
Absalom, Absalom!
As I Lay Dying
Intruder in the Dust
Light in August
The Sound and the Fury

Fielding, Henry
Joseph Andrews
Tom Jones

Fitzgerald, F. Scott
The Great Gatsby
Tender Is the Night

Flaubert, Gustave
Madame Bovary

Forster, E. M.
A Passage to India
A Room With a View

Franklin, Benjamin
*The Autobiography of
   Benjamin Franklin*

Galsworthy, John
The Forsyte Saga

Golding, William
Lord of the Flies

Goldsmith, Oliver
She Stoops to Conquer

Graves, Robert
I, Claudius

Greene, Graham
The Heart of the Matter
The Power and the Glory

Hamilton, Edith
Mythology

Hardy, Thomas
*Far From the Madding
   Crowd*
Jude the Obscure
The Mayor of Casterbridge
The Return of the Native
Tess of the D'Urbervilles

Hawthorne, Nathaniel
The House of Seven Gables
The Scarlet Letter

Hemingway, Ernest
A Farewell to Arms
For Whom the Bell Tolls
The Sun Also Rises

Henry, O.
Stories

Hersey, John
A Single Pebble

Hesse, Hermann
Demian
Siddhartha
Steppenwolf

Peterson's © 1999

Homer
The Iliad
The Odyssey

Hughes, Langston
Poems
The Big Sea

Hugo, Victor
Les Misérables

Huxley, Aldous
Brave New World

Ibsen, Henrik
A Doll's House
An Enemy of the People
Ghosts
Hedda Gabler
The Master Builder
The Wild Duck

James, Henry
The American
Daisy Miller
Portrait of a Lady
The Turn of the Screw

Joyce, James
Dubliners
Portrait of the Artist as a Young Man

Kafka, Franz
The Castle
Metamorphosis
The Trial

Keats, John
Poems

Kerouac, Jack
On the Road

Koestler, Arthur
Darkness at Noon

Lawrence, Jerome, and Robert E. Lee
Inherit the Wind

Lewis, Sinclair
Arrowsmith
Babbitt
Main Street

Llewellyn, Richard
How Green Was My Valley

Machiavelli
The Prince

MacLeish, Archibald
J.B.

Mann, Thomas
Buddenbrooks
The Magic Mountain

Marlowe, Christopher
Dr. Faustus

Maugham, Somerset
Of Human Bondage

McCullers, Carson
The Heart Is a Lonely Hunter

Melville, Herman
Billy Budd
Moby Dick
Typee

Miller, Arthur
The Crucible
Death of a Salesman

Monsarrat, Nicholas
The Cruel Sea

Naylor, Gloria
Bailey's Cafe
The Women of Brewster Place

O'Neill, Eugene
The Emperor Jones
A Long Day's Journey Into Night
Mourning Becomes Electra

Orwell, George
Animal Farm
1984

Pasternak, Boris
Doctor Zhivago

Poe, Edgar Allan
Short Stories

Remarque, Erich
All Quiet on the Western Front

Rolvaag, O. E.
Giants in the Earth

Rostand, Edmond
Cyrano de Bergerac

Salinger, J. D.
The Catcher in the Rye

Sandburg, Carl
Abraham Lincoln: The Prairie Years
Abraham Lincoln: The War Years

Saroyan, William
The Human Comedy

Sayers, Dorothy
The Nine Tailors

Shakespeare, William
Plays and Sonnets

Shaw, George Bernard
Arms and the Man
Major Barbara
Pygmalion
Saint Joan

Sheridan, Richard B.
The School for Scandal

Shute, Nevil
On the Beach

Sinclair, Upton
The Jungle

Sophocles
Antigone
Oedipus Rex

Steinbeck, John
East of Eden
The Grapes of Wrath
Of Mice and Men

Stowe, Harriet Beecher
Uncle Tom's Cabin

Swift, Jonathan
Gulliver's Travels

Thackeray, William M.
Vanity Fair

Thoreau, Henry David
Walden

Tolstoy, Leo
Anna Karenina
War and Peace

Trollope, Anthony
Barchester Towers

Turgenev, Ivan
Fathers and Sons

Twain, Mark
Pudd'nhead Wilson

Updike, John
Rabbit, Run

Vergil
The Aeneid

Voltaire
Candide

Walker, Alice
The Color Purple
Meridian

Warren, Robert Penn
All the King's Men

Waugh, Evelyn
Brideshead Revisited
A Handful of Dust

Wharton, Edith
Age of Innocence

White, T. H.
The Once and Future King
The Sword and the Stone

Wilde, Oscar
The Importance of Being Earnest
The Picture of Dorian Gray

Wilder, Thornton
Our Town

Williams, Tennessee
The Glass Menagerie
A Streetcar Named Desire

Wolfe, Thomas
Look Homeward, Angel

Woolf, Virginia
Mrs. Dalloway
To the Lighthouse

Wouk, Herman
The Caine Mutiny

Wright, Richard
Black Boy
Native Sun

Source: The National Endowment for the Humanities.

NCAA Eligibility Requirements

Most college athletic programs are regulated by the National Collegiate Athletic Association (NCAA), an organization that has established rules on eligibility, recruiting, and financial aid. The NCAA has three membership divisions—Division I, Division II, and Division III. Institutions are members of one or another division according to the size and scope of their athletic programs and whether they provide athletic scholarships.

If you are planning to enroll in college as a freshman and you wish to participate in Division I or Division II athletics, you must be certified by the NCAA Initial-Eligibility Clearinghouse. The Clearinghouse was established as a separate organization by the NCAA member institutions to ensure consistent interpretation of NCAA initial-eligibility requirements for all prospective student athletes at all member institutions.

If you want to participate in Division I or Division II sports in college, you should start the certification process when you are a junior in high school. Check with your counselor to make sure you are taking a core curriculum that meets NCAA requirements. Also, register to take the ACT or SAT as a junior. Submit your Student Release Form (available in your guidance counseling office) to the Clearinghouse by the beginning of your senior year.

Currently, in order to be eligible for practice, participation in regular season competition, and athletically related financial aid during the freshman year of college, a student must meet the following criteria:

Eligibility requirements for Division I NCAA member institutions

Effective August 1, 1996

- Graduate from high school

- Maintain a minimum 2.50 grade point average in a core curriculum of at least thirteen academic courses:
  - 4 units of English
  - 2 units of social science
  - 2 units of mathematics (must be 1 unit of algebra and 1 unit of geometry)
  - 2 units of natural or physical science (including 1 laboratory science)
  - 2 units of additional courses in the above areas and/or foreign language or computer science
  - 1 unit of an additional course in English, mathematics, or natural/physical science
- Receive a minimum score on the SAT or the ACT:
  - SAT (recentered)—Minimum combined score of 820 (verbal + math score)
  - ACT—Minimum combined score of 68 (sum of the four scores)

If you do not meet the 2.50 GPA requirement, you must compensate by making higher standardized test scores:

Core GPA	Minimum SAT Score	Minimum ACT Score
2.500 and higher.........	820	68
2.475.................	830	69
2.450	840/850	70
2.425.................	860	70
2.400.................	860	71
2.375.................	870	72
2.350.................	880	73
2.325.................	890	74
2.300.................	900	75
2.275.................	910	76
2.250.................	920	77
2.225.................	930	78
2.200.................	940	79
2.175.................	950	80
2.150.................	960	80
2.125.................	960	81
2.100.................	970	82
2.075.................	980	83
2.050.................	990	84
2.025.................	1000	85
2.000.................	1010	86

Below 2.000—Not Eligible

Peterson's © 1999

Eligibility requirements for Division II NCAA member institutions

Effective August 1, 1996
- Graduate from high school
- Maintain a minimum 2.00 grade point average in a core curriculum of at least thirteen academic courses:
  - 3 units of English
  - 2 units of social science
  - 2 units of mathematics (algebra/geometry)
  - 2 units of natural or physical science (including 1 laboratory science)
  - 2 units of additional courses in the above areas and/or foreign language or computer science
  - 2 units of additional courses in English, mathematics, or natural/physical science
- Receive a minimum score on the SAT or the ACT:
  - SAT (recentered)—Minimum combined score of 820 (verbal + math score)
  - ACT—Minimum combined score of 68 (sum of the four scores)

Initial eligibility of freshman athletes for Division I and II member institutions

Students who plan to participate in NCAA Division I or II college sports must complete the following steps:
- Obtain the Student Release Form from their high school, complete it, and send it to the NCAA Clearinghouse.
- This form authorizes high schools to release student transcripts, including test scores, proof of grades, and other academic information, to the Clearinghouse.
- The form authorizes the Clearinghouse to release this information to the colleges that request it.
- The Student Release Form and a fee must be received before any documents will be processed. (Fee waivers are available for economically disadvantaged students. Check with your counselor for fee waiver information.)
- Students must also make sure the Clearinghouse receives ACT and/or SAT score reports.
- Students can have score reports sent directly to the Clearinghouse by entering a specific code (9999) printed in the ACT and SAT registration packets.

Once a year, high schools will send an updated Form 48-H, which lists each course offering that meets NCAA core course requirements. The Clearinghouse personnel will validate the form. Thereafter, the Clearinghouse will determine each student's initial eligibility.

Collegiate institutions will request information from the Clearinghouse on the initial eligibility of prospective student-athletes. The Clearinghouse will make a certification decision and report it directly to the institution.

Three types of eligibility are possible

1. Certification of eligibility for expense-paid campus visits.
2. Preliminary certification of eligibility to participate in college sports (appears likely to meet all NCAA requirements but not yet graduated).
3. Final certification granted when proof of graduation is received.

Eligibility requirements for Division III NCAA member institutions

Division III NCAA member institutions, as well as nonmember institutions, are not under the above-mentioned eligibility requirements.

In order to be eligible for practice, participation in regular season competition, and need-based or merit-based financial aid, an entering freshman must satisfy the following:
- The eligibility rules and requirements of the institution
- The eligibility rules of the athletic conference in which the institution holds membership

National Association of Intercollegiate Athletics (NAIA) regulations

The National Association of Intercollegiate Athletics (NAIA) has different eligibility requirements for student-athletes. To be eligible to participate in intercollegiate athletics as an incoming freshman, two of the following three requirements must be met:
- Have a 2.0 (C) or higher cumulative final grade point average in high school;
- Have an 18 composite or higher on the ACT or an 860 total score or higher on the SAT on a single test administered on a national test date; and/or
- Have a top-half final class rank in his/her high school graduating class.

Student-athletes must also have on file at the college an official ACT or SAT score report from the appropriate national testing center. Results reported on the student's high school transcript are not acceptable. Therefore,

Athletic Resume

Name
Address

Height/weight
Footspeed (by specific event)
Position played
Weight classification

GPA
Class rank
ACT or SAT scores (or when you plan to take them)

Athletic records
All state teams
Special awards
Off-season accomplishments

Weightlifting exercises
Vertical jumps
Pushups
Bench jumps
Shuttle run

Leadership characteristics
Former successful athletes from your high school
Outstanding capabilities
Citizenship
Alumni parents/relatives

Team schedule with dates and times
Videotape with jersey number identified
Newspaper clippings about you or your team
High school address and phone number
Coach's name

students must request that their test score report be forwarded to the college's admission office.

If you have questions about the certification process that cannot be answered by your guidance counselor, write to:

NCAA Clearinghouse
P.O. Box 4044
Iowa City, IA 52243-4044
Fax: 319-337-1556
(Transcripts may NOT be sent via fax.)

NCAA Clearinghouse Forms Processing
P.O. Box 4043
Iowa City, IA 52243-4043
Phone: 319-339-3003
    (Voice Response Service)
Fax: 319-337-1556

The National Association for College Admission Counseling has published a 24-page brochure, *High School Planning for College-Bound Athletes*, that provides guidance to the student athlete. Call 703-836-2222 to order. ($6)

Athletic Scholarships

Applying for athletic scholarships has become an important area of college preparation because these scholarships are a way of earning tuition in return for your competitive abilities. Whether you're male or female or interested in baseball, basketball, crew, cross-country, fencing, field hockey, football, golf, gymnastics, lacrosse, sailing, skiing, soccer, softball, swimming and diving, tennis, track and field, volleyball, or wrestling, there may be scholarship dollars available for you.

At the beginning of your junior year, ask your guidance counselor to help you make sure you take the required number and mix of academic courses and to inform you of the SAT and ACT score minimumsthat must be met to play college sports. Also ask your counselor about academic requirements, because you must be certified by the NCAA Initial-Eligibility Clearinghouse, and you must start this process by the end of your junior year.

Questions to ask yourself

Before you begin the search, you must ask yourself if you have what it takes to play college sports. In general, it requires the basic skills and natural ability, a solid knowledge of the sport, overall body strength, speed, and sound

academics. Today's athletes are stronger and faster due to improved methods of training and conditioning. They are coached in skills and techniques, and they begin training in their sport at an early age. Remember, your talents will be compared with those from across the U.S. and around the world.

Another question is, do you want and need an athletic scholarship? Certainly it is prestigious to receive an athletic scholarship, but some athletes compare having an athletic scholarship to having a job—you are expected to perform. Meetings, training sessions, practices, games, and studying take away from social and leisure time. Also, with very few "full ride" scholarships available, you will most likely receive a "partial" scholarship or a one-year renewable contract. If your scholarship is not renewed, you may be left scrambling for financial aid. So ask yourself if you are ready for the demands and roles associated with accepting an athletic scholarship.

Marketing yourself and your talents

College recruiters look for a combination of the following attributes when awarding athletic scholarships: academic excellence, a desire to win, self-motivation, ability to perform as a team player, willingness to help others, cooperation with coaching staff, attitude in practice, attitude in games/matches, toughness, strength, optimal height and weight, and excellence in skill areas.

In order to successfully sell your skills to a college or university, you'll need to take three main steps: locate the colleges and universities that offer scholarships in your sport, contact the institution in a formal manner, and follow up each lead. There are many ways to become familiar with the sports programs a college or university has to offer. You can ask your coach or assistant coaches; learn about the conference or institution from newspaper or television coverage; ask your guidance counselor; review guidebooks, reference books, and the Internet; ask alumni; or attend a tryout or campus visit. You can also write to the NCAA to request a recruiting guide for your sport.

Once you make a list of schools you are interested in, get the name of the head coach and write a letter to the top twenty schools on your list. Then compile a factual resume of your athletic and academic accomplishments, put together 10–15 minutes of video highlights of your athletic performance (with your jersey number noted), get letters of recommendation from your high school coach and your off-season coach, and include a season schedule.

When you meet a recruiter or coach, exhibit self-confidence by using a firm handshake, maintaining eye contact, and making sure that you are well groomed. According to recruiters, the most effective attitude is quiet confidence, respect, sincerity, and enthusiasm. Don't be afraid to probe the recruiter by asking: Do I qualify athletically and academically? If I am recruited, what would the parameters of the scholarship be? For what position am I being considered? Also, it is okay to ask the recruiter to declare what level of interest he or she has in you.

Persistence pays off when it comes to seeking an athletic scholarship. And timing can be everything. There are four good times that a follow-up letter from your coach or a personal letter from you is extremely effective: prior to your senior season, during or just after the senior season, just prior to or after announced conference-affiliated signing dates or national association signing dates, and late summer, in case scholarship offers have been withdrawn or declined.

To sum up, you know yourself better than anyone, so you must look at your skills, both athletic and academic, objectively. Evaluate the skills you need to improve and keep the desire to improve alive within your heart. Develop your leadership skills and keep striving for excellence with your individual achievements. Keep your mind open as to what school you want to attend, and keep plugging away, even when you are tired, sore, and unsure. After all, athletes are trained to be winners!

Athlete's Bookshelf

There are a number of books that focus on athletic scholarships to help student athletes. Some include guides to the recruiting process and/or lists of schools providing sports scholarships.

Look for *Peterson's Sports Scholarships and College Athletic Programs 1997*, 3rd edition. Ron Walker, ed. ($24.95).

What is Proposition 48?

Proposition 48, or the "2.000 rule," was passed in January 1983 and applies to member institutions of the NCAA Division I and II. The rule sets GPA and SAT/ACT score standards that must be met to participate in college athletics and to receive athletically related financial aid as a freshman. NCAA Division III as well as NAIA and National Junior College Athletic Association (NJCAA) college participants are not held to the "2.000" guidelines. These institutions set their own requirements, which may be more or less challenging.

What is Title IX?

Title IX is part of the Education Amendments of 1972. It states that colleges must provide equivalent amounts of athletic scholarship aid to female and male athletes. Also, all resources, support, and opportunity must be shared equally by males and females.

Student Snapshot
Adam's touchdown

Charlotte Thomas
Career and Education Editor, Peterson's

It's hard not to make comparisons between Adam Merrell's high school football career and how he tackled getting into college. Yes, football had a lot to do with the colleges he considered and the one he eventually chose to attend—he is a running back after all. But the same kind of tactics that had won games for his team enabled Adam to find just the right college for him.

Practice, practice, practice

For starters, he trained hard—academically that is. Adam has been a high achiever and in gifted programs all along. Although he has a 3.7 grade point average, he believed he could have done better. However, the fact that he worked 20 hours a week, except during football season, and was involved in extracurricular activities probably had something to do with what he says are disappointing grades. Adam is vice president of the Key Club, is in the National Honor Society, and recently joined Future Educators of America. He says the extra work that all these activities entailed was worth it because they made him look good on college applications.

Indeed they did. Not surprisingly, he was accepted by all the colleges he chose. The rub came in finding which one would give him the juiciest football scholarship and which offered the best courses in his major.

Keeping his eye on his goals

Adam remained flexible about his eventual major and so was able to change directions based on his new-found interests. Originally, Adam thought he wanted to be a computer programmer. However, after taking a community service class in which he assisted an elementary school teacher, he changed tactics and decided to major in education. He realized that he's more of a people person and would rather look at kids' faces than a computer screen all day. With his new career goal in mind he was better able to choose a college that suited him.

Great coaching

Adam also took advantage of great coaching—not from his football coach but from his high school counselor, Mr. Lou Martino, who taught a class in how to apply to college. In the first semester of Adam's senior year, he was writing a resume, filling out application forms, and searching the Web and college guides for scholarships and colleges. Adam enthusiastically plowed into the task.

Attuned to timing

As expected, football played a big part in the timing of Adam's college search. At the beginning of their senior year, he and his team members had their hopes set on football scholarships that would propel them into top colleges. They had every reason to believe they'd get them. They'd just come from a "miracle" season, as he puts it, and after practicing all summer they expected to pull off another winner. Unfortunately, things didn't go as planned when several of the star players were injured early in the season. There went Adam's prospects of getting a

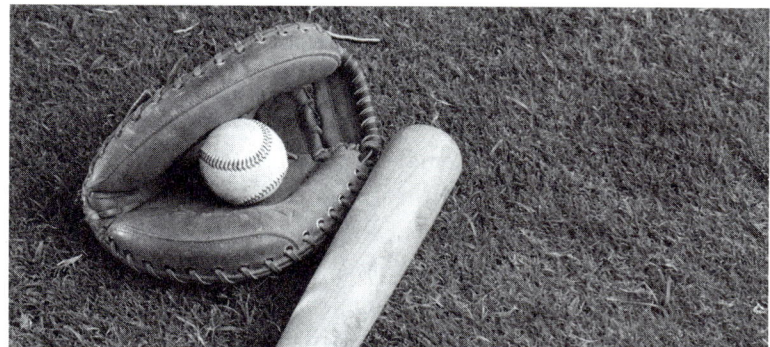

football scholarship at his sister's college, where he had at first wanted to go. The team ran out of time to play the important games and to be seen by the right coaches.

Have a solid game plan

Adam quickly came up with another strategy. He didn't think he could play the pros, but he knew he could leverage his football talents into scholarship money if he looked elsewhere. In the process, he discovered that he didn't want a big sprawling university, and with his change in major, he knew he needed to have a solid education curriculum.

After several fumbles he found Ottawa University in Ottawa, Kansas. It had everything he was looking for and then some:

- Football scholarship. Score!
- Two-hour drive from home. Score!
- Small-school atmosphere. Score!
- Small class sizes. Score!
- Great teaching courses. Score!

Because of his high school counselor's advice, Adam knew never to choose a college without scrutinizing it firsthand. With that in mind when he visited Ottawa's campus, he talked to the dean of the education department, sneaked into some classes, talked to students, and realized that Ottawa had won the game, so to speak.

The hometown atmosphere of Ottawa is what scored with him. The campus size is about fifty more students than are at Adam's high school, so class sizes suited him just fine.

Types of Athletic Scholarships

Colleges and universities offer two basic types of athletic scholarships: the institutional grant, which is an agreement between the athlete and the college, and the conference grant, which also binds the college to the athlete. The difference is that the athlete who signs an institutional grant can change his or her mind and sign with another team. The athlete who signs a conference contract cannot renegotiate another contract with a school that honors conference grants.

Full four-year

Also known as "full ride," these scholarships pay for room, board, tuition, and books. Due to the high cost of awarding scholarships, this type of grant is being discouraged by conferences around the country in favor of the one-year renewable contract or the partial scholarship.

Full one-year renewable contract

This type of scholarship, which has basically replaced the four-year grant, is automatically renewed at the end of each school year for four years if the conditions of the contract are met. The recruiter will probably tell you "in good faith" that the intent is to offer a four-year scholarship, but he is legally only allowed to offer you a one-year grant. You must ask the recruiter as well as other players what the record has been of renewing scholarships for athletes who comply athletically, academically, and socially. Remember—no athlete can receive more than a full scholarship.

One-year trial grant (full or partial)

A verbal agreement between you and the institution that at the end of the year your renewal will be dependent upon your academic and athletic performance.

Partial scholarship

The partial grant is any part of the total scholarship. You may be offered room and board but not tuition and books. Or you may be offered just tuition. The possibility exists for you to negotiate to a full scholarship after your freshman year.

Waiving out-of-state fees

This award is for out-of-state students to attend the college or university at the same fee as an in-state student.

Students routinely call professors by their first names, a detail which Adam liked very much. He was looking for the same kind of camaraderie that he had with his high school football buddies and didn't want to give that up. By attending Ottawa, it looks like he won't have to.

Tips from a pro

Adam has a lot of tips to pass along. On the surface it seems like he had a wide-open field and faced no opposition in getting into college. However, looking closer it's evident that he put a lot into finding and choosing the right college. Just as a coach does a play-by-play evaluation, a look at how Adam applied to college indicates some really spectacular plays.

- Know what you want and who you are. Adam took the time to find out what he really wanted to major in, not just the first hot career to come along. He also assessed his personal likes and dislikes, realizing that he wanted to be close to home and to duplicate the same kind of comfortable feeling he'd had in high school. Basically, he was looking for a home away from home.
- Take advantage of courses and teachers who can coach you through the college application process. Adam went through all the exercises his high school counselor threw at him—searching the Net, pouring through college guides, filling out practice applications. It was time-consuming, but Adam used all the resources at his disposal, including online personality surveys, college guides, college Web sites, and search engines for scholarships.
- Be flexible. The disappointing football season that scratched Adam's hopes of a scholarship at the college he thought he wanted to attend could have been a big stumbling block. Instead, he sought more options and kept on going. Personal contact pays off. Adam didn't hesitate to pick up the phone and call deans and coaches at colleges he was considering. Not content to just send letters, he got his name in front of them while pumping them for information. Visit each campus you're really serious about and know what you're looking for. Adam looked at the campus surroundings and checked out class sizes. He wanted to make sure teachers would know him by name. Because he was sure about his major, he researched exactly what the education curriculum was and how long it would take him to complete a degree.

CHAPTER 3

Tackling the TESTS

Test Talk

What is the PLAN?

The PLAN is an instrument designed for use by sophomores to help guide them in their postsecondary planning and preparation. The test measures the same academic skills as the ACT Assessment (English, mathematics, reading, and science reasoning) but measures them at the tenth-grade level. The PLAN includes an interest inventory, a study skills assessment, an educational/occupational planning section, and a student needs profile. The PLAN also provides the student with an "estimated ACT composite score range." Students can use the "Skills Diagnosis" section to focus on academic weaknesses that need attention prior to taking the ACT Assessment.

Test Format—*Achievement Tests*
120 questions, 1 hour 55 minutes

- Writing Skills Test
- Mathematics Test
- Reading Test
- Science Reasoning Test

Nonacademic Sections
120 items, 50 minutes

- Interest Inventory
- High School Course Information
- Educational/Occupational Plans
- Needs Assessment Profile

What is the ACT?

The ACT Assessment is a standardized college entrance examination that measures knowledge and skills in English, mathematics, reading, and science reasoning and the application of these skills to future academic tasks. The ACT consists of four multiple-choice tests.

Test Format—*Test 1—English*
75 questions, 45 minutes

- Punctuation
- Grammar and Usage
- Sentence Structure
- Strategy
- Organization
- Style

Test 2—Mathematics
60 questions, 60 minutes

- Prealgebra
- Elementary Algebra
- Intermediate Algebra
- Coordinate Geometry
- Plane Geometry
- Trigonometry

Test 3—Reading
40 questions, 35 minutes

- Prose Fiction
- Humanities
- Social Studies
- Natural Sciences

Test 4—Science Reasoning
40 questions, 35 minutes

- Biology
- Physical Science
- Chemistry
- Physics

Test Scores

Each section is scored from 1 to 36 and scaled for slight variations in difficulty. Students are not penalized for incorrect responses. The composite score is the average of the four scaled scores.

What Is the PSAT/NMSQT?

(Preliminary SAT/National Merit Scholarship Qualifying Test)

The PSAT is a practice test for the SAT I, which is one of the tests often required for college admission. Many students take the PSAT more than once because scores tend to increase with repetition and it allows students to become more comfortable with taking standardized tests. During the junior year, the PSAT is also used as a qualifying test for the National Merit Scholarship Program and the National Scholarship Service and Fund for Negro Students. It is also used in designating students for the National Hispanic Scholar Recognition Program. The PSAT includes a Writing Skills Section, which consists entirely of multiple-choice questions. This section does not currently appear on the SAT.

Test Format

The PSAT has the same format as the SAT I but is a shorter version.

Verbal Reasoning

Approximately 50 questions, two 25-minute sections

- Analogies
- Sentence Completion
- Critical Reading Passages

Mathematical Reasoning

40 questions, two 25-minute sections

- Student-Produced Responses
- Quantitative Comparisons
- Regular Math

Writing Skills

39 questions, one 30-minute section

- Identifying Sentence Errors
- Improving Sentences
- Improving paragraphs

Test Scores

Students receive a score in each content area (verbal, math, and writing). Each score ranges from 20–80 and is totaled with the others for the combined score. The total score ranges from 60–240.

Selection Index
(used for National Merit Scholarship purposes)

Verbal + Math + Writing Scores
   Score Range: 60–240
Mean Junior Score: 147

National Merit Scholarship Program

Semifinalist Status:
   Selection Index of 201–222 (recentered)
Commended Student:
   Selection Index of 199 (recentered)

What Is the SAT I?

The SAT I measures developed verbal and mathematical reasoning abilities as they relate to successful performance

1998 Test Scores for College-Bound Seniors

STATE	SAT I			ACT
	Verbal	Math	Overall	Average Composite
California	497	516	1013	21.2
Florida	500	501	1001	20.8
Idaho	545	544	1089	22.5
Illinois	564	581	1145	21.4
Massachusetts	508	508	1016	21.6
Michigan	558	569	1127	21.3
Ohio	536	540	1076	21.4
Pennsylvania	497	495	992	21.4
South Carolina	478	473	951	19.0
Texas	494	501	995	20.3
USA	505	512	1017	21.0

in college. It is intended to supplement the secondary school record and other information about the student in assessing readiness for college. There is one unscored experimental section on the exam, which is used for equating and/or pretesting purposes.

Test Format—Verbal Reasoning

78 questions, 75 minutes

- Analogies
- Sentence Completions
- Critical Reading Passages

Experimental Section

30 minutes

Mathematical Reasoning

60 questions, 75 minutes

- Student-Produced Responses
- Quantitative Comparisons
- Regular Math

Test Scores

Students receive one point for each correct response and lose a fraction of a point for each incorrect response (except for student-produced responses). These points are totaled to produce the raw scores, which are then scaled to equalize the scores for slight variations in difficulty for various editions of the test. Both the Verbal Scaled Score

Range and the Math Scaled Score Range are from 200 to 800. The Total Scaled Score Range is from 400 to 1600.

Recentered Scores Explained

Until April 1995, SAT I scores were scaled based on the results of the April 1941 exam, which was taken by 10,654 students, many of whom were white males attending private Northeastern colleges. Due to the increased number of students taking the test and the culturally diverse nature of the population, the average SAT I score has fallen since 1941. The College Board decided to recenter the scores, and scores are now scaled based on the results of a much larger group that took the SAT I in 1990.

As a result, the midpoint, or 50th percentile, has shifted upward. However, students should not assume that a recentered score will result in a higher ranking among prospective admission applicants. College admission officers take the recentered scores into account, realizing that higher scores are generally due to the new measurement tool, not necessarily the performance of the student.

What Are the SAT II Subject Tests?

Subject Tests are required by some institutions for admission and/or placement in freshman courses. Each Subject Test measures one's knowledge of a specific subject and the ability to apply that knowledge. Students should check with each institution for its specific requirements. In general, students are required to take three Subject Tests (one English, one mathematics, and one of their choice).

Upcoming Test Dates

SAT I	SAT II	ACT
May 1, 1999	May 1, 1999	
June 5, 1999	June 5, 1999	June 12, 1999
		September 25, 1999 (not in all states)
October 9, 1999	October 9, 1999	October 23, 1999
November 6, 1999	November 6, 1999	
December 4, 1999	December 4, 1999	December 11, 1999
January 22, 2000	January 22, 2000	
		February 12, 2000
April 8, 2000		April 1, 2000
May 6, 2000	May 6, 2000	
June 3, 2000	June 3, 2000	June 10, 2000

Subject Tests are given in the following areas: writing, literature, American history and social studies, world history, mathematics level IC, mathematics level IIC, biology (administered for the last time in May 1999), biology E/M, chemistry, physics, French—reading only, French with listening, German—reading only, German with listening, Spanish—reading only, Spanish with listening, Italian—reading only, modern Hebrew—reading only, Latin—reading only, Chinese with listening, Japanese

What Does It Take to Get In?

College Admission Policy	Class Rank	ACT Range (Average) Range: 1–36	SAT Range (Average) Range: 400–1600
Highly Selective	Rank in top 10 percent of class, very strong academic record	27–31	1220–1380
Selective	Rank in top 25 percent of class, strong academic record	22–27	1150–1230
Traditional	Rank in top 50 percent of class, good academic record	20–23	950–1070
Liberal	Many accepted from lower half of class	18–21	870–990
Open	All accepted to limit of capacity	17–20	830–950

Visit: www.petersons.com

with listening, Korean with listening, and the English language proficiency. These tests are designed to measure knowledge and the ability to apply that knowledge in specific subject areas. They are 1-hour, primarily multiple-choice tests. Three SAT II Subject Tests may be taken on one test date.

Test Scores

The SAT II Subject Tests are scored like the SAT I, with a point awarded for each correct answer and a fraction of a point deducted for each incorrect answer. The raw scores are then converted to scaled scores that range from 200 to 800.

What Is the TOEFL?

The Test of English as a Foreign Language is designed to help assess a foreign-born student's grasp of English if English is not the student's first language. Performance on the TOEFL may help interpret scores on the verbal section of the SAT I.

The purpose of TOEFL is to evaluate the English proficiency of people whose native language is not English. The 3-hour test consists of three sections: listening comprehension, structure and written expression, and reading comprehension. The test is given at more than 1,260 centers in 180 countries and areas and is administered by Educational Testing Service (ETS). For further information, visit http://www.toefl.org.

Recommended Test-Taking Dates

Sophomore

October	PSAT/NMSQT and PLAN *For practice, planning, and preparation*
May–June	SAT II Subject Tests (if necessary)

Junior

October	PSAT/NMSQT *For the National Merit Scholarship Program and practice*
January–June	ACT and/or SAT I, SAT II Subject Tests (if necessary) *For college admission*

Senior

October–December	ACT and/or SAT I, SAT II Subject Tests (if necessary) *For college admission*

Recommendations

It is recommended that students take both the ACT and the SAT I. This assures that they will have the test scores required for admission to all schools, because some colleges accept the results of one test and not the other. Some institutions use test results for proper placement of students in English and math courses.

Students should take the ACT and SAT I during the spring of their junior year. This enables students to retake the test in the fall of their senior year if they are not satisfied with their test scores. Also, this makes it possible for institutions to have all test scores before the end of January. Institutions generally consider the better score when determining admission/placement. Because most scholarship applications are processed between December and April during the senior year, the best score results can then be included in the application.

What Is the Advanced Placement (AP) Program?

The Advanced Placement Program allows high school students to try college-level work and build valuable skills and study habits in the process. Subject matter is explored in more depth in AP courses than in other high school classes. A qualifying score on an AP test—which varies from school to school—can earn you college credit or advanced placement. Getting qualifying grades on enough exams can even earn you a full year's credit and sophomore standing at more than 1,400 higher education institutions. There are currently thirty-two AP courses in eighteen different subject areas, including art, biology, and computer science. Speak to your guidance counselor for information about your school's offerings.

What Is the College-Level Examination Program (CLEP)?

The College-Level Examination Program enables students to earn college credit for what they already know, whether it was learned in school, through independent study, or other experiences outside of the classroom. More than 2,800 colleges and universities now award credit for qualifying scores on one or more of the thirty-four CLEP exams. The exams, 90 minutes in length and primarily multiple-choice, are administered at participating colleges and universities. For more information check out the Web site at

http://www.collegeboard.org/clep/students/html/student.html.

What is the ASVAB?

ASVAB stands for the Armed Services Vocational Aptitude Battery, which is a career exploration program. A multiaptitude test battery helps students explore their interests, abilities, and personal preferences. A career exploration workbook gives students information about the world of work. And a career information resource book helps students match their personal characteristics to the working world. Finally, an occupational outlook handbook describes in detail approximately 250 civilian and military occupations. Students can use ASVAB scores for military enlistment up to two years after they take the test. A student can take the ASVAB as a sophomore, junior, or senior, but students cannot use their sophomore scores to enter the armed forces. Ask your guidance counselor or your local recruiting office for more information.

Test-Prep Bookshelf

There are a variety of ways to prepare for standardized tests. Find a method that fits your schedule and your budget, but you should definitely prepare. Far too many students walk into these tests "cold," either because they find standardized tests frightening or annoying or they just couldn't find time to study. The key is that these exams are *standardized*; think about it. That means these tests are largely the same from administration to administration; they always test the same concepts. They have to, or else you couldn't compare the scores of people who took the tests on different dates. The numbers or words may change, but the underlying content doesn't.

So how do you prepare? At the very least, you should review relevant material, such as math formulas and commonly tested vocabulary words, and know the direc-

Here's what Peterson's offers to help you test your best:

Peterson's SAT Success	$14.95
Peterson's SAT Math Flash	$ 8.95
Peterson's SAT Word Flash	$ 8.95
Peterson's Panic Plan for the SAT	$ 9.95
Peterson's ACT Success....................	$14.95
Peterson's ACT Math Flash.................	$ 8.95
Peterson's ACT Word Flash...............	$ 8.95
Peterson's Panic Plan for the ACT.........	$ 9.95

Visit: www.petersons.com

Test Scorekeeper

Use this chart to keep track of your test scores. Use the second column if you take a test more than once or if you take more than two SAT II's.

PSAT	**PSAT**
Test date	Test date
Verbal score	Verbal score
Mathematics score	Mathematics score
Writing score	Writing score
SAT I	**SAT I**
Test date	Test date
Verbal score	Verbal score
Mathematics score	Mathematics score
SAT II	**SAT II**
Test date	Test date
Subject	Subject
Score	Score
SAT II	**SAT II**
Test date	Test date
Subject	Subject
Score	Score
ACT	**ACT**
Test date	Test date
Composite score	Composite score

tions for each question type or test section. You should take at least one practice test and review your mistakes, so you don't make them again on test day. Beyond that, you know best how much preparation you need. You'll find lots of material in libraries or bookstores to help you: books and software (from the test makers and from other publishers); or live courses (ranging from national test-preparation companies to teachers at your high school who give classes).

Preparing for Standardized Tests

Here are the answers to some commonly asked questions about standardized tests.

Q. *What kinds of short-term things can I do to prepare?*

College Score Requirements

When you begin applying to schools, use this chart to keep track of the test score requirements of your top schools. Then compare your actual scores to the requirements.

	College 1	College 2	College 3	College 4
ACT				
SAT				
Verbal				
Math				
Required GPA				

A. Know what to expect. Get familiar with how the test is structured, how much time is allowed, and the directions for each type of question. Get plenty of rest the night before the test and eat breakfast that morning.

Q. *What are good ways to prepare for the SAT I?*

A. Take the PSAT/NMSQT. Spend time going over sample questions and take sample SAT I's. You should carefully review *Taking the SAT I: Reasoning Test* (free to students who take the SAT I) and know the content of the test. Also, most libraries and bookstores stock a large selection of material about the SAT I and all standardized tests.

Q. *What resources are available for the ACT?*

A. Ask your guidance counselor for a free guidebook called *Preparing for the ACT Assessment.* Besides providing general test-preparation information and additional test-taking strategies, this guidebook describes the content and format of the four ACT subject area tests, summarizes test administration procedures followed at ACT test centers, and includes a practice test.

Q. *What about computer software and other preparation materials?*

A. It is important to prepare for the SAT and ACT. The good news is that there are a variety of prodcts from books to software to videos available to help you. Find the learning style that suits you best. As for which products to buy, there are two major categories—those created by the test makers and those created by private companies. The best approach is to talk to someone who has been through the process and find out which product or products he or she recommends.

Q. *Do coaching programs help?*

A. Some students report significant increases in scores after participating in coaching programs. Longer-term programs (40 hours) seem to raise scores more than short-term programs (20 hours), but beyond 40 hours, score gains are minor. Math scores appear to benefit more from coaching than do verbal scores.

Homeschoolers Go to College

If you've been learning at home for the last few years, you might have some concerns about selecting the right college or university, the application process, and the overall change in learning environments. With an estimated 1.23 million students being homeschooled nationwide, these are valid concerns for the many institutions of higher education as well.

According to homeschooling consultant Rich Fairchild, "The bottom line is: Can you do the work and can you pay the bill?" If so, the process of being admitted to college is no different for homeschoolers than it is for other students. At present, there are simply no set rules for admitting homeschoolers to the country's many colleges and universities. In fact, the phenomenon is so new that many of the institutions of higher learning are only now in the process of establishing some guidelines in this area.

Cafi Cohen, homeschooling enthusiast and author of a book on the topic, agrees. "Ninety-five percent of the colleges and universities have no protocol for evaluating applications from homeschoolers," she says. Cohen's book, *And What About College?: How Home Schooling Leads to Admissions to the Best Colleges and Universities*, offers homeschoolers some specific advice on the topic while sharing the experiences of getting her own children admitted to college.

Peterson's © 1999

Home Schooling Resources

Home Education Magazine
http://www.home-ed-press.com/wlcm_HEM.html

Home Education League of Parents (HELP)
P.O. Box 14296
Columbus, OH 43214

Clonlara School
http://www.grfn.org/education/clonlara/

Homeschool World
http://www.home-school.com

Miningco Guide to Homeschooling
http://homeschooling.miningco.com/

National Homeschool Association
http://www.n-h-a.org

Cohen's son and daughter were homeschooled since the sixth and seventh grades. Her son recently graduated from the Air Force Academy, while her daughter is attending California Polytechnic Institute. "Homeschoolers apply to college like anyone else," she emphasizes. Cohen cautions, however, that the SAT I is more important for homeschoolers because it is the one benchmark that is used to compare homeschoolers with other students. Some admission officers say they require homeschoolers to also take several SAT IIs, which are achievement tests in specific subjects.

Cohen doesn't recommend that homeschoolers take the GED exam—see "General Educational Development (GED) Test" below—unless a college specifically asks for it. Instead, homeschoolers should create a transcript that resembles those from area high schools. According to Cohen, it's probably best to use a portfolio for the smaller, more specialized schools, conforming your document to what they are used to seeing. In her experiences with both children, she was never asked for a diploma.

Cohen believes that in five to ten years, most colleges and universities will have developed admission policies for homeschoolers. In the meantime, homeschooled students should take advantage of the same resources that regular students use—namely, high school guidance counselors, some of whom work on a freelance basis.

For more information on Cohen's book, access her Web site via http://www.home-ed-press.com.

General Educational Development (GED) Test

If you have not completed your high school education, you may earn an equivalence by taking the GED test, sponsored by your state Department of Education. However, taking the GED test is not a legitimate reason for dropping out of school. In fact, it is more difficult to get into the armed services with only a GED, and some employees have difficulty getting promoted without a high school diploma.

You are eligible to take the GED if you are not enrolled in high school, have not yet graduated from high school, are at least 16 years old, and meet your local requirements regarding age, residency, and length of time since leaving school. Contact your local GED office to arrange to take the exam. Call 800-62-MYGED to find your local GED office.

There are five sections to the GED test, covering writing skills, social studies, science, interpreting literature and the arts, and mathematics. Part II of the Writing Skills Test requires writing an essay. The GED costs an average of $35 but can vary from state to state, but the application fee may be waived under certain circumstances. Again, contact your local office for more information.

CHAPTER 4

Student RESOURCES

Stress Management

In the rapidly changing world in which we live, stress has become a way of life. Students in particular experience lots of pressure and stress when preparing for life after high school. Some people enjoy stress and say that it makes them perform to their potential; others say stress prevents them from moving forward in a productive, efficient manner.

Stress can be defined as the body's reaction to change. You may react emotionally (with anger, irritability, anxiety, depression), experience muscular problems (headache, back pain, jaw pain), have stomach disturbances, or feel "stressed out" as a result of an elevation in blood pressure, a rapid heartbeat, sweaty palms, dizziness, or shortness of breath. Obviously, this is not your optimal state of performance.

Stress prevention measures

Healthy behaviors and resources are your first line of defense against stress. We'll talk about how to handle stress later, but first let's talk about how to prevent it.

- Eat at least one hot, balanced meal per day. An ongoing diet of fast food or inconsistent meals will leave you vulnerable to stress.
- Get 7–8 hours of sleep at least four nights per week. This is easier said than done. When you're in high school, you get pulled in a lot of different directions—a job, several extracurricular activities, study requirements, college preparation, and the demands of maintaining a social and home life. Many times, sleep gets the short end of the stick. But if you make yourself get enough sleep, stress will have a harder time staking its claim on you.
- Give and receive affection regularly. Hug your mom, your dog, or your significant other. Don't leave yourself feeling lonely and isolated.
- Exercise. For some people, this comes naturally. For others, it takes discipline. Exercise releases stress, relaxes you, and gives your body the physical stamina to withstand stress. Exercise to the point of perspiration at least three times a week.
- Don't smoke, drink, or use excessive amounts of caffeine. You may think that a good way to relax is to party, but nicotine and alcohol deplete your body, so you actually take two steps back in fighting stress. Besides, the negative consequences of smoking and drinking can add stress.
- Make sure you are the appropriate weight for your height. This has less to do with physical appearance than being in good shape. If you are physically fit, you'll be better able to ward off the effects of stress. Believe it or not, good posture helps, too.
- Make sure you have income or allowance sufficient to meet your basic needs. Money is a big stress factor, especially for high school seniors who have a lot of extra expenses. Simplify your life so that the money you do have is not stretched too far. Share resources. Sell personal items you no longer use. Be creative.
- Cultivate a network of friends and acquaintances. Even though attending clubs and social activities takes time, in moderation it is time well spent. Maintain a social network and do something fun at least once a week.

- Speak openly about your feelings when you are angry or worried. Don't waste time and energy on keeping your feelings inside. Often the problem can be solved, and you can move on to more productive things. Have regular conversations with your parents and siblings about domestic problems (chores, money, daily living issues).
- Organize your time effectively. The next section offers several time-management strategies to help you prioritize, plan, delegate, use teamwork, and enlist support to maximize your time.
- Try to have an optimistic outlook. Use humor to see the lighter side of life. The decisions you make during high school are important, but very few are irreversible.

What stresses you out?

It is important to get in touch with exactly what makes you stressed and then review your options for change.

Once you identify what causes stress in your life, you can reduce stress by doing one of three things:

1. Alter the situation. If you have too much on your plate and can't possibly do all of it well, you can make the decision to do less. Or you can make the decision to be assertive and say no to extra demands on your time. Remember, there are things you can't control and things that you can. Change the ones you can.
2. Avoid the situation. If you are worried, feel scared, or are uncomfortable about completing a task, make a conscious decision to do it later, when you are more prepared to handle it. Don't confuse avoiding with procrastination. Instead, think of avoiding as "buying time." Take a break and do more research, talk to others, or make a different decision later.
3. Accept the situation. Sometimes what makes people stressed is their perception. A person may think he or she "should" or "ought" to do something, make a certain decision, or behave in a particular way. Reevaluate that perception. Think clearly, focus rationally, and reduce your emotional involvement. Then reassess the situation from a personal values position. Do what feels right to you. Adapt when possible.

Skills that make you "stress hardy"

Most people get stressed when things are out of control, for example, if there are too many things to do, too many decisions to make, or too much information to digest. If you add not having enough time, enough money, or enough energy to get it all done, you have the perfect recipe for stress. Just as it takes several individual players to make a good team, you can more easily reduce stress if you strengthen certain skill areas. Like other skills, each area takes practice.

- Organizational skills. You don't want to be too organized, because that causes stress, too. But you want to be organized enough to keep up with papers, deadlines, money, car keys, and life's other details.
- Time-management skills. Keep moving forward. Be realistic. Don't overcommit. Stay disciplined.
- Goal-setting skills. Know yourself. Set short-term and long-term goals. Take the steps necessary to achieve both kinds of goals.
- Communication skills. Talk. Listen. Learn.
- Conflict resolution skills. Negotiate. Agree. Implement.
- Flexibility skills. When Plan A goes wrong, have a Plan B and put it into effect. Concentrate on what is important and don't sweat the details. Learn to solve problems.

- Self-esteem skills. Have the confidence to make decisions. Know when to let something roll off your back. Believe in yourself.
- Reality-testing skills. Is this really a problem? Do I need to solve it now?

Self-control is the key to coping with stress

Even if you employ the preventative measures and practice stress-hardy skills, there still may be times when you will feel stressed out. Stress is a good thing, within reason. But if you feel it getting out of hand, take a few minutes to gain control of yourself and the situation. Here are a few tips.

- Quiet time. When things feel out of control, go somewhere you can think. Take a walk. Listen to soft music. Take a shower. Try to gain some balance by making the world slow down for a few minutes.
- Deep breathing. It is very soothing to be aware of the rhythm of your breathing. Lie or sit down for 15 minutes and concentrate on relaxing. If you need to take a power nap, that's okay, too.
- Muscle relaxation. Release the stress in your body by progressively relaxing your head, shoulders, arms, and legs until you feel yourself begin to calm down.
- Meditation. Calming your mind is as important as calming your body. Close your eyes and think of nothing. Clear your mind and don't let nagging thoughts sneak in while you are trying to get rid of the clutter.
- Imagery. Picture yourself achieving your goals. See the success. Feel the satisfaction. Turn those positive feelings into energy to make it happen.
- When all else fails, laugh. Watch a funny movie. Read the comics. Put yourself in a frame of mind in which you can tackle life's challenges with a smile on your face.

Winning the Time Management Game

What is the value of time? Six dollars an hour? The price of a scholarship because the application is a day late? Time can be a very expensive resource or an ace in your pocket. Even if you recognize the value of time, managing it is a challenge. Time either flies by or drags on. But time marches on, with or without you. The key is to be ahead of time, not forever trying to catch up.

When you live with enough time, life is relaxed and balanced. In order to find that balance, you have to prioritize and plan. Decide what you want and what is important to you. Organize logically and schedule realistically. Overcome obstacles. Change bad habits. Simplify and streamline. Save time when you can. Sound impossible? It's not easy, but you can do it. The secret is held in a Chinese proverb: "The wisdom of life is the elimination of nonessentials."

Managing time is all about control

The good thing about time is that most of it is yours to do with as you wish. You may feel out of control and that you must run to keep up with the conflicting demands and expectations of your life. But we all have the same number of hours in each day. The key is in how we spend them. The following tips are designed to help you spend your time wisely and to keep you in control of your life.

- Prepare a list of your goals and the tasks necessary to accomplish them. This could be by day, week, month, semester, or year. You may also want to break the list into sections, such as friends and family, school, work, sports, health and fitness, home, personal development, and college preparation.
- Prioritize based on time-sensitive deadlines.
- Use a grading system to code how important each task is. A is "Do It Now," B is "Do It Soon," C is "Do It Later." Understand the difference between "important" and "urgent."
- Be realistic about how much you can really do. Analyze how you spend your time now. What can you cut out? How much time do you truly have for each task?
- Think ahead. How many times have you underestimated how long it will take to do something? Plan for roadblocks and give yourself some breathing space.
- Accept responsibility. Once you decide to do something, commit yourself to it. That doesn't mean that a task that was on the "A" list can't be moved to the "C" list. But be consistent and specific about what you want to accomplish.
- Divide and conquer. You may need to form a committee, delegate tasks to your parents, or ask for help from a friend. That is why it is called time management.
- Take advantage of your personal prime time. Don't schedule yourself to get up and do homework at 6 a.m. if you are a night owl. It won't work. Instead, plan complex tasks when you are most efficient.
- Avoid procrastination. There are a million ways to procrastinate. And not one of them is a good reason if you really want to get something done. Have you ever noticed that you always find time to do the things you enjoy?

Prioritizing Chart

This chart can be used to help manage your time. Fill in your goals in each of the time-commitment areas. Prioritize the goals and put time deadlines on each. Then transfer the deadlines to your date book. Each week, look ahead in your date book to see what is coming up so that you are not surprised as an important deadline approaches. Periodically, review your goals and update them as needed.

Time Commitments	Goals	Tasks	Priority (A/B/C)	Due Dates	Time Needed	Start Date
Friends and Family	1	1	1	1	1	1
	2	2	2	2	2	2
	3	3	3	3	3	3
	4	4	4	4	4	4
School	1	1	1	1	1	1
	2	2	2	2	2	2
	3	3	3	3	3	3
	4	4	4	4	4	4
Sports	1	1	1	1	1	1
	2	2	2	2	2	2
	3	3	3	3	3	3
	4	4	4	4	4	4
Health and Fitness	1	1	1	1	1	1
	2	2	2	2	2	2
	3	3	3	3	3	3
	4	4	4	4	4	4
Home	1	1	1	1	1	1
	2	2	2	2	2	2
	3	3	3	3	3	3
	4	4	4	4	4	4
Work	1	1	1	1	1	1
	2	2	2	2	2	2
	3	3	3	3	3	3
	4	4	4	4	4	4
Personal Development	1	1	1	1	1	1
	2	2	2	2	2	2
	3	3	3	3	3	3
	4	4	4	4	4	4
College Preparation	1	1	1	1	1	1
	2	2	2	2	2	2
	3	3	3	3	3	3
	4	4	4	4	4	4

Sources: You Can Find More Time For Yourself Every Day, Time Power, Time Management For Dummies, Manage Your Time, Your Work, Yourself.

- Do the most unpleasant task first. Get it over with. Then it will be all downhill from there.
- Don't over prepare. That is just another way to procrastinate.
- Learn to say no to the demands on your time that you cannot afford.
- Be enthusiastic and share your goals with others.

Goals are the building blocks of better time utilization

If you set too many goals at once, you will overwhelm yourself from the start. Remember, what is important is the quality of the time you spend, not the quantity. It doesn't make any difference if you study for 10 hours if you don't study efficiently. The overall goal is to be productive, efficient, and effective, not just busy. You'll also need to pace yourself. All work and no play makes for an unbalanced person.

Utilize all the benefits of modern technology to help you manage time. You can save lots of time by using a fax, e-mail, or voice mail. If you don't already use a day planner or calendar, you would be wise to invest in one. Write in all the important deadlines and refer to it often. Block out commitments you know you have so you won't over schedule yourself. When you do over schedule yourself or underestimate the time it takes to accomplish a task, learn from your mistakes. But don't get too down on yourself. Give yourself a pep talk every now and then to keep yourself positive and motivated.

Here's What Students Have to Say

The following quotes are from students who attend a college that offers services for learning disabled students.

"I have delayed development. I need help getting things done. I need extra time for tests. As long as I'm able to go up to teachers and ask questions, I do well on tests." —**Anita**

"I have dyslexia. I thought the term 'disabilities services' was for people with visual and hearing impairments. When I got here, I found it covered a variety of disabilities. It was like Christmas. You got everything you wanted and more." —**Debra**

"I was always afraid I wouldn't be able to hear what [teachers] said. It's hard to read lips and listen at the same time. With note takers, I still get what I need even if the teacher moves around. They want you to make it through." —**Jeannette**

Students with Disabilities

Current estimates indicate that more than 49 million American citizens have been identified as having disabilities. With increased public awareness of the laws requiring access to every facet of community life, there has been an apparent rise in the number of students identified as having disabilities. Often those students enter early intervention programs as infants or toddlers. Elementary and secondary programs for some disabilities continue through age 21.

Legal rights of students with disabilities

Section 504 of the Rehabilitation Act of 1973 states that "no otherwise qualified individual . . . shall, solely by reason of . . . handicap, be excluded from participation in, be denied the benefits of, or be subject to discrimination under any program or activity receiving federal financial assistance."

Passage of that legislation mandated that colleges and universities receiving federal financial assistance could not discriminate in the recruitment, admission, or treatment of students.

In 1990, the Americans with Disabilities Act (ADA) extended and made more specific the rights and antidiscrimination legislation provided by Section 504. The ADA requires educational institutions at all levels, public and private, to provide equal access to programs, services, and facilities. Schools must be accessible to students, as well as to employees and the public, regardless of any disability. To ensure such accessibility, they must follow specific requirements for new construction, alterations or renovations, academic programs, and institutional policies, practices, and procedures.

Students with specific disabilities have the right to request and expect accommodations, including auxiliary aids and services, that enable them to participate in and benefit from all programs and activities offered by or related to the school.

To comply with ADA requirements, many high schools and universities offer programs and information to answer questions for students with disabilities and to assist them both in selecting appropriate colleges and in attaining full inclusion once they enter college. And most colleges and universities have disabilities services offices to help students negotiate the system.

What is a disability?

A person is considered to have a disability if he or she meets at least one of three conditions. The individual must:

- have a documented physical or mental impairment that substantially limits one or more major life activities, such as personal self-care, walking, seeing, hearing, speaking, breathing, learning, working, or performing manual tasks;
- have a record of such an impairment; or
- be perceived as having such an impairment.

Physical disabilities include impairments of speech, vision, hearing, and mobility. Other disabilities, while less obvious, are similarly limiting; they include diabetes, asthma, multiple sclerosis, heart disease, cancer, mental illness, mental retardation, cerebral palsy, and learning disabilities.

Learning disabilities refer to an array of biological conditions that impede a person's ability to process and disseminate information. A learning disability is commonly recognized as a significant deficiency in one or more of the following areas: oral expression, listening comprehension, written expression, basic reading skills, reading comprehension, mathematical calculation, or problem solving. Individuals with learning disabilities also may have difficulty with sustained attention, time management, or social skills.

According to a 1994 study by the Health Resource Center of the American Council on Education, 3 percent of the nation's 1.5 million full-time college freshmen identified themselves as having a learning disability.

Auxiliary aids and services

The ADA requires educational institutions to provide auxiliary aids and services to ensure that no individual is excluded or denied access to a program. Auxiliary aids and services encompass a wide range of devices and assistance, including acquisition or modification of equipment, devices, or action. Examples include but are not limited to the following items for specific disabilities:

Deaf/hard of hearing:
- qualified interpreter
- note takers
- computer-aided transcription services (real-time captioning)
- written materials
- telephone handset amplifiers
- assistive listening devices and systems
- telephones compatible with hearing aids
- closed-caption decoders
- open and closed captioning
- telecommunication devices for deaf persons (TDDs/TTYs)
- videotext displays

The ADA slightly revised the definition of a "qualified interpreter" as one who is able to interpret effectively, accurately, and impartially both receptively and expressively, using any necessary specialized language. A qualified interpreter does not need to be a certified interpreter, and a certified interpreter may or may not be qualified in a given circumstance. The definition applies on a case-by-case basis.

Blind/visually impaired:
- qualified readers
- taped texts
- audio recordings
- Braille materials
- large print
- tactile and high-contrast signage or documents

Architectural barrier removal, especially for those with physical impairments, is also required and may include items such as:
- ramps
- curb cuts of sidewalks or entrances
- repositioning or rearranging of furniture or equipment
- installation of visual and auditory alarms
- renovation or construction of restrooms for accessibility (grab bars, widened stalls, raised toilet seats, lowered urinals, insulated pipes, lever handles, etc.)

Schools must provide what is adequate for inclusion at all levels, though the aids or services do not necessarily have to be the most expensive or complex.

Many of the auxiliary aids and services listed are actually assistive technology (AT). An AT device is any item, piece of equipment, or product system, whether acquired off-the-shelf, modified, or customized, that is used to increase, maintain, or improve functional capabilities of an individual with a disability. An AT service is any service that directly assists an individual with a disability in the selection, acquisition, or use of an assistive technology device.

The ADA opens doors for inclusion and educational success. Assistive technology devices and services are enablers that help you function once you get inside the door.

Special services for students with learning disabilities

Some students with learning disabilities need only to connect with instructors who will afford them extra attention or extra time for assignments. Others need additional services, which may include tutoring, alternative test arrangements, note-taking, taped textbooks, basic skills remediation, diagnostic testing, priority registration, and advocates. Services change and are added regularly, so check with the school(s) that you are interested in to see if special services are offered.

Tips for Students with Disabilities

- Document your disability with letters from your physician(s), therapist, case manager, school psychologist, and other service providers.
- Get letters of support from teachers, family, friends, and service providers that detail how you have learned to work despite your disability.
- Learn the federal laws that apply to students with disabilities.
- Research support groups for peer information and advocacy.
- Visit several campuses.
- Determine the best point in the admissions process at which to identify yourself as having a disability.
- Look into the services available, the pace of campus life, and the college's expectations for students with disabilities.
- Ask about orientation programs, including specialized introductions for or about students with disabilities.
- Ask about flexible, individualized study plans.
- Ask if the school offers technology such as voice synthesizers, voice recognition, and/or visual learning equipment.
- Ask about adapted intramural/social activities.
- Ask to talk with other students who have similar disabilities to hear about their experiences on campus.
- Once you select a college, get a map of the campus and learn the entire layout.
- If you have a physical disability, make sure the buildings you need to be in most are accessible to you. Some, even though they comply with the ADA, aren't as accessible as others.
- Be realistic. If you use a wheelchair, for example, a school with an exceptionally hilly campus may not be your best choice, no matter what other accommodations it has.

Comprehensive programs for students with learning disabilities

A comprehensive program is one that is especially designed for students with learning disabilities. Often special admissions procedures must be followed for students to be admitted to colleges with these programs.

Such a program may be more than some students need, however. Services change from year to year, and even from semester to semester, so be sure to check with schools to see what they provide. You may also want to check the following Internet address for a listing of almost every national organization associated with learning disabilities: http://www.tiac.net/users/poorrich/nationalorgs.html.

Directory for students with disabilities

The following resources can provide assistance to students, families, and schools regarding legal requirements for accommodations for the rights of students with disabilities. They can also link you with other groups and individuals knowledgeable in students' rights and the process of transition into postsecondary education.

Also, there are special interest, education, support, and advocacy organizations for persons with particular disabilities. Check with your guidance counselor or contact one of the following organizations for further information.

Association on Higher Education and Disability (AHEAD)
P.O. Box 21192
Columbus, Ohio 43221-0192
614-488-4972
Fax: 614-488-1174
http://www.ahead.org/

Attention Deficit Disorder Association (ADDA)
P.O. Box 972
West Newbury, Massachusetts 01985
800-487-2282 (toll-free)
http://www.add.org/

Attention Deficit Information Network, Inc. (AD-IN)
475 Hillside Avenue
Needham, Massachusetts 02194
617-455-0585 or 444-5466

Children and Adults with Attention Deficit Disorders (CHADD)
499 Northwest 70th Avenue
Suite 101
Plantation, Florida 33317
305-587-3700
800-233-4050 (toll-free)
Fax: 305-587-4599
http://www.chadd.org/

Council for Exceptional Children (CEC)
Division for Learning Disabilities (DLD)
1920 Association Drive
Reston, Virginia 22091-1589
703-620-3660
800-328-0272 (toll-free)
Fax: 703-264-9494
http://www.cec.sped.org/

Sample Letter Requesting Information

Student's street address
City, State Zip
Date

Name of College Contact
Name of College or University
Address
City, State Zip

Dear (Dr., Mr., or Ms.)
        (last name of contact):

I am a student with a learning disability (attention deficit disorder) and am completing my (junior or senior) year at (name of high school). I expect to graduate in (date) and then go on to college.

Please send me information about the assistance you offer to students with learning disabilities. Also send admission forms, a catalog, and any other specific information that you believe will be helpful to me.

Thank you for your assistance.

Sincerely,

Name of student

Sample Letter Requesting a Campus Visit

Student's street address
City, State Zip
Date

Name of College Contact
Name of College or University
Address
City, State Zip

Dear (Dr., Mr., or Ms.)
        (last name of contact):

I am a student with a learning disability (attention deficit disorder) who has been accepted to your college (university). To help me make a final decision about attending, I wish to visit your campus. During this visit I hope to talk to you regarding the assistance available to students with learning disabilities (attention deficit disorder). I also hope to see the campus and meet some of the students with learning disabilities (attention deficit disorder) who attend your college (university). If possible, would you please arrange a visit for me on any of the following dates: (list two or three available dates)?

I look forward to hearing from you and visiting your campus.

Sincerely,

Name of student

Council for Learning Disabilities (CLD)
P.O. Box 40303
Overland Park, Kansas 66204
913-492-8755
Fax: 913-492-2546
http://www1.winthrop.edu/cld/

HEATH Resource Center
National Clearinghouse on Postsecondary Education for
   Individuals with Disabilities
American Council on Education
One Dupont Circle, NW, Suite 800
Washington, D.C. 20036-1193
202-939-9322
800-544-3284 (toll-free)
Fax: 202-833-4760
http://ace-info-server.nche.edu/Programs/HEATH/

International Dyslexia Association
The Chester Building,
8600 LaSalle Road
Suite 382
Baltimore, Maryland 21286-2044
410-296-0232
800-222-3123 (toll-free)
Fax: 410-321-5069
http://www.interdys.org/

**Learning Disabilities Association of America, Inc.
   (LDA)**
4156 Library Road
Pittsburgh, Pennsylvania 15234-1349
412-341-1515
Fax: 412-344-0224
http://www.ldanatl.org/

Learning Disabilities Association of Canada (LDAC)
323 Chapel Street,
Ottawa, Ontario K1N 7Z2
613-238-5721
http://edu-ss10.educ.queensu.ca/lda/

Learning Disabilities Center
331 Milledge Hall
University of Georgia
Athens, Georgia 30602-5875
706 542-4589
Fax: 706 542-4532
http://www.coe.uga.edu/ldcenter/

Learning Disabilities Network
72 Sharp Street
Suite A-2
Hingham, Massachusetts 02043
617-340-5605
Fax: 617-340-5603

National Adult Literacy and Learning Disabilities Center (National ALLD Center)
Academy for Educational Development
1875 Connecticut Avenue, NW
Washington, D.C. 20009-1202
202-884-8185
800-953-2553 (toll-free)
Fax: 202-884-8422
http://www.nifl.gov/nalldtop.htm/

National Center for Law and Learning Disabilities (NCLLD)
P.O. Box 368
Cabin John, Maryland 20818
301-469-8308
Fax: 301-469-9466

National Center for Learning Disabilities (NCLD)
381 Park Avenue
Suite 1420
New York, New York 10016
212-545-7510
Fax: 212-545-9665
http://www.ncld.org/

National Information Center for Children and Youth with Disabilities (NICHCY)
P.O. Box 1492
Washington, D.C. 20013
202-884-8200
800-695-0285 (toll-free)
Fax: 202-884-8441
http://www.nichcy.org/

Ask Questions

All students should write a list of questions to take with them on college campus visits. Use the following list as a guide for writing your own:

1. Is the campus attractive?
2. Are the residence halls appealing?
3. Do I have a choice of meal plans?
4. Is there a good library?
5. What is the surrounding community like?
6. Can I keep a car on campus?
7. Is travel between college and home easy?
8. Are there good recreational facilities?
9. Is there a comprehensive student health center?
10. Overall, is this a place where I would like to spend my college days? Would I feel comfortable here?

Information about nonstandard testing arrangements for the ACT and SAT may be obtained from:

ACT Test Administration
P.O. Box 4028
Iowa City, Iowa 52243
319-337-1332
Fax: 319-339-3020

SAT Services for Students with Disabilities
College Board
P.O. Box 6226
Princeton, New Jersey 08541-6226
609-771-7137
Fax: 609-771-7681

Information about obtaining recorded textbooks may be obtained from:

Recording for the Blind & Dyslexic
20 Roszel Road
Princeton, New Jersey 08540
609-452-0606
Fax: 609-520-7990
http://www.rfbd.org/

Peterson's Colleges with Programs for Students with Learning Disabilities or Attention Deficit Disorders provides information on more than 1,000 programs.

A final word

If you have a disability, you will take the same steps to choose and apply to a college as other students, but you will also evaluate each college based on your special need(s). Get organized and meet with campus specialists to discuss your specific requirements. Then explore whether the programs, policies, procedures, and facilities meet your specific situation.

It is usually best to describe your disability in a letter attached to the application so the proper fit can be made between you and the school. You may even want to have your psychoeducational evaluation and testing record sent to the school. Some colleges help with schedules and offer transition courses, reduced course loads, extra access to professors, and special study areas to help address your needs.

Remember, admission to college is a realistic goal for any motivated student. If you invest the time and effort, you can make it happen.

Community Service

You can try different careers, gain valuable skills and experience, and help others by getting involved in community service. However, you can't meet the community's needs and contribute to the American tradition of community service if you don't know where community service opportunities exist.

No matter what your area of interest, there are unlimited ways for students to serve their community. Assess your areas of interest and then apply that interest to the lives of others. For instance, if you love to read, volunteer at the library or Literacy Council. If you have an interest in animals, you might volunteer at the zoo or your local animal shelter.

Online Help

In today's technological world it is not surprising to find that a lot of college selection material, scholarship information, and student information is now available on line or on CD-ROM. While this list is not comprehensive, it will lead you to some of the high-tech resources available to students today.

World Wide Web sites

CollegeView
CollegeView is a database that contains information on 3,368 colleges and universities. Some colleges on the database have multimedia presentations, accept electronic requests for information, and accept electronic applications. CollegeView can be found in some high school guidance offices, or you can find it on the Internet at http://www.collegeview.com:80/search/search.

Peterson's Education Center
Peterson's publications offer some of the most comprehensive information available to students about all aspects of preparation for higher education. Now Petersons.com brings this information together at one central address, offering consistently organized information about educational opportunities at all levels. Hundreds of private schools, camps, study-abroad programs, colleges, universities, and employers have their own sites in Petersons.com, which permits each to develop a full array of information and communication tools. A searchable database leads Webusers to applicable institutional sites, where they will find an overview of the institution. Features and functions include online view books and campus tours, applications, and "instant inquiry" e-mail queries. Visit Peterson's Education Center, the most comprehensive education resource on the Web, at http://www.petersons.com.

CollegeQuest
One of the most comprehensive Web resources for college-bound students can be found at CollegeQuest.com. CollegeQuest provides information and tools that will help you prepare, search, apply, and pay for college. If you are preparing for the SAT or ACT, you will find test dates, valuable test-taking tips, and full-length practice tests that you can download for free. You can search through Peterson's complete college database to find the colleges that best fit your needs and then view in-depth profiles or do a side-by-side comparison of selected colleges. The site will keep you on track with a personal organizer and college calendar that provides general reminders, test dates, and key dates for every college that you add to your personal list. The financial aid section provides a complete overview of how financial aid works, a free scholarship search using Peterson's database of more than 800,000 awards, and an EFC estimator that will help your family calculate how much you will be expected to contribute

Peterson's © 1999

toward the cost of college. Once you are ready to apply, you can use CollegeQuest eApply to fill out one application that is accepted at more than 1,200 colleges. All of these tools are supplemented with informative articles throughout each section as well as an Expert Forum, where admissions and financial aid experts are available to answer your questions. http://www.collegequest.com.

College Board Online

Gives advice on how to prepare and pay for college. You can also order resource materials to help you with the AP and SAT. Find all this and more at http://www.college-board.org.

ETS Net

This site is brought to you by the Educational Testing Service, the folks who prepare the SAT. Order materials to study for the tests and subscribe to an online magazine by and for high school students. Surf to http://www.ets.org/.

The Free Application for Federal Student Aid

This document can be downloaded from the U.S. Department of Education's World Wide Web page and filed electronically. The address is http://www.ed.gov/offices/OPE/express.html.

The National Association for College Admission Counseling

This home page offers information for professionals, students, and parents. The Internet address is http://www.NACAC.com/.

U.S. Department of Education

The department's National Center for Education Statistics produces reports on every level of education, from elementary to postgraduate. Dozens are available for downloading. Hook up with these and other links at http://www.ed.gov.

The Education Resource Institute (TERI)

TERI is a private, not-for-profit organization that was founded to help middle-income Americans afford a college education. One impressive feature of the site is a database describing more than 150 programs that aim to increase college attendance from underrepresented groups. (The target population includes students from low-income families and those who are the first in their family to pursue postsecondary education.) The Web site provides a wealth of helpful material, including background information, student handouts, and activities. Visit TERI's Web site at http://www.teri.org.

Visit Peterson's http://collegequest.com

CollegeQuest — FIND YOUR COLLEGE. FIND YOURSELF.℠

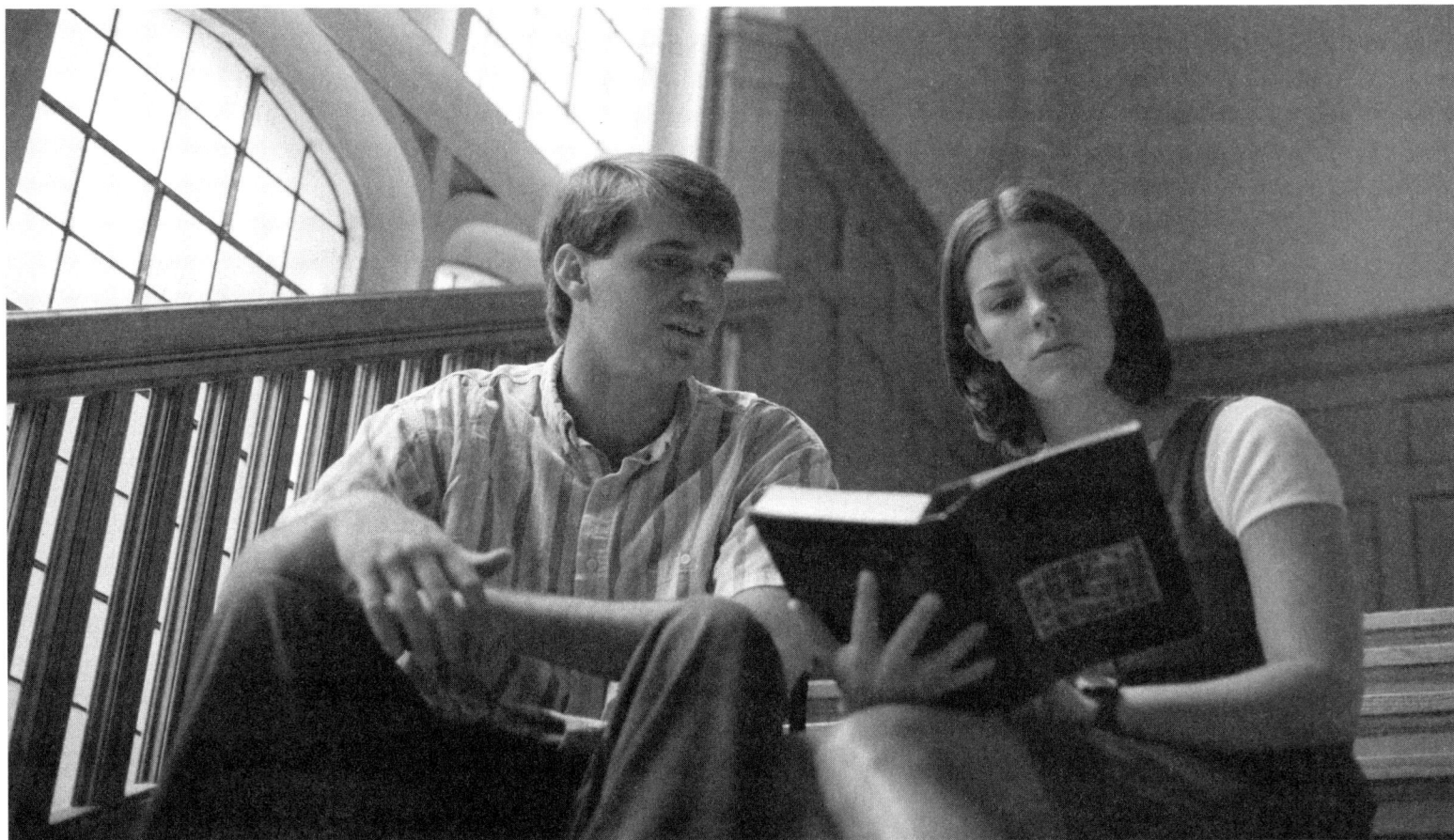

Guidance Counselor Tips

"Find a good match. Visit schools when students are in class. Walk the campus, eat in the cafeteria, visit the student union, and look at the other students. Be sure you feel comfortable."

—Henry Winkler, Guidance Counselor, Overbrook High School, Philadelphia, Pennsylvania

"I like to stress to my students that this is an exciting time in their lives. The choices they are about to make should not be taken lightly. Regardless of their past history they can still do or become whatever they set their sights on. You can't change your past, so learn from it: take control of your future—it belongs to you!"

—Dan Shay, Counselor, Princeton High School, Cincinnati, Ohio

"If there is a school you have always wanted to go to but fear that you don't fit the profile, GO FOR IT! You might be just the person they are looking for. If you apply, all that can happen is you may not get in. It would feel worse to be forty years old and wonder whether or not you would have been accepted to that school had you tried."

—Lynn Caldwell, Highland Park ISD, Highland Park, Texas

Minority Students

In an effort to diversify views and experiences, to respond to the social and economic disadvantages of certain groups of Americans, and to reflect the globalization of our economy and communications network, recruitment of special groups is a task that all schools take seriously. In fact, most colleges have at least one member of the admissions staff who specializes in the recruitment of minorities.

African-American students often opt to attend a historically black college or university. According to *U.S. News & World Report*, enrollment in the nation's 103 historically black colleges or universities grew 31 percent between 1984 and 1993. Overall, some 230,000 of the 1.4 million blacks now seeking college degrees attend these schools, where up to 40 percent of students are the first in their families to attend college.

According to the Hispanic Market Report, the Hispanic population in the U.S. is growing at an unprecedented rate—by the year 2000, Hispanics will comprise 11 percent of the total population. Reflecting this growth, between 1991 and 1995, the number of Hispanic undergraduates at U.S. colleges and universities increased by 25.8 percent.

Minority students should check with the colleges and universities they are interested in to connect with minority affairs offices and student groups.

Academic and financial resources for minority students

In addition to churches, sororities and fraternities, and college minority affairs offices, minority students can receive information and assistance from the following organizations:

ASPIRA of America, Inc.
1444 I Street, NW, Suite 800
Washington, DC 20005
202-835-3600

ASPIRA is an association of community-based organizations providing leadership, development, and educational services to Latino youths.

INROADS
2501 South Congress
Austin, Texas 78704
512-442-3998
Fax: 512-442-3983

INROADS is a national career development organization that places and develops talented minority students (African American, Hispanic American, and Native American) in business and industry. INROADS also has offices in Dallas and Houston.

National Action Council for Minorities in Engineering (NACME)
3 West Thirty-fifth Street
New York, New York 10001
212-279-2626

NACME aims to increase the number of minorities who earn bachelor's degrees in engineering by offering an Incentive Grants Program, Summer Engineering Employment Project, field services, and publications for parents and students.

National Association for the Advancement of Colored People (NAACP)
4805 Mt. Hope Drive
Baltimore, Maryland 21205
410-358-8900

The purpose of the NAACP is to improve the political, educational, social, and economic status of minority groups; to eliminate racial prejudice; to keep the public aware of the adverse effects of racial discrimination; and to take lawful action to secure its elimination, consistent with the efforts of the national organization. Contact your local branch of the NAACP to find out more about the resources available through this organization.

National Scholarship Service and Fund for Negro Students (NSSFNS)
250 Auburn Avenue, NE
Suite 500
Atlanta, Georgia 30314
404-577-3990

NSSFNS acts as a clearinghouse for financial aid and provides tutorial services and educational, career, and financial aid counseling for African-American students.

Urban Leagues

The Education and Youth Services Department of the Urban League provides services for African Americans and economically disadvantaged people. These services include basic academic development, GED test preparation for youths and adults, after-school tutoring for children, parent training classes, scholarships, an annual tour of historically black colleges and universities, and summer

employment for youths. For further information, call the Urban League in these cities: Austin, Dallas, and Houston.

United Negro College Fund (UNCF)
9401 LBJ Freeway, Suite 401
Dallas, Texas 75243
972-234-1007
Fax: 972-234-8605

The United Negro College Fund provides scholarships for undergraduates who attend one of forty private, historically black colleges. Students must be accepted first and then nominated by the college's financial aid director. Programs and services include summer learning programs, internships, precollege and mentoring programs, and international programs.

Scholarships

The following is just a sample of the many scholarships available to minority students.

NAACP Agnes Jones Jackson Scholarship
Students with 2.5 GPA or better.
Undergraduates, $1,500; graduate students, $2,500.
Call 410-358-8900.

Roy Wilkins Scholarships
$1,000
Call 410-358-8900.

College Access Programs

The National College Access Network (NCAN) is a nationwide federation of college access programs. All participating member organizations have a common goal—to help students from low-income backgrounds go to college. Students are guided through each step of the process: making the decision to pursue postsecondary education; designing an appropriate high school curriculum; researching schools; filling out applications; and ultimately enrolling in a two- or four-year college. State programs share two fundamental characteristics: each offers students school-based advising and awards "last-dollar" scholarships that close the gap between regular financial aid and the real cost of attending college.

For information on the programs available in your state, talk to your guidance counselor or order a directory of state offices by calling 410-244-7218.

Sutton Education Scholarships
Undergraduates, $1,000; graduate students, $2,000.
Call 410-358-8900.

Financial Need Culturally Disadvantaged Scholarship
National Scholars Foundation (NSF)
Undergraduate and graduate students, minimum 2.3 GPA. Awards range from $250 to $3,000.
Write to the NSF, P.O. Box 2534, Lafayette, LA 70502-2534.

Jackie Robinson Foundation Scholarship, Jackie Robinson Foundation
For minority students accepted to a four-year college and with demonstrated academic achievement and financial need. Award up to $5,000.
Call 212-290-8600.

Online resources

Historically Black Colleges and Universities
    http://www.acq.osd.mil/ddre/edugate/hbcumi.html

Minority Scholarships and Fellowships
http://Web.fie.com/htbin/cashe.pl

Minority On-Line Information Service (MOLIS)
    his federal information exchange site contains information on minority institutions as well as a minority scholarship database.

United Negro College Fund
    http://www.bin.com/assocorg/uncf/uncf.html

Other resources

The Big Book of Minority Opportunities
Garrett Park Press
P.O. Box 190A
Garrett Park, Maryland 20896.

Financial Aid for Minority Students
Garrett Park Press
P.O. Box 190A
Garrett Park, Maryland 20896

The Minority Guide to Scholarships and Financial Aid
Tinsley Communications, Inc.
100 Bridge Street, Suite A-3
Hampton, Virginia 23669

Summer Opportunities for Students

There's the kind of summer when you get bored a few weeks after school lets out. When you've listened to all of your CDs, aced all of your video games, watched one too many soaps, hung out at the same old mall. But summer doesn't have to be this way. You could windsurf on a cool, clear New England lake. Perfect your backhand or golf swing. Horseback ride along breathtaking mountain trails. Parlez français in Paris. Trek through spectacular canyon lands or live with a family in Costa Rica, Spain, Switzerland, or Japan. Get a jump on next year's classes. Explore college majors or maybe even careers. Help out on an archeological dig or community-service project. And along the way, meet some wonderful people, maybe even make a couple of lifelong friends.

Interested? Get ready to pack your bags and join the 5 million kids and teens who'll be having the summer of a lifetime at thousands of terrific camps, academic programs, sports clinics, arts workshops, internships, volunteer opportunities, and travel adventures throughout North America and abroad. Don't have a lump-sum inheritance? Not to worry. There are programs to meet every budget, from $50 workshops to $4,500 world treks, with sessions varying in length from a couple of days to a couple of months.

Abilene Christian University–Kadesh Life Camp/Learning to Lead/MPulse

Abilene Christian University
Box 29004
Abilene, Texas 79699-9004
General Information
Coed residential Bible camp.
Contact
Jan Meyer, Director of Leadership Camps, ACU Box 29004, 127 McKinzie Hall, Abilene, Texas 79699-9004.

American Computer Experience-Summer Computer Camp–Rice University/Southern Methodist University/University of Texas

American Computer Experience
Dallas/Houston, Texas
General Information
Coed day academic program.
Contact
American Computer Experience, PO Box 15367, Atlanta, Georgia 30333.

Arts on the Lake

Saint Stephen's Episcopal School
PO Box 1868
Austin, Texas 78767
General Information
Coed residential and day arts program established in 1996.
Contact
Elizabeth Hansing, Director, main address above.

A.S.C. Kicking Camp at St. Edward's University

A.S.C. Football Camps, L.L.C.
St. Edward's University
Austin, Texas 78704
General Information
Boys' residential and day sports camp established in 1986.
Contact
Howard Berman, Director, 28 Oxbow Lane, Basking Ridge, New Jersey 07920.

Austin Nature and Science Center

301 Nature Center Drive
Austin, Texas 78746
General Information
Coed day academic program and wilderness program.
Contact
Rachel Moyer-Trimyer, Public Programs Coordinator, main address above.

Camp Invention–Texas

Inventure Place, The National Inventor's Hall of Fame
General Information
Coed day academic program established in 1990.
Contact
Reservationist, 221 South Broadway, Akron, Ohio 44308-1505.

Camp Val Verde

Tejas Council of Camp Fire, Inc.
1007 Camp Road
McGregor, Texas 76657

General Information
Coed residential outdoor program and traditional camp established in 1948.
Contact
Pat McKee, Executive Director, 1826 Morrow, Waco, Texas 76707.

Hockaday Coed Summer Session

The Hockaday School
11600 Welch Road
PO Box 29900
Dallas, Texas 75229
General Information
Girls' residential academic program, arts program, and sports camp established in 1986.
Contact
Claudia Todd, Director of Summer Programs, main address above.

Junior Statesmen Summer School–University of Texas at Austin

Junior Statesmen Foundation
University of Texas at Austin
Austin, Texas 78712
General Information
Coed residential academic program established in 1991.
Contact
Ms. Karen Prosser, Program Director, 60 East Third Avenue, Suite 320, San Mateo, California 94401.

Marine Military Academy Summer Military Training Camp

Marine Military Academy
320 Iwo Jima Boulevard

Harlingen, Texas 78550
General Information
Boys' residential academic program
established in 1977.
Contact
Tee Recore, Recruiting, main address
above.

Outward Bound–Texas
Outward Bound, USA
Big Bend Area
El Paso, Texas
General Information
Community service program, outdoor
program, and wilderness program
established in 1964.
Contact
Voyageur Outward Bound School, 111
3rd Avenue, South, Minneapolis,
Minnesota 55401-2551.

Parent/Youth Golf School
The Academy of Golf Dynamics
45 Club Estates Parkway
Austin, Texas 78738
General Information
Coed day family program and sports camp.
Contact
Kevin Hunt or Bill Moretti, main address
above.

Professional Kicking Services, Inc.–Texas
Professional Kicking Services, Inc.
General Information
Coed residential sports camp established
in 1979.
Contact
Fran Cumpton, Registrar, PO Box 2747,
Sparks, Nevada 89432.

Sea Camp
Texas A&M University at Galveston
PO Box 1675
Galveston, Texas 77553
General Information
Coed residential academic program
established in 1986.
Contact
Sylvia Turrubiate, Registrar, main address
above.

SMU–College Experience
Southern Methodist University
PO Box 750383
Dallas, Texas 75275
General Information
Coed residential academic program
established in 1978.
Contact
Dr. Kathy Hargrove, Director of Pre-
College Programs, main address above.

Summer Super Start
College of the Mainland
1200 Amburn Road
Texas City, Texas 77591
General Information
Coed day academic program established
in 1987.
Contact
Jess Olive, Summer Super Start
Coordinator, main address above.

SWT Summer Creative Writing Camp
Southwest Texas State University
Department of English
San Marcos, Texas 78666
General Information
Arts program and academic program
established in 1988.
Contact
Steve Wilson, Director, main address above.

TAG (Talented and Gifted)
Southern Methodist University
PO Box 750383
Dallas, Texas 75275
General Information
Coed residential academic program
established in 1978.
Contact
Dr. Kathy Hargrove, Director of Pre-
College Programs, main address above.

Upward Bound–Summer Science and Mathematics Program for High School Students
Wiley College
Marshall, Texas 75670
General Information
Coed residential academic program
established in 1992.
Contact
Leonard Wilmer, Program Director, main
address above.

Weather Camp
Weather Research Center
3227 Audley Street
Houston, Texas 77098
General Information
Coed day academic program established
in 1993.
Contact
Ms. Dorri Breher, Meteorologist/Program
Coordinator, main address above.

Westinghouse Talent Search Research and Science Fair Preparation (Science and Math)–Texas
International Education Center
General Information
Coed residential academic program
established in 1993.
Contact
Jack Scheckner, Director, PO Box 4400,
Flushing, New York 11356.

Picking the Ideal Summer Program

It's important to look beyond the location, facilities, and activities when choosing a summer camp. Both you and your parents will want to look at possible programs carefully—though your concerns and considerations may differ. Here are some guidelines to help your family through the search process, along with a few sample questions.

Talk to the people who run the camp

- How is the day structured?
- Can counselors articulate the program's underlying philosophy?
- What happens when rules are violated?

Scrutinize the staff

- What are the maturity and experience levels of the counselors?
- Does the staff have a high turnover rate?
- How are counselors trained?

Talk to parents and campers

- Were their expectations met?
- What did they like about the program?
- What didn't they like about the program?

Visit the camp while it's in session

- Look around; what do you see happening?
- Are you comfortable in that kind of environment?
- Does the program fit your interests?

Examine what you want to get out of the experience

- Do you like and trust the people who run the program?
- Why do you want to participate; what do you hope to learn?
- Can you picture yourself being in the program and having a good time?

Endless Summer Fun

Classic Camping
You can find camps in some of America's most spectacular natural settings—from the rugged Atlantic coastline of Maine to the Blue Ridge Mountains of North Carolina to the canyons and the temperate rain forests of the Pacific Northwest.

Summer on Campus
When you're studying under the shady trees of a prep school or college campus, attending small classes, getting individual attention in the company of kids from different parts of the country or around the world, learning takes on a new meaning.

Extra Credit?
Why not take advantage of the rich curricula many private schools and college programs offer by tackling a course? Looking ahead, you may want to get a preview of what college life will be like.

For the Sports Fan
There's a camp for just about every sport imaginable. There are camps for baseball, basketball, figure skating, golf, gymnastics, hockey, horseback riding, sailing, soccer, tennis, volleyball, and wrestling—to name just a few!

Feeling Adventurous?
Why just sit there when you can hike, bike, sail, paddle, or climb your way through summer. There are adventure programs that will take you trekking through mountain wilderness, down white-water rapids, and over rugged canyons.

Career Interests
Summer may also be a great time to check out some possible career paths before you have to start thinking about choosing colleges or majors. Look for paid or unpaid internships in a field that interests you.

International Experiences and Opportunities Abroad
If languages are your focus, a world of choices awaits. You can sharpen Spanish skills in Mexico City or Barcelona, learn Japanese in Tokyo, and study French in Geneva or Paris.

CHAPTER 5

Life after HIGH SCHOOL

College Is Not a Career

Some students spend a few years working before going to college. Others begin their career with a high school diploma, a vocational certificate, or up to two years of education or training after high school. Listed below are some general areas where opportunities exist. Put a check next to or circle the careers that interest you and then talk to your guidance counselor, teacher, librarian, or career counselor for more information.

Education and Related Services

High School/Vocational
Nursery School Attendant
Teacher Aide

Social and Government

High School/Vocational
Corrections Officer
Police Officer
Security Guard
Store Detective

Up to two years beyond high school
Detective (police)
Hazardous Waste Technician
Recreation Leader

Personal/Customer Services

High School/Vocational
Barber
Bartender
Beautician
Child-care Worker
Counter Attendant
Dining Room Attendant
Electrologist
Flight Attendant
Host/Hostess
Houseparent
Manicurist
Parking Lot Attendant
Porter
Private Household Worker
Waiter/Waitress

Marketing and Sales

High School/Vocational
Auctioneer
Bill Collector
Driver (route)
Fashion Model
Product Demonstrator
Salesperson (general)
Sample Distributor

Up to two years beyond high school
Claims Adjuster
Insurance Worker
Manufacturer's Representative
Real Estate Agent

Sales Manager
Travel Agent
Travel Guide

Management and Planning

High School/Vocational
Administrative Assistant
Food Service Supervisor
Postmaster
Service Station Manager

Up to two years beyond high school
Benefits Manager
Building Manager
Caterer
Contractor
Credit Manager
Customer Service Coordinator
Employment Interviewer
Executive Housekeeper
Funeral Director
Hotel/Motel Manager
Importer/Exporter
Insurance Manager
Manager (small business)
Office Manager
Personnel Manager
Restaurant/Bar Manager
Store Manager
Supermarket Manager

Records and Communications

High School/Vocational
Billing Clerk
Clerk (general)
File Clerk
Foreign Trade Clerk
Hotel Clerk
Meter Reader
Postal Clerk
Receptionist
Stenographer

Up to two years beyond high school
Court Reporter
Legal Secretary
Library Assistant
Library Technician
Medical Records Technician
Medical Secretary
Personnel Assistant
Secretary
Travel Clerk

Financial Transactions

High School/Vocational
Accounting Clerk
Bank Teller
Cashier
Check-out Clerk
Payroll Clerk
Reservations Agent
Travel Agent

Up to two years beyond high school
Bookkeeper
Loan Officer

Storage and Dispatching

High School/Vocational
Dispatcher
Mail Carrier
Railroad Conductor
Shipping/Receiving Clerk
Stock Clerk
Tool Crib Attendant
Warehouse Worker

Up to two years beyond high school
Warehouse Supervisor

Business Machine/Computer Operation

High School/Vocational
Data Entry
Key Punch Operator
Office Machine Operator
Statistical Clerk
Telephone Operator
Typist

Up to two years beyond high school
Computer Operator
Computer Printer Operator
Motion Picture Projectionist
Word Processing Machine Operator

Vehicle Operation and Repair

High School/Vocational
Automotive Painter
Bus Driver
Chauffeur
Diesel Mechanic
Farm Equipment Mechanic
Fork Lift Operator
Heavy Equipment Mechanic
Locomotive Engineer
Railroad Braker
Refuse Collector
Service Station Attendant
Taxicab Driver
Truck Driver

Up to two years beyond high school
Aircraft Mechanic
Airplane Pilot
Auto Body Repairer
Automotive Mechanic
Garage Supervisor
Motorcycle Mechanic

Construction and Maintenance

High School/Vocational
Bricklayer
Construction Laborer
Drywall Installer
Elevator Mechanic
Floor Covering Installer
Glazier
Heavy Equipment Operator
Janitor
Maintenance Mechanic

Up to two years beyond high school
Building Inspector
Carpenter
Cement Mason
Electrician (construction)
Electrician (maintenance)
Insulation Worker
Lather
Painter (construction)
Paper Hanger
Pipefitter
Plasterer
Plumber
Roofer
Sheet Metal Worker
Stone Cutter

Structural Steel Worker
Tile Setter

Agriculture and Natural Resources

High School/Vocational
Fisher
Groundskeeper
Horticulture Worker
Logger
Pest Controller

Up to two years beyond high school
Fish and Game Warden
Forestry Technician
Tree Surgeon

Crafts and Related Services

High School/Vocational
Baker
Blacksmith
Butcher
Cook/Chef
Furniture Upholsterer
Housekeeper (hotel)
Kitchen Helper
Tailor/Dressmaker

Up to two years beyond high school
Drycleaner
Jeweler
Locksmith
Musical Instrument Repairer
Shoe Repairer
Watch Repairer

Home/Business Equipment Repair

High School/Vocational
Air-Conditioning/Refrigeration/
    Heating Mechanic
Appliance Servicer
Coin Machine Mechanic

Up to two years beyond high school
Communications Equipment
    Mechanic
Line Installer/Splicer
Office Machine Servicer
Radio/TV Repairer
Telephone Installer

Industrial Equipment Operations and Repair

High School/Vocational
Assembler
Blaster
Boilermaker
Coal Equipment Operator
Compressor House Operator
Crater
Dock Worker
Forging Press Operator
Furnace Operator
Heat Treater
Machine Tool Operator
Material Handler
Miner
Sailor
Sewing Machine Operator

Up to two years beyond high school
Bookbinder
Compositor/Typesetter
Electronic Equipment Repairer
Electroplater
Firefighter
Instrument Mechanic
Job and Die Setter
Lithographer
Machine Repairer
Machinist
Millwright
Molder
Nuclear Reactor Operator
Patternmaker
Photoengraver
Power House Mechanic
Power Plant Operator
Printing Press Operator
Stationery Engineer
Tool and Die Maker
Water Plant Operator
Welder
Wire Drawer

Medical Specialties and Technologies

High School/Vocational
Dialysis Technician

Up to two years beyond high school
Dental Hygienist
Dental Laboratory Technician
EEG Technologist
EKG Technician
Emergency Medical Technician
Medical Laboratory Technician
Medical Technologist
Nuclear Medicine Technologist
Operating Room Technician
Optician
Radiation Therapy Technologist
Radiologic Technologist
Respiratory Therapist
Sonographer

Engineering and Related Technologies

High School/Vocational
Biomedical Equipment Technician
Laser Technician

Up to two years beyond high school
Aerospace Engineer Technician
Avionics Technician
Broadcast Technician
Chemical Laboratory Technician
Civil Engineering Technician
Computer Programmer
Computer Service Technician
Drafter
Electronic Technician
Energy Conservation Technician
Industrial Engineering Technician
Laboratory Tester
Mechanical Engineering Technician
Metallurgical Technician
Pollution Control Technician
Quality Control Technician
Robot Technician
Surveyor (land)
Technical Illustrator
Test Engineer
Textile Technician
Tool Designer
Tool Programmer
Weather Observer

Applied Arts (visual)

High School/Vocational
Floral Arranger
Merchandise Displayer
Painter (artist)
Photographic Process Worker

Up to two years beyond high school
Cartoonist
Commercial Artist
Fashion Artist
Fashion Designer
Interior Decorator
Photographer/Camera Operator
Photograph Retoucher

Creative/Performing Arts

High School/Vocational
Singer
Stunt Performer

Up to two years beyond high school
Actor/Actress
Dancer/Choreographer
Musician
Writer/Author

Applied Arts (written and spoken)

High School/Vocational
Proofreader

Up to two years beyond high school
Advertising copywriter
Legal assistant

General Health Care

High School/Vocational
Dental Assistant
Medical Assistant
Nursing/Psychiatric Aide

Up to two years beyond high school
Dietetic Technician
Nurse (practical)
Nurse (registered)
Optometric Assistant
Physical Therapist's Assistant
Physician's Assistant
Recreation Therapist

The Armed Services

There are three paths that a high school student can take into the armed services—enlisted personnel, reserve officers' training, and officer candidate school—all of which provide opportunities for financial assistance for college. See Chapter 7, "Dollars and Cents," for more information about financing your education through the U.S. Armed Forces.

Enlisted personnel

All five branches of the armed services offer college-credit courses on base. Enlisted personnel can also take college courses at civilian colleges while on active duty.

Officer training

More than 40,000 college students participate in Reserve Officers' Training Corps (ROTC). Some students participate to receive ROTC scholarships. However, even those students who participate without scholarships learn the following skills that prepare them for life after college:
- Earn the respect of others
- Make tough decisions under pressure
- Confidently express yourself
- Speak effectively to groups of people
- Motivate others to get a job done
- Learn teamwork

Two-, three-, and four-year ROTC scholarships are available to outstanding students. If ROTC is not offered at your home college, you may be able to take it at a nearby college. You can try ROTC at no obligation for two years or, if you have a four-year scholarship, for one year. Normally, all ROTC classes, uniforms, and books are free. ROTC graduates will incur some form of required military service, either full-time on active duty or part-time in the Reserve or National Guard. Qualifying graduates can delay their service to go to graduate or professional school first.

Officer Candidate School

Openings at the U.S. service academies are few, so it pays to get information early. Every student is on a full scholarship, but free does not mean easy—these intense programs train graduates to meet the demands of leadership and success.

West Point

The U.S. Army Academy offers a broad-based academic program with nineteen majors in twenty-five fields of study. Extensive training and leadership experience go hand in hand with academics.

Annapolis

The U.S. Naval Academy is a unique blend of tradition and state-of-the-art technology. Its core curriculum includes eighteen major fields of study, and classroom work is supported by practical experience in leadership and professional operations.

Air Force Academy

The U.S. Air Force Academy prepares and motivates cadets for careers as Air Force officers. The academy offers a Bachelor of Science degree in twenty-six majors. Graduates receive a reserve commission as a second lieutenant in the Air Force.

Coast Guard Academy

This broad-based education, which leads to a Bachelor of Science degree in one of eight technical or professional majors, includes thorough grounding in the professional skills necessary to the Coast Guard's work.

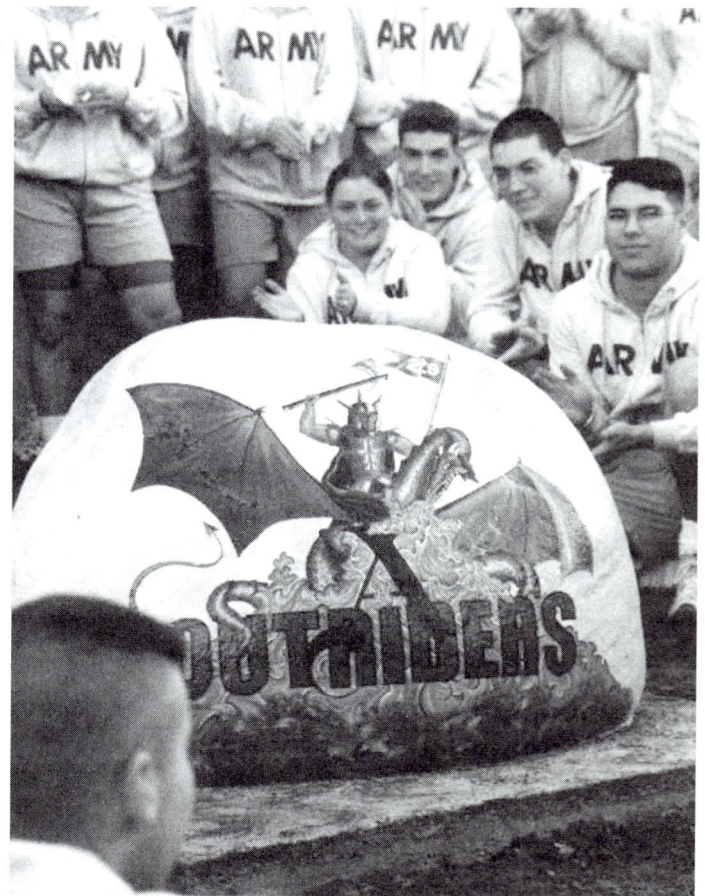

Photograph by Specialist Anderson, Ingrid, Defense Language Institute, Monterey, CA.

Peterson's © 1999

Apprenticeships

Kenneth Edwards
Director of Research and Technical Services,
International Brotherhood of Electrical Workers

Some students enjoy working with their hands and have the skill, patience, and temperament to become expert mechanics, carpenters, electronics repairmen, or computer maintenance people. If you would enjoy a profession like this and feel that college training is not for you, then perhaps you should consider an occupation that requires vocational or apprenticeship training.

If you are looking for a soft job, forget it. Apprenticeship is no snap. It demands hard work and has tough competition, so you've got to have the will to see it through. An apprenticeship is a program formally agreed upon between a worker and an employer in which the employee learns a skilled trade through theoretical classroom work and practical on-the-job training. Apprenticeship programs vary in length, rate of pay, and intensity between the various trades. A person completing an apprenticeship program generally becomes a "journeyman" (skilled craftsman) in that trade.

Apprenticeships: Valuable training for higher-paying jobs

To remain competitive, America needs highly skilled workers. One of the best possible ways for you to obtain the skills that will lead to a career in a high-paying occupation is through a formal apprenticeship program.

Apprenticeship provides structured on-the-job training under the supervision of a qualified craftsperson, technician, or professional. This training is supplemented by related classroom instruction conducted either by the sponsor or by an educational institution.

The advantages of apprenticeships are numerous. First and foremost, apprenticeship leads to a lasting lifetime skill. As a highly trained worker, you can take your skill anywhere. The more creative, exciting, and challenging jobs are put in the hands of the fully skilled worker, the all-around person who knows his or her trade inside out.

Skilled workers advance much faster than those who are semiskilled or whose skills are not broad enough to equip them to assume additional responsibilities. Those who complete an apprenticeship have also acquired the skills and judgment necessary to go into business for themselves if they choose.

Visit: www.petersons.com

About apprenticeships

Although there are more than 20,000 occupations listed in the *Dictionary of Occupational Titles*, the Bureau of Apprenticeship and Training and state apprenticeship councils consider only 813 of these to be "apprenticeable." To be apprenticeable, an occupation must be commonly practiced in industry and must lend itself to sequential learning experiences accompanied by a program of related instruction.

Currently, 394,064 apprentices are being trained by 35,948 programs registered with either the Bureau of Apprenticeship and Training or with state apprenticeship councils. Sixty to 65 percent of these apprentices are in the construction industry, with electricians and carpenters leading the industry in the use of apprentices.

How apprenticeships are regulated

Registration of an apprenticeship program with the Bureau of Apprenticeship and Training or with a state apprenticeship council is purely voluntary. Having such status is significant, however, as a "registered apprenticeship" must meet certain minimum standards of training established by federal regulations. Registration thus serves as an official stamp of approval. Virtually all apprenticeships in the construction industry are registered; in the printing, metal, and utilities trades, one third to one half of these programs are registered.

This does not mean, however, that nonregistered apprenticeships are not quality programs. Quite a number of major corporations have outstanding apprenticeship programs that have never been registered. If you want to inquire about the validity of a certain apprenticeship, you should contact a state apprenticeship agency or a regional office of the Bureau of Apprenticeship and Training; addresses of regional offices are listed at the end of this article.

National standards are in place for 160 recognized apprenticeable occupations. These standards are established in each field by a nationally recognized association of employers or by a recognized labor organization and an employer association. For example, the International Brotherhood of Electrical Workers and the National Electrical Contractors Association have established national standards for the training of apprentices in the electrical construction industry. National standards ensure uniformity of training across the country, so an apprentice can seek employment anywhere in the United States and have his or her training accepted without question.

In general, apprenticeship is legally recognized only if it is recorded in a written contract or agreement called an "indenture," in which the employer promises to teach the worker the processes of his or her trade in return for services rendered to the employer. Recognized standards of training must be stated in the contract; these standards include qualifications that the apprentice must meet, the term of the apprenticeship, a work schedule listing the hours that the apprentice will spend learning each work process, safety instruction to be provided, and a statement that a certificate of completion will be awarded to each apprentice who finishes the prescribed training.

What to do if you're interested in an apprenticeship

A person seeking an apprenticeship fills out what amounts to an application for employment. These applications may be available year-round or at certain times during the year. Because an apprentice must be trained in an area where work actually exists and where a certain pay scale is guaranteed upon completion of the program, the wait for application acceptance may be quite lengthy in areas of low employment. Such a standard works to the advantage of the potential apprentice; certainly no one would want to encourage you to spend one to six years of your life learning an occupation where no work exists or where the wage is the same as, or a little above, that of common labor.

Federal regulations prohibit anyone under 16 from being considered as an apprentice. Some programs require that the individual has received a high school degree or has completed certain course work. Other requirements may include passing certain validated aptitude tests, proof of physical ability to perform the duties of the trade, and possession of a valid driver's license.

Once the applicant has met the basic program entrance requirements, he or she is interviewed to determine interest in the trade, to discover his or her attitude toward work in general, and to observe personal

Peterson's © 1999

traits such as appearance, sincerity, character, and habits. Points are assigned for these items as well as for any additional education and experience. Openings are awarded to those who have achieved the most points.

For more information

If you're considering an apprenticeship, the best sources of assistance and information are vocational or career counselors, local state employment security agencies, field offices of state apprenticeship agencies, and regional offices of the Bureau of Apprenticeship and Training. Addresses and phone numbers for these regional offices are listed below. You can also visit the Bureau's Web site at http://www.doleta.gov/bat.

Bureau of Apprenticeship and Training Offices

National Office:
U.S. Department of Labor
Frances Perkins Building
200 Constitution Avenue, NW
Washington, D.C. 20210
202-219-5943

Region 3 Office (including Delaware, Maryland, Pennsylvania, Virginia, and West Virginia):
Room 13240
3535 Market Street
Philadelphia, Pennsylvania 19104
215-596-6417 or 6418

Region 4 Office (including Alabama, Florida, Georgia, Kentucky, Mississippi, North Carolina, South Carolina, and Tennessee):
Room 6T71
61 Forsyth Street, SW
Atlanta, Georgia 30303
404-562-2335

Region 5 Office (including Illinois, Indiana, Michigan, Minnesota, Ohio, and Wisconsin):
Room 708
230 South Dearborn Street
Chicago, Illinois 60604
312-353-7205

Region 6 Office (including Arkansas, Louisiana, New Mexico, Oklahoma, and Texas):
Room 311
Federal Building
525 Griffin Street
Dallas, Texas 75202
214-767-4993

How to Choose a Major

A major is the area that you will study in-depth in college. You will take up to two thirds of your classes in that subject. However, your major is only part of your undergraduate studies, as colleges and universities generally require a core curriculum in addition to your major course work.

You can choose from hundreds of majors—accounting to zoology—but which is right for you? Should you choose something traditional or select a major from an emerging area? Perhaps you already know what career you want to have, so you can work backward to decide which major will best help you achieve your goals.

If you know what you want to do early, you will have more time to plan your high school curriculum, extracurricular activities, jobs, and community service to coincide with your major. Your selection of a college may also depend upon the college providing a strong academic program in a certain major.

What if I don't know what I want to do with my life?

It's okay if you have not decided upon a major yet. In fact, more than half of all college freshmen are "undecided" and prefer to get a feel for what's available at college before making a decision. Most four-year colleges do not require students to formally declare a major until the end of their sophomore year or beginning of their junior year.

Can I change my major if I change my mind?

Choosing a major does not set your future in stone, nor does it necessarily disrupt your life if you need to change your major. However, there are advantages to choosing a major sooner rather than later. If you wait too long to choose, you may have to take additional classes to satisfy the requirements, which may cost you additional time and money.

Where do I start?

Choosing a major usually begins with an assessment of your career interests. Once you have taken the self-assessment test provided in this book, you should have a clearer understanding of your interests, talents, values, and goals. Then review the majors and try several on for size. Picture yourself taking classes, writing papers, making presentations, conducting research, or working in a related field. Talk to people you know who work in your fields of interest and see if you like what you hear. Also, try reading the classified ads in your local newspaper. What jobs sound interesting to you? Which ones pay the salary that you'd like to make? What level of education is required in the ads you find interesting? Select a few jobs that you think you'd like and then consult the following list of majors to see what major(s) coincide.

Agriculture

Agricultural Business and Production
Agricultural Business and Management
Agricultural Mechanization
Agricultural Supplies and Related Services
Horticulture Services Operations and Management

Agricultural Sciences
Agriculture/Agricultural Sciences
Animal Sciences
Food Sciences and Technology
Plant Sciences

There are many different kinds of programs in the area of agriculture, ranging from animal sciences to problems of crop productivity.

Many agriculture majors apply their knowledge directly on farms and ranches. Others work in industry (food, farm equipment, and agricultural supply companies), federal agencies (primarily in the Departments of Agriculture and the Interior), and state and local farm and agricultural agencies. Jobs might be in research and lab work, marketing and sales, advertising and public relations, or journalism and radio/TV (for farm communications media).

Agriculture majors also pursue further training in biological sciences, animal health, veterinary medicine, agribusiness, management, vocational agriculture education, nutrition and dietetics, and rural sociology.

Architecture

Architecture and Related Programs
Architectural Environmental Design
Architecture
City/Urban, Community, and Regional Planning
Landscape Architecture

Architecture and related design fields focus on the built environment as distinct from the natural environment of the agriculturist or the conservationist. The four-year architecture degree is a preprofessional one; professional

Peterson's © 1999

practice requires a five-year bachelor's degree or a six-year program leading to a master's degree.

Career possibilities include drafting, design, and project administration in architectural, engineering, landscape design, interior design, industrial design, planning, real estate, and construction firms; government agencies involved in construction, housing, highways, and parks and recreation; and government and nonprofit organizations interested in historic or architectural preservation.

These studies also provide a good background for further training in architectural, civil, and structural engineering; public administration; city management; and business management.

Area/Ethnic Studies

Area, Ethnic, and Cultural Studies
  Area Studies
  Ethnic and Cultural Studies

Area and ethnic studies majors provide a background that is useful in a wide variety of work settings. The important skills that are acquired through these majors—research, writing, analysis, critical thinking, cultural awareness— combined with the expertise gained in a particular area

make this group of majors valuable in a number of professional careers. Area and ethnic studies majors who are familiar with the language of the area they study are often viewed more favorably by prospective employers.

Positions in administration, education, public relations, and communications in such organizations as cultural, government, international, and (ethnic) community agencies; international trade (import-export); social service agencies; and the communications media (journalism, radio, and TV) utilize the skills of an area and ethnic studies major.

These studies also provide a good background for further training in law, business management, public administration, education, social work, museum and library work, and international relations.

Arts

Visual and Performing Arts
  Crafts, Folk Art, and Artisanry
  Dance
  Design and Applied Arts
  Dramatic/Theater Arts and Stagecraft
  Film/Video and Photographic Arts
  Fine Arts and Art Studies
  Music
  Visual and Performing Arts

Art majors most often use their training to become practicing artists, though the settings in which they work are varied. Knowledge and appreciation of the arts can be applied in both the business and the not-for-profit sectors. In addition, many people with art training ultimately work in non-art-related fields or fields in which art is useful but not essential. An advanced degree is necessary for research and scholarship.

Aside from the most obvious art-related career, that of the self-employed artist or craftperson, there are many fields that utilize the skills of visual artists: advertising; public relations; publishing; journalism; museum work; television, movies, and theater, which need designers of many types; community and social service agencies concerned with education, recreation, and entertainment; and teaching, both in schools (which usually require education courses) and independently.

There are many career possibilities in the performing arts beyond being "on stage" and many areas of the performing arts in which knowledge and appreciation can be used in both the commercial and the nonprofit sectors.

Actors, dancers, and musicians find work in radio/TV; community and social service agencies concerned with education, recreation, and entertainment; and teaching, both in schools (usually requiring education courses), and independently.

A background in art is also useful if a student wishes to pursue art therapy, arts or museum administration, or library work.

Biological Sciences

Biological Sciences/Life Sciences
Biochemistry and Biophysics
Biology, General
Botany
Cell and Molecular Biology
Microbiology/Bacteriology
Miscellaneous Biological Specializations
Zoology

The biological sciences include the study of living organisms from the level of molecules to that of populations. A bachelor's degree is adequate preparation for some beginning jobs, but a career in the biological sciences often requires an advanced degree in either a life science specialty or a related discipline within the fields of agriculture, engineering, health, physical science, or social science.

Biological science majors find jobs in industry; government agencies; technical writing, editing, or illustrating; science reporting; secondary school teaching (which usually requires education courses); and research and laboratory analysis and testing.

Biological sciences are also a sound foundation for further study in medicine, psychology, health and hospital administration, and biologically oriented engineering.

Business

Business Management and Administrative Services
Accounting
Administrative and Secretarial Services
Business
Business Administration and Management
Business Communications
Business Information and Data Processing Services
Business Quantitative Methods and Management Science
Business/Managerial Economics
Enterprise Management and Operation
Financial Management and Services
Hospitality Services Management
Human Resources Management
International Business
Marketing Management and Research
Real Estate

Marketing Operations/Marketing and Distribution

Apparel and Accessories Marketing Operations
Entrepreneurship
Food Products Retailing and Wholesaling Operations
Hospitality and Recreation Marketing Operations
Tourism and Travel Services Marketing Operations

The business majors comprise all the basic business disciplines. At the undergraduate level, students can major in a general business administration program or specialize in a particular area such as marketing or accounting. These studies lead of course to positions in business and industry, but they are also applicable to management positions in other sectors.

Management-related studies include the general management areas (accounting, finance, marketing, management) as well as special studies related to a particular type of organization or industry. Management-related majors may be offered in a business school or in a department dealing with the area in which the management skills are to be applied.

Career possibilities exist in almost any organization in which financial and administrative activities take place and where management principles can be applied. This includes business firms; educational, cultural, and health institutions; city, state, and federal government agencies; and nonprofit organizations. Jobs may be found in such areas as accounting, advertising and public relations, marketing and sales, banking, data processing, financial or investments analysis, human resources (personnel, employee relations, labor relations), international trade (import-export), market research, purchasing, real estate, retailing, securities sales, secretarial work, travel and tourism, underwriting (insurance), and secondary school business/secretarial teaching (with education courses).

Business studies also provide a good background for further training in business or management-related studies at the M.B.A. level, law, public accounting (CPA), actuarial work (insurance), and training and management development.

Communication

Communications

Advertising
Communications, General
Journalism and Mass Communications
Public Relations and Organizational Communications
Radio and Television Broadcasting

Guidance Counselor Tips

"When applying to college you want to include a 'stretch' school. If you don't receive a rejection letter from any school, you might wonder if you made a big enough stretch when you first applied."

—Lynn Caldwell, Highland Park ISD, Highland Park, Texas

"Often, when students come in for a counseling session to discuss issues surrounding academics, or even personal concerns, there is a great deal of frustration and worry. While some worry is healthy, too much is dangerous. I never let a student leave my office until I've shared the wise words from Charlie Chan, the crime-fighting suspense character. Like Chan, I always tell my students that no matter the situation, they should always do their 'humble best.'"

—Elmer Booth, Guidance Department Head, Blake Senior High School, Tampa, Florida

"Your counselors can be neutral sounding boards for you. They can help in your career, college, family, and even personal decisions. Use them—theye don't have all the answers, but they know where to get information to help you make informed decisions."

—Dan Shay, Counselor, Princeton High School, Cincinnati, Ohio

Communications Technologies
Communications Technologies

Majors in communication tend to focus on either print media (journalism, publishing) or electronic media (radio, TV). Career areas tend to follow this split and to further divide into the creative side (writing, editing, programming) and the business side (sales, marketing, advertising, finance, management). An M.B.A. is becoming increasingly necessary for advancement on the business side, whereas experience still seems to be the best upward route on the creative side (although a master's degree may help you get your first job).

Jobs in communication range from reporting (news, special features), copywriting, technical writing, copyediting, and programming to advertising, public relations, media sales, and market research. Such positions can be found at newspapers, radio and TV stations, publishing houses (book and magazine), advertising agencies, corporate communications departments, government agencies, universities, and firms that specialize in educational and training materials. Free-lance work is an alternative way to get started.

Communication students also go on for further training in law, business management, public administration, arts management, social work, educational media, journalism, radio/TV, and library and archival work.

Computer, Information, and Library Sciences

Computer and Information Sciences
Computer and Information Sciences, General
Computer Programming
Computer Science
Data Processing Technology
Information Sciences and Systems

Library Science
Library Science/Librarianship

Computer and information science and systems majors stress the theoretical aspects of the computer and emphasize mathematical and scientific disciplines. Data processing, programming, and computer technology programs tend to be more practical; they are more oriented to business than to scientific applications and to working directly with the computer or with peripheral equipment.

Career possibilities for computer and information sciences include data processing, programming, and systems work in almost any setting: business and industry, banking and finance, government, colleges and universities, libraries software firms, service bureaus, computer manufacturers, publishing, and communications.

Library science gives preprofessional background in library work and provides valuable knowledge of research sources, indexing, abstracting, computer technology, and media technology, which is useful for further study in any professional field.

In most cases, a master's degree in library science is necessary to obtain a job as a librarian.

Library science majors find positions in public, school, college, corporate, and government libraries and research centers; book publishing (especially reference books); database and information retrieval services; and communications (especially audiovisual media).

Computer, information, and library sciences all provide good backgrounds for further training in management-related areas (business, government, health, non-profit organizations), engineering, archival work, and systems analysis.

Education

Education
Bilingual/Bicultural Education
Education Administration and Supervision
Education, General
Educational/Instructional Media Design
General Teacher Education
Special Education
Student Counseling and Personnel Services
Teacher Assistant/Aide
Teacher Education, Specific Academic and Vocational Programs
Teaching English as a Second Language/Foreign Language

If you want to teach a particular subject at the elementary or secondary level, you will generally have to become certified to teach in your field. This is not necessarily the case for private and parochial schools, where the pay is more often lower. Nevertheless, even in these settings, certification is usually preferred. Generally, if you are interested in teaching as a career, you would go to a college that offers certification sequences—education, secondary education, or elementary education—and the academic major you wish to teach. So, if you wanted to teach secondary-level English, you would look into colleges that offer either education or secondary education and also offer English. Certification is done by state, so you will also want to find out whether the program at a specific college will be acceptable preparation for the state in which you plan to teach.

On the other hand, if the education field you are interested in requires extensive or very specialized course work in education and relatively little advanced study in other areas (such as physical, reading, or special education), you should choose only the specific education major that applies.

Students who major in education should be prepared to consider working in related fields (of which there are many) in case jobs are scarce in their particular teaching specialty. Although the current situation is competitive in most teaching fields, there is highest demand for teachers of math, science, special education, and vocational subjects. Master's degrees are recommended for teachers and almost always required for positions as guidance counselors, principals, and curriculum specialists. Teacher aids, who are assistants to the classroom teacher, work with children directly and do clerical work.

Positions as teachers in public elementary and secondary schools, private day and boarding schools, religious and parochial schools, vocational schools, and proprietary schools are the jobs most often filled by education majors. However, there are also teaching positions in noneducational institutions, such as museums, historical societies, prisons, hospitals, and nursing homes as well as jobs as educators and trainers in government and industry. Administrative (nonteaching) positions in employee relations and personnel, public relations, marketing and sales, educational publishing, TV and film media, test development firms, and government and community social service agencies also tap the skills and interests of education majors.

Course work in education also provides a good background for further training in school psychology, social work, library and museum work, personnel and labor relations, public administration, business management, college student personnel work (admissions, financial aid, student activities), and training and management development.

Engineering and Engineering Technologies

Engineering
Aerospace, Aeronautical, and Astronautical Engineering
Agricultural Engineering
Architectural Engineering
Bioengineering and Biomedical Engineering
Ceramic Sciences and Engineering
Chemical Engineering
Civil Engineering
Computer Engineering
Electrical, Electronics, and Communications Engineering
Engineering Design
Engineering Mechanics
Engineering Physics
Engineering Science
Engineering, General
Engineering/Industrial Management
Environmental/Environmental Health Engineering
Geological Engineering
Industrial/Manufacturing Engineering
Materials Engineering
Materials Science
Mechanical Engineering
Metallurgical Engineering
Nuclear Engineering
Petroleum Engineering
Polymer/Plastics Engineering
Systems Engineering

Engineering–Related Technologies
Architectural Engineering Technology
Civil Engineering/Civil Technology
Construction/Building Technology
Electrical and Electronic Engineering–Related Technology
Electromechanical Instrumentation and Maintenance Technology Environmental Control Technologies
Industrial Production Technologies
Mechanical Engineering-Related Technologies
Mining and Petroleum Technologies
Miscellaneous Engineering-Related Technologies
Quality Control and Safety Technologies

Engineering is one of the few professional fields in which a bachelor's degree is sufficient career preparation. Many engineers, however, do go on for a master's degree in a new technology or in order to move into management. A Ph.D. is generally necessary for teaching positions in colleges and universities.

Engineering technology and science technology majors prepare students for practical design and production work rather than for jobs that require more theoretical, scientific, and mathematical knowledge.

Industry, research labs, and government agencies where technology plays a key role, such as in manufacturing, electronics, construction communications, transportation, and utilities, hire engineering as well as engineering technology and science technology graduates regularly.

Work may be in technical activities (research, development, design, production, testing, scientific programming, systems analysis) or in nontechnical areas where a technical degree is needed, such as marketing, sales, or administration.

These studies provide a good background for further training in the disciplines listed above, as well as in business management, public administration, urban planning, city management, medicine, public health, environmental design, and law (especially patent law).

Foreign Languages

Foreign Languages and Literatures

Classical and Ancient Near Eastern Languages and Literatures
East and Southeast Asian Languages and Literatures
East European Languages and Literatures
Foreign Languages and Literatures
Germanic Languages and Literatures
Greek Languages and Literatures (Modern)
Middle Eastern Languages and Literatures
Romance Languages and Literatures

A knowledge of foreign languages and cultures is becoming increasingly recognized as important in today's international world. The language major possesses a skill that is used in organizations that have international dealings as well as in career fields (e.g., hotel services) and geographical areas (e.g., New York City, Montreal, the Southwest), where languages other than English are prominent. However, a greater variety of career possibilities exists if facility with a foreign language is combined with other skills, knowledge, and interests than if it is relied on alone as an entry to the job market. You might want to consider a dual major or a concentration of courses in another field as well as a language major to enhance your job prospects. A Ph.D. is generally necessary for college teaching and research positions in these disciplines.

Career possibilities include positions with business firms with international subsidiaries; import-export firms; international banking; travel agencies; airlines; tourist services; government and international agencies dealing with international affairs, foreign trade, diplomacy, customs, or immigration; secondary school foreign language teaching and bilingual education (which usually require education courses); freelance translating and interpreting (high level of skill necessary); foreign language publishing; and computer programming (especially for linguistics majors).

Foreign languages also provide a good background for further training in law, international affairs and diplomacy, international trade, international social service, professional specialized translating and interpreting, library and archival work, and museum work.

Health Sciences

Health Professions and Related Sciences

Communication Disorders Sciences and Services
Dental Services
Health and Medical Administrative Services
Health and Medical Assistants
Health and Medical Diagnostic and Treatment Services
Health and Medical Laboratory Technologies
Health and Medical Preparatory Programs
Mental Health Services
Miscellaneous Health Professions
Nursing
Pharmacy
Public Health
Rehabilitation/Therapeutic Services

Health professions majors, while having a scientific core, are more focused on applying the results of scientific investigation than on the scientific disciplines themselves. A bachelor's degree is adequate preparation for some beginning-level jobs, but a master's degree is increasingly necessary for career advancement. Allied health majors prepare graduates to assist health professionals in providing diagnostics, therapeutics, and rehabilitation.

The medical science majors, such as optometry, pharmacy, and the premedical profession sequences, are, for the most part, preprofessional studies comprising the scientific disciplines necessary for admission to graduate or professional school in the health or medical fields. A bachelor's degree is adequate for some beginning-level jobs, but a career in these major fields requires an advanced degree.

The health service and technology majors prepare students for positions in the health fields that primarily involve services to patients or working with complex machinery and materials. Medical technologies covers a wide range of fields, such as cytotechnology, biomedical technologies, and operating room technology.

Administrative, professional, or research assistant positions in health agencies, hospitals, occupational health units in industry, community and school health departments, government agencies (public health, environmental protection), and international health organizations are available to majors in health fields as are jobs in marketing and sales of health-related products and services, health education (with education courses), advertising and public relations, journalism and publishing, and technical writing.

Home Economics and Social Services

Home Economics
Family and Community Studies
Family/Consumer Resource Management
Foods and Nutrition Studies
Home Economics, General
Housing Studies
Individual and Family Development Studies

Public Administration and Services
Community Organization, Resources, and Services
Public Administration
Public Policy Analysis
Social Work

Vocational Home Economics
Consumer and Homemaking
Education

Home economics encompasses many different fields—basic studies in foods and textiles as well as new areas, such as consumer economics and leisure studies, that overlap with aspects of agriculture, social science, and education. Career areas are emerging in which a background in home economics provides the advantage of an interdisciplinary viewpoint.

Jobs for home economics majors can be found in government and community agencies (especially those concerned with education, health, housing, or human services), nursing homes, child-care centers, journalism, radio/TV, educational media, and publishing. Types of work also include marketing, sales, and customer service in consumer-related industries, such as food processing and packaging, appliance manufacturing, utilities, textiles, and secondary school home economics teaching (which usually requires education courses).

Majors in social services find administrative aide or assistant positions in government and community health, welfare, and social service agencies, such as hospitals, clinics, YMCAs and YWCAs, recreation commissions, welfare agencies, and employment services. See the Law and Legal Studies section for information on more law-related social services.

Home economics and social services studies also provide a good background for further training in business management, hotel and institutional management, public health, food technology, environmental design and urban planning, social work, marriage and family counseling, public administration, and personnel.

Humanities (Miscellaneous)

English Language and Literature/Letters
Comparative Literature
English Creative Writing
English Language and Literature, General
English Technical and Business Writing
Speech and Rhetorical Studies

Liberal Arts and Sciences, General Studies and Humanities

Liberal Arts and Sciences, General Studies and Humanities
Philosophy

The majors that constitute the humanities (sometimes called "letters") are the most general and widely applicable and the least vocationally oriented of the liberal arts. They are essentially studies of the ideas and concerns of human kind. These include classics, history of philosophy, history of science, linguistics, and medieval studies, among others.

The skills and knowledge that the study of these subjects imparts are truly enduring and relevant to any field of endeavor, especially where the ability to understand ideas, think logically, and write and speak clearly is crucial. A major in philosophy—or in any other of the humanities—does not lead automatically to a job labeled "philosopher" or "writer," but these majors provide an excellent foundation for many generalized careers and for further training in a variety of fields. Some think the humanities are the ideal preprofessional preparation for law school. Research and teaching in any of these fields at the university level usually require a Ph.D.

Career possibilities for humanities majors can be found in business firms, government and community agencies, advertising and public relations, marketing and sales, publishing, journalism and radio/TV, secondary school teaching in English and literature (which usually requires education courses), freelance writing and editing, and computer programming (especially for those with a background in logic or linguistics).

Law and Legal Studies

Students of legal studies can use their knowledge of law and government in fields involving the making, breaking, and enforcement of laws; the crimes, trials, and punishment of law breakers; and the running of all branches of government at local, state, and federal levels. Advanced degrees are needed for research and scholarship and for practicing law.

Students in legal areas find positions in all types in law firms, legal departments of other organizations, the court or prison system, government agencies (such as law enforcement agencies or offices of state and federal attorneys general), and police departments.

In addition, the skills acquired in this field, such as research and writing, can be useful in most careers, especially those listed in the Social Sciences section.

Mathematics and Physical Sciences

Mathematics

Applied Mathematics
Mathematical Statistics
Mathematics

Physical Sciences

Astronomy
Atmospheric Sciences and Meteorology
Chemistry
Geological and Related Sciences
Miscellaneous Physical Sciences
Physical Sciences, General
Physics

Mathematics is the science of numbers and the abstract formulation of their operations. Physical sciences involve the study of the laws and structures of physical matter. A bachelor's degree is adequate preparation for some beginning jobs, but for career advancement to high-level positions a graduate degree is necessary in either a physical science specialty or a related discipline within the fields of biological sciences, engineering, health and medicine, or social sciences. The quantitative skills acquired through the study of science and mathematics are especially useful for computer-related careers.

Career possibilities include positions in industry (manufacturing and processing companies, electronics firms, defense contractors, consulting firms); government agencies (defense, environmental protection, law enforcement); scientific/technical writing, editing, or illustrating; journalism (science reporting); secondary school teaching (usually requiring education courses); research and laboratory analysis and testing; statistical analysis; computer programming; systems analysis; surveying and mapping; weather forecasting; and technical sales.

These studies also provide a good background for further training in engineering (any field), actuarial work (insurance), operations research, business management, and public administration.

Miscellaneous

Multidisciplinary/Interdisciplinary Studies

Biological and Physical Sciences
Gerontology
Historic Preservation, Conservation and Architectural History
Medieval and Renaissance Studies
Peace and Conflict Studies
Science, Technology, and Society
Systems Science and Theory

Peterson's © 1999

Protective Services

Criminal Justice and Corrections
Fire Protection

Reserve Officers' Training Corps (R.O.T.C.)

Army R.O.T.C.

There are more majors in more areas than you probably imagined. They don't all fit into neat categories, and the organization and majors can vary greatly from institution to institution. Branching out and approaching subjects from a number of angles—the interdisciplinary approach—are important parts of what makes postsecondary education so exciting.

Natural Resources

Conservation and Renewable Natural Resources

Fishing and Fisheries Sciences and Management
Forest Production and Processing
Forestry and Related Sciences
Natural Resources Conversation
Natural Resources Management and Protective Services
Wildlife and Wildlands Management

Parks, Recreation, Leisure, and Fitness Studies

Health and Physical Education/Fitness
Parks, Recreation, and Leisure Facilities Management
Parks, Recreation, and Leisure Studies

A major in the natural resources field prepares students for work in a variety of areas. These can be as generalized as environmental conservation and as specialized as groundwater contamination.

Jobs are available in industry (food, energy, natural resources, and pulp and paper companies), consulting firms, state and federal government agencies (primarily the Departments of Agriculture and the Interior), and public and private conservation agencies. Also see the Agriculture and Biological Sciences sections for more information on natural resources-related fields.

Course work in natural resources provides a good background for further training in biological sciences, environmental education, environmental or natural resources engineering, and resources management.

Psychology

Psychology

Clinical Psychology
Cognitive Psychology and Psycholinguistics
Developmental and Child Psychology
Experimental Psychology
Industrial and Organizational Psychology
Physiological Psychology/Psychobiology
Psychology

Psychology majors involve the study of behavior and can range from the biological to the sociological. Students can study individual behavior, usually that of humans, or the behavior of crowds. Students of psychology do not always go into the more obvious clinical fields, the fields in which psychologists work with patients. Certain areas of psychology, such as industrial/organizational, experimental, and social, are not clinically oriented.

Psychology and counseling careers can be in government (such as mental health agencies), schools, hospitals, clinics, private practice, industry, test development firms, social work, and personnel. The careers listed in the general Social Sciences section are also pursued by psychology and counseling majors.

With advanced study, psychology graduates teach at the college level, do research, and become psychiatrists (M.D. required) and psychologists.

Religion

Religion

Religion/Religious Studies

Theological Studies and Religious Vocations

Bible/Biblical Studies
Biblical and Other Theological Languages and Literatures
Missions/Missionary Studies and Missiology
Pastoral Counseling and Specialized Ministries
Religious Education
Religious/Sacred Music
Theological and Ministerial Studies

Religion majors are usually seen as preprofessional studies for those who are interested in entering the ministry. Graduate study in a seminary is required for practice in most religious denominations. However, other professional fields, as well as the career opportunities listed below, are open to those who want to pursue these majors at the bachelor's level only. In contrast to the academic study of religion, which takes a neutral stance, theology is usually studied from the perspective of those committed to a particular religious belief.

Career possibilities for religion include case work, youth counseling, administration in community and social service organizations, teaching in religious educational institutions, and writing for religious and lay publications. Religious studies also prepare students for the kinds of jobs other humanities majors often pursue.

Social Sciences (Miscellaneous)

Social Sciences and History

Anthropology
Archaeology
Criminology
Economics
Geography
History
International Relations and Affairs
Political Science and Government
Social Sciences, General
Sociology
Urban Affairs/Studies

Social sciences is the study of people in relation to their society. Thus, social science majors can apply their education to a wide range of occupations that deal with social issues and activities. A Ph.D. is required for research and teaching positions in most of the social sciences.

Career opportunities are varied. Positions are available in government, business, community agencies (serving children, youth, senior citizens), advertising and public relations, marketing and sales, secondary school social studies teaching (with education courses), case work, law enforcement, parks and recreation, museum work (especially for anthropology, archaeology, geography, history majors), preservation (especially for anthropology, archaeology, geography, history majors), banking and finance (especially for economics majors), market and survey research, statistical analysis, publishing, fund-raising and development, and political campaigning. For more specific information, see the sections on Area/Ethnic Studies, Home Economics and Social Services, Law and Legal Studies, and Psychology.

The Social sciences are also useful for further training in law, business management, public administration, city management, counseling (vocational, school, rehabilitation, family, personal), international relations, journalism and radio/TV, library and archival work, personnel and labor relations, medicine, urban planning, student personnel work, public health, and criminology.

Technologies

Science Technologies

Biological Technology
Nuclear and Industrial Radiologic Technologies

Technology Education/Industrial Arts

Technology Education/Industrial Arts

Technology majors, along with trade fields, are the areas that are most often offered as two-year programs. Majors in technology fields prepare students directly for jobs. However, positions are in practical design and production work rather than in areas that require more theoretical, scientific, and mathematical knowledge.

Technology fields are also very diverse. Engineering technologies prepare students with the basic training in specific fields (e.g., electronics, mechanics, chemistry) necessary to become technicians on the support staffs of engineers. Other technology majors center more on maintenance and repair. Work may be in technical activities, such as production or testing, or in nontechnical areas where a technical degree is needed, such as marketing, sales, or administration.

In any case, a technology major, more than the liberal studies majors mentioned earlier, can provide the training necessary for graduates to work in that field after only two years of courses. However, some technology-oriented majors, such as nuclear technology and aircraft and missile maintenance, may require additional study or certification for many positions. In addition, more training is generally required for complex technical areas, such as research, development, design, scientific programming, and systems analysis. However, technology program credits do not necessarily transfer to upper-level programs, so finding out about specific programs before you enroll is important.

Industries, research labs, and government agencies in which technology plays a key role—such as in manufacturing, electronics, construction, communications, transportation, and utilities—hire technology graduates regularly. Also see the Health Sciences section for information on health-related technologies.

Technological studies also provide a good background for further training in the disciplines listed above as well as in specific engineering fields, business management, public administration, urban planning, city management, public health, and environmental design.

Trades

Construction Trades

Construction and Building Finishers and Managers

Mechanics and Repairers

Electrical and Electronics Equipment Installers and Repairers

Heating, Air-Conditioning, and Refrigeration Mechanics and Repairers

Industrial Equipment Maintenance and Repairers

Vehicle and Mobile Equipment Mechanics and Repairers

Personal and Miscellaneous Services

Cosmetic Services

Culinary Arts and Related Services

Funeral Services and Mortuary Science

Precision Production Trades

Drafting

Graphic and Printing Equipment Operators

Precision Metal Workers

Transportation and Materials Moving Workers

Air Transportation Workers

Majors in trade specialties are as straightforward as they are diverse. For the most part, graduates of a particular trade program go on to practice that trade. Carpentry majors work as carpenters, culinary arts majors as cooks and chefs.

Though for most vocational positions an associate degree is sufficient to start in the field, some jobs might require further study or some kind of licensing or certification. Sometimes this special licensing can be obtained through a college program. In addition, a period of apprenticeship must be served for most trade specialties before a worker can practice independently.

Nontraditional Career Opportunities

Unlike previous generations, today's young people have a full range of career choices based upon their individual interests and abilities and unlimited by narrow role expectations. With approximately 35,000 occupations available in the United States, students have a lot of careers from which to choose, and not all of these occupations are traditional. Let's explore some nontraditional possibilities that you might consider.

Unique careers

Medical Illustrator

By combining the talents of an artist, a scientist, and an educator, medical illustrators convey information through a variety of mediums, from pen and ink to computers. Professionals in this field must have a background not only in anatomy, but also in pathology and physiology so that they can reach audiences that range from doctors and scientists to elementary school students. There are currently about 800 medical illustrators in this country, with an additional thirty or more entering the market each year. They find work in medical schools, medical centers, and publishing houses, while others freelance.

Music Therapist

Music therapy is a form of emotional, physical, and psychological treatment using music. Some music therapists work primarily with children, others work with adults in settings such as nursing homes, mental hospitals, and clinics for the abused. Some music therapists are hired as consultants or work with day-care facilities, substance abuse treatment centers, prisons, rehabilitation centers, and hospices.

There are very few undergraduate programs for music therapy; consequently, most music therapists earn a master's degree after getting a bachelor's in psychology, social work, education, or special education. There are roughly 5,000 practicing music therapists in the United States.

Herpetologist

If you shake at the sight of snakes, lizards, and crocodiles, the field of herpetology is not for you. Herpetology is the study of reptiles, and a herpetologist is a specialist in these animals. Although a true herpetologist holds a doctorate in the field, zoos across the country hire a number of individuals who have experience working with reptiles.

Many have majored in zoology, the branch of biology concerned with the animal kingdom.

Work in this field involves much more than cleaning out cages and ranges from designing new exhibits and developing special diets to breeding many of the animals. Very little is known about the reptile world, so herpetologists spend a great deal of time sharing their observations with scientists.

Forensic Psychophysiologist

Never lie to a forensic psychophysiologist; this person makes a living by identifying lies and confirming truths through the use of special examinations. Once known as polygraph exams because of the special equipment used, today they are more aptly titled "psychophysiological detection of deception exams."

The majority of those in the occupation start with experience in law enforcement or private investigation; however, a college education in areas such as criminal justice or psychology can sometimes substitute for investigative experience. Others acquire a bachelor's degree in public safety. By contacting the American Polygraph Association (APA) at 800-272-8037 (toll-free), you can obtain a list of the small number of schools that offer specialized training. Currently there are approximately 3,000 forensic psychophysiologists in this country.

Cartographer

Cartography is the art and science of mapmaking. Cartographers often come from backgrounds as diverse as art and environmental planning. Students can earn a cartographer's certificate from the geography departments of many colleges and universities, where they study different mapping sciences, such as photogrammetry (mapping from aerial photographs) and remote sensing (interpreting satellite imagery), and typography (the use of different kinds of type).

Cartographers may need to acquire knowledge in a specific area, such as the environment, transportation systems, or geopolitics. An organization like the National Geographic Society employs numerous cartographers. With an ever-growing global society, the need for cartographers should continue well into the future.

Women and nontraditional work

Nontraditional jobs for women are defined as those jobs in which 25 percent or less of those employed are women. Because only twenty out of 440 broad occupational classifications have women concentrated in them, this qualifies many occupations as nontraditional for women. Women working in nontraditional jobs typically earn 20 to 30 percent more than women in traditional occupations. In an effort to rectify this inequity and to help women achieve a firm footing in today's economically challenging world, several programs are available to promote growth and independence.

Students can explore a variety of nontraditional career options in fields such as law enforcement, telecommunications, auto and truck mechanics, fire services, auto body repair, carpentry, welding, and electronics. For more information on programs like these, contact your State Department of Education.

How to Choose a College

You have examined your interests, talents, wants, and needs in great detail. Now it's time to begin investigating the colleges you are interested in attending. Each college offers its own advantages, but only a handful will be perfect matches for you. To help narrow your choices to a manageable number, decide which of the following college characteristics are most important to you. Then use the most important characteristics to fill out the College Comparison Worksheet that appears later in this chapter.

Academic program

- University—usually has a liberal arts college as well as several other specialized colleges, such as business, engineering, education, agriculture, law, and medicine. Each of these individual colleges may have its own set of entrance requirements.
- Four-year college—an institution of higher learning that offers a curriculum leading to a four-year Bachelor of Arts or Bachelor of Science degree.
- Two-year college (community college, technical college, or university regional campus)—offers associate degree programs that serve as the first two years of a bachelor's degree and/or provide skills needed for entry into technical career fields.
- Vocational/trade school—offers career-oriented programs that may last from a few months to a couple of years. These schools, which are often proprietary (for-profit) institutions, generally do not offer transfer programs or programs parallel to those of four-year colleges.

Affiliation

- Public
- Private independent
- Private church affiliated
- Proprietary

Size

- Very small (fewer than 1,000 students)
- Small (1,000–3,999 students)
- Medium (4,000–8,999 students)
- Large (9,000–19,999 students)
- Very large (more than 20,000 students)

Community

- Rural
- Small town
- Suburban
- Urban

Location

- In your hometown
- Less than 3 hours from home
- More than 3 hours from home

Housing

- Dorm
- Off-campus apartment
- Home
- Facilities and services for students with disabilities

Student body

- All male
- All female
- Coed
- Minority representation
- Primarily one religious denomination
- Primarily full-time students
- Primarily part-time students
- Primarily commuter students
- Primarily residential students

Admissions

- Highly selective—students rank in top 10 percent of class and have a very strong academic record.
- Selective—students rank in top 25 percent of class and have a strong academic record.
- Traditional—students rank in top 50 percent of class and have a good academic record.
- Liberal—many students are accepted from lower half of class.
- Open—all students are accepted to limit of capacity.

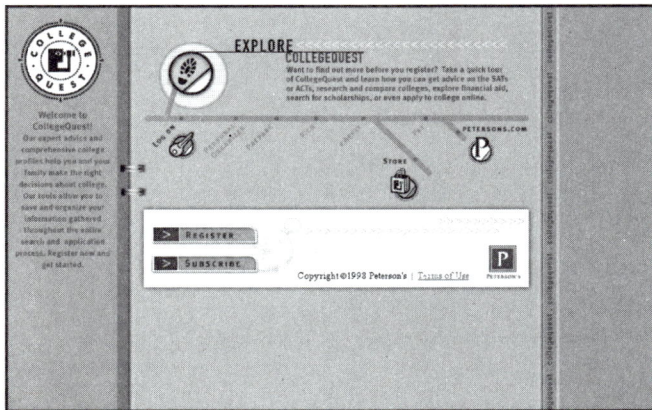

With CollegeQuest.com—Point! Click and Discover 3,400 Colleges

It's that simple! **Explore all** your college choices. **Check out** financial aid opportunities. And fill out only one electronic application for over 1,000 colleges—all through **CollegeQuest.com**. Talk with admissions deans, keep track of your applications, and enjoy the Quest.

Academic environment

- Is your major offered
- Student-faculty ratio
- Faculty teaching reputation
- Instruction by professors versus teaching assistants
- Facilities (such as classrooms and labs)
- Libraries
- Independent study available
- International study available
- Internships available

Cost

Colleges vary greatly in cost. Do not automatically pass over an institution that appears to be too expensive. You may be able to receive financial aid that will make your education affordable.

When estimating cost, remember tuition and fees, room and board, miscellaneous personal expenses, and transportation costs.

Financial aid

- Scholarships
- Grants
- Loans
- Work-study program
- Part-time or full-time jobs

Support services

- Academic counseling
- Career/placement counseling
- Personal counseling
- Student health facilities

Activities/social clubs

- Clubs, organizations
- Greek life
- Athletics, intramurals
- Other

Athletics

- Division I, II, or III
- Sports offered
- Scholarships available

Specialized programs

- Gifted student services
- Services for students with disabilities or special needs

CollegeQuest

Did you know there's one place you can go to get help with every aspect of the application process? That place is CollegeQuest, and you can find it on the Internet at http://www.collegequest.com.

If you need help finding colleges, ask CollegeQuest's Personal Counselor to narrow your search to the schools that fit you best. Want to spend four years in a bustling city or a suburban area? What about housing? Do you want to live in a single-sex or coed dorm? These are just a few of the questions that the Personal Counselor will help you explore.

CollegeQuest also offers a personal organizer that acts like a virtual filing cabinet, monitoring your applications in progress. It helps you build and maintain your list of potential colleges. You can enter personal and academic information into the organizer and it will be transferred into any online application that you open on CollegeQuest. The Personal Organizer also keeps track of application deadlines and other key dates in your calendar.

If you already know the schools that you are interested in, you can do a quick keyword or alphabetical search to find your preferred schools, then add them to your Personal Organizer. You can narrow your college choices by reading in-depth descriptions of schools, making side-by-side comparisons of different institutions, or by looking at profiles from the *Yale Daily News Insider's Guide to the Colleges*, written by current college students. You can even send instant inquiries to get more information from the schools of your choice.

CollegeQuest also helps students understand and prepare for standardized tests. The site offers test dates, helpful test-taking tips, and full-length downloadable practice tests for the SAT I and ACT. In addition, this section provides tips and sample questions for the TOEFL and TWE.

You can also read daily campus news articles and feature articles that address many facets of college preparation—including tips on summer jobs, choosing the right classes, and more. Students who have specific questions can go to CollegeQuest's Ask the Experts forum. This forum allows you to ask admissions and financial aid experts about any college concerns. Answers to students' questions are posted on a regular basis and archived for everyone to read.

We know that attending college is very expensive. That is why CollegeQuest provides an extensive financial aid section that explains aid in terms that are easy to understand. This part of the site helps you organize your financial materials, estimate how much your family will have to contribute to college bills, and figure out how to budget your expenses and possibly lower the monthly cost of attending college. You can tell CollegeQuest about your financial situation, your personal characteristics, and your college choices, and it will provide results tailored to your individual needs.

CollegeQuest also offers an extensive scholarship search featuring more than 850,000 awards. Once you input your personal data, the program will give you information about the need-based and merit scholarships for which you qualify.

You can apply to more than 1,000 colleges right from CollegeQuest, using the eApply feature, which houses the Universal Application, the Common Application, and other custom college applications. Your profile in the Personal Organizer will be used to fill out part of your applications. You can print the application, fill in the supplementary information, and mail it, or you can submit the application electronically. The Application Manager helps monitor your applications and gives you a checklist of important steps to complete along the way.

As you can see, CollegeQuest makes the entire college application process easier by helping you prepare, search, apply, and pay for college all in one place.

THE BEST ADVICE.
THE BEST TOOLS.
THE RIGHT CHOICE.

"One of the very best . . . . .perfect . . . " **College Bound**

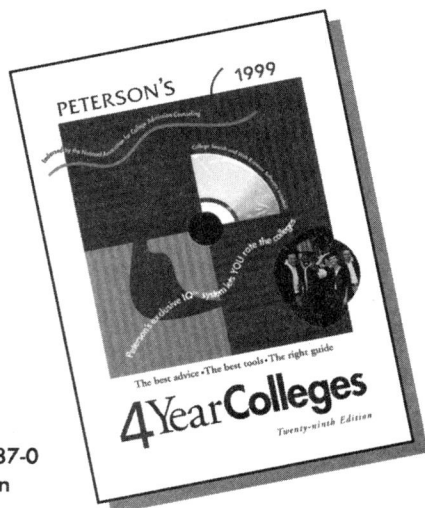

PETERSON'S 1999

4 Year Colleges
Twenty-ninth Edition

The best advice • The best tools • The right guide

ISBN
1-56079-987-0
29th edition
$24.95

Everything you need is here in one place! Over 2,000 college and university profiles! Plus—complete information on majors, costs, entrance requirements, and financial aid.

The World's Leading College Guide—Endorsed by the National Association for College Admission Counseling

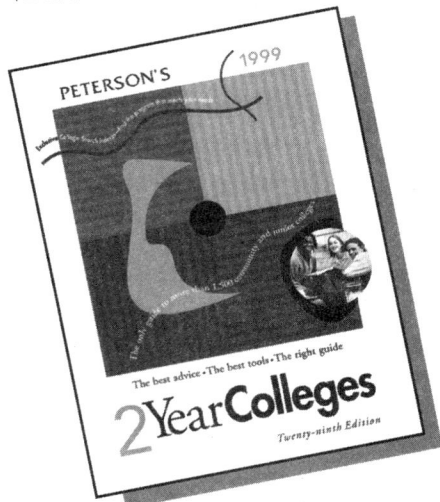

PETERSON'S 1999

The best advice • The best tools • The right guide

2 Year Colleges
Twenty-ninth Edition

ISBN
1-56079-993-5
29th edition
$24.95

With complete information on program offerings at 1,500 junior and community colleges, this guide **makes it easy** for you to compare programs, requirements, costs, and facilities. Full-time, part-time, weekend, and co-op degree programs are highlighted.

P PETERSON'S
Princeton, New Jersey
www.petersons.com

At fine bookstores near you.
To order from our online store,visit
http://bookstore.petersons.com

TEXAS

The comprehensive data in this section will help you identify colleges by various factors, such as geographical location and size of school. The maps below indicate the location of two- and four-year colleges in Texas. On the following pages, alphabetical lists of schools include statistics that can help you determine which institutions might be a good match for you. Starting on page 64 you will find a list of majors; look them over for areas that may interest you.

2-Year Colleges

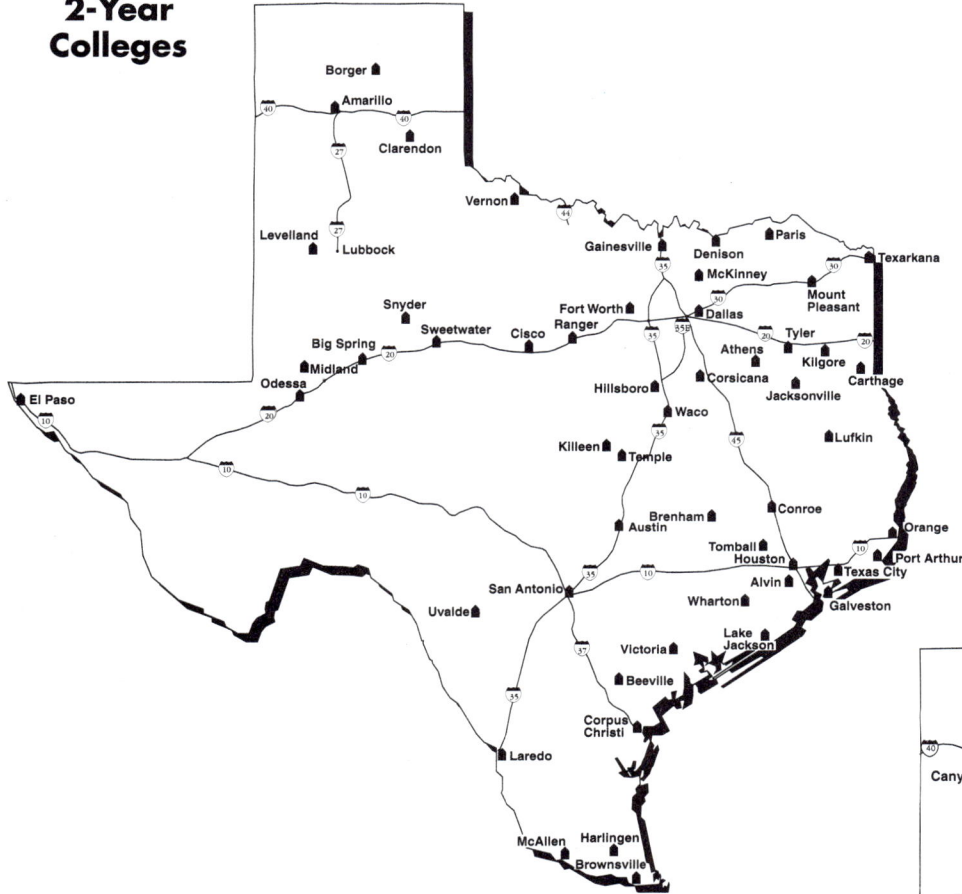

Borger
Amarillo
Clarendon
Vernon
Levelland
Lubbock
Gainesville
Paris
Denison
McKinney
Texarkana
Mount Pleasant
Snyder
Fort Worth
Ranger
Dallas
Tyler
Sweetwater
Cisco
Athens
Kilgore
Carthage
Big Spring
Midland
Corsicana
Jacksonville
Odessa
Hillsboro
Waco
El Paso
Lufkin
Killeen
Temple
Brenham
Conroe
Austin
Orange
Tomball
Houston
Port Arthur
San Antonio
Alvin
Texas City
Wharton
Galveston
Uvalde
Victoria
Lake Jackson
Beeville
Corpus Christi
Laredo
McAllen
Harlingen
Brownsville

4-Year Colleges

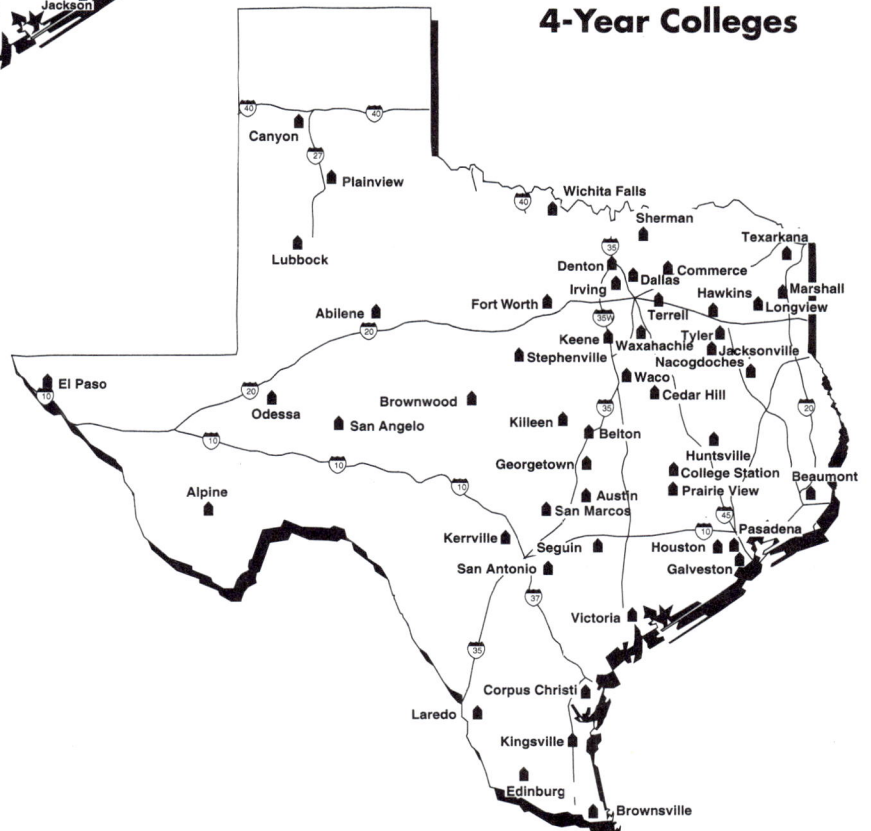

Canyon
Plainview
Wichita Falls
Sherman
Texarkana
Lubbock
Denton
Dallas
Commerce
Marshall
Irving
Hawkins
Longview
Abilene
Fort Worth
Terrell
Keene
Waxahachie
Tyler
Jacksonville
El Paso
Stephenville
Nacogdoches
Odessa
Brownwood
Waco
Cedar Hill
San Angelo
Killeen
Belton
Huntsville
Georgetown
College Station
Beaumont
Alpine
Austin
Prairie View
San Marcos
Kerrville
Pasadena
Seguin
Houston
San Antonio
Galveston
Victoria
Laredo
Corpus Christi
Kingsville
Edinburg
Brownsville

The Dallas/Fort Worth area includes the towns of Arlington, Farmers Branch, Garland, Irving, Lancaster, Mesquite, Richardson, and Weatherford.

The Houston area includes the towns of Baytown, Friendswood, Kingwood, and Pasadena.

Two-Year Colleges

This index includes the names and locations of accredited two-year colleges in Texas and shows responses to Peterson's 1998 Survey of Undergraduate Institutions. If an institution submitted incomplete or no data, one or more columns opposite the institution's name is blank.

Y—Yes; N—No; R—Recommended; S—For Some

		Degrees Awarded: Transfer Associate (C), Terminal Associate (T), Bachelor's (B), Master's (M), Doctoral (D), First Professional (F)	Undergraduate Enrollment Fall 1997	Percent Attending Part-Time	Percent 25 Years of Age or Older	Percent of Grads Going on to 4-Year Colleges	Open Admissions	High School Equivalency Certificate Accepted	High School Transcript Required	Entrance Test(s) Required	Need-based Aid Available	Non-need-based Aid Available	Part-Time Jobs Available	Career Counseling Available	Job Placement Services Available	College Housing Available	Number of Sports Offered	Number of Majors Offered
Alvin Community College	Alvin	C,T	2,765	62	45		Y	Y		Y	Y	Y	Y	Y	Y	N	4	32
Amarillo College	Amarillo	C,T	5,810	64	43	52	Y		Y	Y		Y	Y	Y	Y	Y	3	84
Angelina College	Lufkin	C,T	3,942	74	58		Y	Y	Y	Y		Y	Y	Y	Y	Y	10	50
The Art Institute of Dallas	Dallas	T	1,200		5		Y	Y	Y	Y	Y	Y	Y	Y	Y	Y		5
The Art Institute of Houston	Houston	C,T	1,437	32	0		N	Y	Y	R,S	Y	Y	Y	Y	Y	Y		9
Austin Business College	Austin	T	191					Y	Y	Y								1
Austin Community College	Austin	C,T	26,000		28		Y	Y	R	R,S		Y	Y	Y	Y	Y	N	6	69
Blinn College	Brenham	C,T	9,927	41	18	55	Y	Y	Y	Y	Y	Y	Y	Y			Y	7	23
Brazosport College	Lake Jackson	C,T	3,561	74	40		Y	Y	S	S	Y	Y	Y	Y	Y		N	6	51
Brookhaven College	Farmers Branch	C,T	1,026	80	55		Y			Y		Y	Y	Y	Y	Y	N	9	7
Cedar Valley College	Lancaster	C,T	1,148	63			Y	Y	R	R,S	Y	Y	Y	Y	Y		N	3	13
Central Texas College	Killeen	C,T	15,041	86	55		Y	Y	Y	Y	Y	Y	Y	Y	Y	Y	Y	10	50
Cisco Junior College	Cisco	C,T	2,583	56	45		Y	Y			Y	Y	Y	Y	Y		Y	7	35
Clarendon College	Clarendon	C,T	800		43		Y	Y	Y	Y	Y	Y	Y	Y	Y	Y	Y	7	12
Coastal Bend College	Beeville	C,T	2,209	45	58		Y	Y	Y	Y	Y	Y	Y	Y	Y	Y	Y	12	56
The College of Saint Thomas More	Fort Worth	C,T	25	0	65	80	N	Y	Y	Y	Y	Y	Y	Y	Y	Y			1
College of the Mainland	Texas City	C,T	3,546		60		Y	Y		S		Y	Y	Y	Y		N	8	17
Collin County Community College District	McKinney	C,T	10,784	67	46	52	Y			Y	Y	Y	Y	Y	Y	Y	N	9	30
Commonwealth Institute of Funeral Service	Houston	T	82		41		N	Y	Y	R,S	Y	Y		Y	Y	N		1
Computer Career Center	El Paso	C																
Dallas Institute of Funeral Service	Dallas	C,T	220				Y	Y						Y				1
Del Mar College	Corpus Christi	C,T	10,424	67	68		Y	Y		Y	Y	Y	Y	Y	Y	Y	N	14	77
Eastfield College	Mesquite	C,T	2,154	67	51		Y	Y		Y	Y	Y	Y	Y	Y	Y	N	7	22

Two-Year Colleges

This index includes the names and locations of accredited two-year colleges in Texas and shows responses to Peterson's 1998 Survey of Undergraduate Institutions. If an institution submitted incomplete or no data, one or more columns opposite the institution's name is blank.

Y—Yes; N—No; R—Recommended; S—For Some

		Degrees Awarded: Transfer Associate (C), Terminal Associate (T), Bachelor's (B), Master's (M), Doctoral (D), First Professional (F)	Undergraduate Enrollment Fall 1997	Percent Attending Part-Time	Percent 25 Years of Age or Older	Percent of Grads Going on to 4-Year Colleges	Open Admissions	High School Equivalency Certificate Accepted	High School Transcript Required	Entrance Test(s) Required	Need-based Aid Available	Non-need-based Aid Available	Part-Time Jobs Available	Career Counseling Available	Job Placement Services Available	College Housing Available	Number of Sports Offered	Number of Majors Offered
El Centro College	Dallas	C,T																
El Paso Community College	El Paso	C,T	19,845		48	39	Y	Y		R	Y	Y	Y	Y	Y	N	9	62
Executive Secretarial School	Dallas	C,T	539	30	15		N	Y	Y	Y	Y		Y	Y	Y	Y		4
Frank Phillips College	Borger	C,T	1,101		26		Y	Y	Y	Y	Y	Y	Y	Y	Y	Y	4	62
Galveston College	Galveston	C,T	1,955	68	51		Y	Y	S	Y	Y	Y	Y	Y	Y	N	4	27
Grayson County College	Denison	C,T	2,873	63	53		Y	Y		Y	Y	Y	Y	Y		Y	2	48
Hallmark Institute of Technology	San Antonio	T	450		85			Y	Y					Y	Y	N		2
Hill College of the Hill Junior College District	Hillsboro	C,T	2,682	63	32	60	Y	Y			Y	Y	Y	Y	Y	Y	5	84
Houston Community College System	Houston	C,T	30,710	71	61	23	Y	Y			Y	Y	Y	Y	Y	N		62
Howard College	Big Spring	C,T	1,674	49	26		Y	Y	Y	Y	Y	Y	Y	Y	Y	Y	7	37
ITT Technical Institute	Arlington	T	392		63		N	Y		Y				Y	Y	N		2
ITT Technical Institute	Austin	T	536		35		N	Y	Y	Y	Y	Y	Y	Y	Y	N		2
ITT Technical Institute	Garland	T	391				N	Y	Y	Y	Y	Y	Y	Y	Y	N		2
ITT Technical Institute	Houston	C,T	480		22	7	N	Y	S	Y			Y	Y	Y	N	4	2
ITT Technical Institute	Houston	T																
ITT Technical Institute	San Antonio	T	602		32		N	Y	Y	Y	Y		Y	Y	Y	N		2
Jacksonville College	Jacksonville	C,T	320		20	85	Y	Y		Y		Y	Y	Y		Y	4	2
KD Studio	Dallas	T	145		24		Y	Y	Y		Y	Y		Y		N		1
Kilgore College	Kilgore	C,T	4,206	47	35		Y	Y	Y	Y	Y	Y	Y	Y	Y	Y	7	65
Kingwood College	Kingwood	C,T	2,405	61	45		Y	Y		S	Y	Y	Y	Y		N		17
Lamar University–Orange	Orange	C,T	1,561	62	45		Y	Y	Y		Y	Y	Y	Y		N		16
Lamar University–Port Arthur	Port Arthur	C,T	2,362		45		Y		Y	Y	Y	Y	Y	Y	Y	N		21
Laredo Community College	Laredo	C,T	7,319	55			Y		Y	R	Y	Y	Y	Y	Y	Y	7	23

Two-Year Colleges

This index includes the names and locations of accredited two-year colleges in Texas and shows responses to Peterson's 1998 Survey of Undergraduate Institutions. If an institution submitted incomplete or no data, one or more columns opposite the institution's name is blank.

		Degrees Awarded: Transfer Associate (C), Terminal Associate (T), Bachelor's (B), Master's (M), Doctoral (D), First Professional (F)	Undergraduate Enrollment Fall 1997	Percent Attending Part-Time	Percent 25 Years of Age or Older	Percent of Grads Going on to 4-Year Colleges	Open Admissions	High School Equivalency Certificate Accepted	High School Transcript Required	Entrance Test(s) Required	Need-based Aid Available	Non-need-based Aid Available	Part-Time Jobs Available	Career Counseling Available	Job Placement Services Available	College Housing Available	Number of Sports Offered	Number of Majors Offered
Lee College	Baytown	C,T	6,010	71	52	6	Y		S	Y	Y	Y	Y	Y	Y	N	7	60
Lon Morris College	Jacksonville	C	375	19	4		N	Y	Y	Y	Y	Y	Y	Y		Y	10	49
McLennan Community College	Waco	C,T	5,493	55			Y	Y	Y	Y	Y	Y	Y	Y	Y	N	7	29
Midland College	Midland	C,T	4,000	38	80		Y		Y	Y	Y	Y	Y	Y	Y	N	7	58
Miss Wade's Fashion Merchandising College	Dallas	C	181	13	35		N	Y	Y		Y		Y	Y	Y	Y		3
Montgomery College	Conroe	C,T	3,860	38			Y	Y			Y	Y	Y	Y		N		18
Mountain View College	Dallas	C,T	5,340	41			Y	Y	Y	Y	Y	Y	Y	Y	Y	N	6	14
MTI College of Business and Technology	Friendswood	T	226	60			N	Y	Y		Y		Y	Y	Y	N		2
Navarro College	Corsicana	C,T	3,467	44	35		Y	Y		Y	Y	Y	Y	Y	Y	Y	9	56
North Central Texas College	Gainesville	C,T	2,987	59	38		Y	Y	Y	Y	Y	Y	Y	Y		Y	9	28
Northeast Texas Community College	Mount Pleasant	C,T	2,027	52	48		Y	Y		S	Y	Y	Y	Y	Y	Y	4	16
North Harris College	Houston	C,T	7,516	68	45		Y	Y	Y	Y	Y	Y	Y	Y	Y	N	9	41
North Lake College	Irving	C,T	6,233	51			Y	Y	R		Y	Y	Y	Y	Y	N	4	15
Odessa College	Odessa	C,T	5,051	44	42		Y	Y		S	Y	Y	Y	Y	Y	Y	12	57
Palo Alto College	San Antonio	C,T																
Panola College	Carthage	C,T	1,694	46	43		Y	Y	R,S	Y	Y	Y	Y	Y		Y	5	5
Paris Junior College	Paris	C,T	2,764	57	41		Y	Y	Y	Y	Y	Y	Y	Y	Y	Y	8	22
Ranger College	Ranger	C,T	861				Y	Y		R,S		Y	Y	Y	Y	Y	8	6
Richland College	Dallas	C,T																
St. Philip's College	San Antonio	C,T	5,810	58	55		Y	Y	Y	R,S	Y	Y	Y	Y	Y	N	5	58
San Antonio College	San Antonio																	

Two-Year Colleges

This index includes the names and locations of accredited two-year colleges in Texas and shows responses to Peterson's 1998 Survey of Undergraduate Institutions. If an institution submitted incomplete or no data, one or more columns opposite the institution's name is blank.

Y—Yes; N—No; R—Recommended; S—For Some

Name	Location	Degrees Awarded: Transfer Associate (C), Terminal Associate (T), Bachelor's (B), Master's (M), Doctoral (D), First Professional (F)	Undergraduate Enrollment Fall 1997	Percent Attending Part-Time	Percent 25 Years of Age or Older	Percent of Grads Going on to 4-Year Colleges	Open Admissions	High School Equivalency Certificate Accepted	High School Transcript Required	Entrance Test(s) Required	Need-based Aid Available	Non-need-based Aid Available	Part-Time Jobs Available	Career Counseling Available	Job Placement Services Available	College Housing Available	Number of Sports Offered	Number of Majors Offered
San Jacinto College–Central Campus	Pasadena	C,T																
San Jacinto College–North Campus	Houston	C,T	3,727	63	41		Y	Y	Y	R,S	Y	Y	Y	Y	Y	N	8	39
San Jacinto College–South Campus	Houston	C,T	4,608	72	50		Y	Y		Y	Y	Y	Y	Y	Y	N	10	38
South Plains College	Levelland	C,T	5,955	46	39	90	Y	Y		Y	Y	Y	Y	Y	Y	Y	10	59
South Texas Community College	McAllen	C,T																
Southwest Texas Junior College	Uvalde	C,T	3,452				Y	Y		Y	Y	Y	Y	Y	Y	Y	7	14
Tarrant County Junior College	Fort Worth	C,T	15,647	67	44	65	Y			Y		Y	Y	Y	Y	N	6	43
Temple College	Temple	C,T	2,897		54		Y		S	R,S		Y	Y	Y	Y	Y	6	20
Texarkana College	Texarkana	C,T	3,733	62	42	25	Y	Y		Y	Y	Y	Y	Y	Y	N	7	32
Texas Southmost College	Brownsville																	
Texas State Tech Coll	Sweetwater	T	992	23	50		Y	Y	Y	Y	Y	Y	Y	Y	Y	Y	6	16
Texas State Tech Coll–Harlingen	Harlingen	T	2,746	42	31		Y	Y	Y	Y	Y	Y	Y	Y	Y	Y	14	31
Texas State Tech Coll– Waco/Marshall Campus	Waco	C,T	4,232	23	33		Y	Y	Y	Y	Y	Y	Y	Y	Y	Y	7	46
Tomball College	Tomball	C,T	2,735	62	45	77	Y	Y		R	Y	Y	Y	Y		N		21
Trinity Valley Community College	Athens	C,T	4,382		51		Y	Y		Y	Y	Y	Y	Y	Y	Y	6	54
Tyler Junior College	Tyler	C,T	8,224		38		Y	Y		Y	Y	Y	Y	Y	Y	Y	9	53
Vernon Regional Junior College	Vernon	C,T	1,750	56	43		Y	Y		Y	Y	Y	Y	Y	Y	Y	9	13
Victoria College	Victoria	C,T	3,822		49		Y	Y		Y	Y	Y	Y	Y	Y	N	2	11
Weatherford College	Weatherford	C,T	2,175	42	56		Y	Y		Y	Y	Y	Y	Y	Y	Y	3	13
Western Texas College	Snyder	C,T	745	50	39		Y	Y	Y	Y		Y	Y	Y	Y	Y	11	22
Wharton County Junior College	Wharton	C,T																

Four-Year Colleges

This index includes the names and locations of accredited four-year colleges and universities in Texas and shows responses to Peterson's 1998 Survey of Undergraduate Institutions. If an institution submitted incomplete or no data, one or more columns opposite the institution's name is blank.

STANDARDIZED TEST SCORE RANGES FOR 1997–98
% of freshmen scoring within each interval

Institution	City	Degrees Awarded (A, B, M, D, P)	Undergraduate Enrollment Fall 1997	Number of Computers on Campus for General Student Use	ACT Composite Scores 1-5	6-11	12-17	18-23	24-29	30-36	SAT I Verbal Scores 200-299	300-399	400-499	500-599	600-699	700-800	SAT I Math Scores 200-299	300-399	400-499	500-599	600-699	700-800
Abilene Christian University	Abilene	A,B,M,D,P	3,840	500	0	0	10	47	36	7	0	5	24	41	23	7	0	5	29	36	24	6
Amber University	Garland	B,M	571	30																		
Angelo State University	San Angelo	A,B,M	5,720	250	0	0	17	54	26	3	1	10	40	35	12	2	0	10	39	33	15	3
Arlington Baptist College	Arlington	B	172	6																		
Austin College	Sherman	B,M	1,154	110	0	0	0	19	57	24	0	0	9	40	36	15	0	0	6	34	48	12
Baptist Missionary Assoc Theol Sem	Jacksonville	A,B,M	21	5																		
Baylor College of Dentistry	Dallas	B,M,P	62	24																		
Baylor University	Waco	B,M,D,P	10,486	917	0	0	2	50	42	6	0	1	15	49	28	7	0	0	11	45	35	9
Concordia University at Austin	Austin	A,B	757	40	0	0	26	46	26	2	1	13	43	27	14	2	0	8	46	32	13	1
The Criswell College	Dallas	A,B,M,P	374	25																		
Dallas Baptist University	Dallas	A,B,M	2,695	100							1	7	41	30	17	4	0	16	36	28	17	3
Dallas Christian College	Dallas	A,B	274	15	0	0	23	54	23	0												
DeVry Institute of Technology	Irving	A,B	2,634	287																		
East Texas Baptist University	Marshall	A,B,M	1,245	106	0	0	11	51	30	8												
Hardin-Simmons University	Abilene	B,M,P	1,971	140	0	0	12	58	26	4	0	5	29	46	18	2	0	7	35	39	16	3
Houston Baptist University	Houston	A,B,M	1,686	115							0	1	44	40	13	2	0	2	33	42	20	3
Howard Payne University	Brownwood	B	1,489	220	0	0	28	44	25	3	2	16	35	33	12	2	2	15	37	30	14	2
Huston-Tillotson College	Austin	B	698	103							16	42	32	10	0	0	0	10	49	32	9	0
ICI University	Irving	A,B,M		0																		
Institute for Christian Studies	Austin	B	21	5																		
Jarvis Christian College	Hawkins	B		75																		
Lamar University	Beaumont	A,B,M,D	8,305	120							0	0	76	22	1	1	0	0	77	21	1	1
LeTourneau University	Longview	A,B,M	1,756	120	0	2	7	34	41	16	0	4	22	31	29	14	1	3	14	35	34	13
Lubbock Christian University	Lubbock	B,M		60																		
McMurry University	Abilene	B	1,348	172	0	0	16	55	26	3	0	7	39	40	13	1	0	10	36	38	13	3
Midwestern State University	Wichita Falls	A,B,M	5,093	220																		
Northwood University, Texas Campus	Cedar Hill	A,B	808	20	0	0	39	54	7	0	3	9	48	29	9	2	0	14	45	30	11	0
Our Lady of the Lake University of San Antonio	San Antonio	B,M,D	2,462	200	0	0	21	62	17	0	0	8	48	36	7	1	0	11	52	31	5	1
Paul Quinn College	Dallas	B		50																		
Prairie View A&M University	Prairie View	B,M	4,776	102							29	41	24	5	1	0	15	44	27	11	2	1
Rice University	Houston	B,M,D,P	2,714	185	0	0	0	16	18	66	0	0	2	7	31	60	0	0	1	7	24	68
St. Edward's University	Austin	B,M	2,477	275	0	0	19	52	26	3	0	4	36	45	14	1	1	7	40	39	12	1
St. Mary's University of San Antonio	San Antonio	B,M,D,P	2,565	100	0	0	6	60	33	1	0	2	27	51	17	3	0	1	20	57	20	2
Sam Houston State University	Huntsville	B,M,D	11,223	200	0	0	31	57	11	1	1	14	46	29	9	1	1	16	44	32	7	0
Schreiner College	Kerrville	A,B,M	647	52	0	0	15	49	32	4	0	14	29	42	15	0	0	9	36	34	21	0
Southern Methodist University	Dallas	B,M,D,P	5,314	409	0	0	2	41	48	9	0	1	17	44	30	8	0	1	15	44	31	9
Southwestern Adventist University	Keene	A,B,M	818	50	0	1	28	52	17	2	2	10	36	36	15	1	5	18	41	29	7	0
Southwestern Assemblies of God University	Waxahachie	A,B,M	1,450	45	0	0	30	53	16	1	0	12	32	36	12	8	0	12	40	28	16	4
Southwestern Christian College	Terrell	A,B		40																		
Southwestern University	Georgetown	B	1,189	150	0	0	1	23	60	16	0	0	6	38	41	15	0	0	6	40	40	14
Southwest Texas State University	San Marcos	B,M,D	17,533	729	0	0	11	65	23	1	0	5	36	47	11	1	0	4	36	47	12	1
Stephen F. Austin State University	Nacogdoches	B,M,D	10,544	800																		
Sul Ross State University	Alpine	A,B,M		124																		

Four-Year Colleges

This index includes the names and locations of accredited four-year colleges and universities in Texas and shows responses to Peterson's 1998 Survey of Undergraduate Institutions. If an institution submitted incomplete or no data, one or more columns opposite the institution's name is blank.

STANDARDIZED TEST SCORE RANGES FOR 1997–98
% of freshmen scoring within each interval

Institution	Location	Degrees Awarded	Undergrad Enrollment Fall 1997	# Computers	ACT 1-5	6-11	12-17	18-23	24-29	30-36	SATV 200-299	300-399	400-499	500-599	600-699	700-800	SATM 200-299	300-399	400-499	500-599	600-699	700-800
Tarleton State University	Stephenville	A,B,M		450																		
Texas A&M International University	Laredo	B,M		200																		
Texas A&M University	College Station	B,M,D,P	33,926	1,500	0	0	0	28	58	14	0	1	14	48	30	7	0	0	8	38	42	12
Texas A&M University at Galveston	Galveston	B	1,095	72	0	0	0	54	38	8	0	0	33	41	23	3	0	0	24	50	24	2
Texas A&M University–Commerce	Commerce	B,M,D	4,785	405																		
Texas A&M University–Corpus Christi	Corpus Christi	B,M,D	4,120	300	0	1	18	60	20	1	1	10	33	40	13	3	1	9	40	38	11	1
Texas A&M University–Kingsville	Kingsville	B,M,D	4,854	600																		
Texas A&M University–Texarkana	Texarkana	B,M	682	104																		
Texas Chiropractic College	Pasadena	B,P		NR																		
Texas Christian University	Fort Worth	B,M,D,P	6,163	1,336																		
Texas Lutheran University	Seguin	B	1,344	50							0	6	28	40	22	4	0	5	34	39	18	4
Texas Southern University	Houston	B,M,D,P	4,130	410																		
Texas Tech University	Lubbock	B,M,D,P	20,806	1,460	0	0	7	55	34	4	0	3	30	47	17	3	0	3	26	47	20	4
Texas Wesleyan University	Fort Worth	B,M,P	1,899	65	0	1	23	54	21	1	0	15	42	30	13	0	1	13	38	35	12	1
Texas Woman's University	Denton	B,M,D	4,984	332																		
Trinity University	San Antonio	B,M	2,298	100	0	0	0	3	69	28	0	0	3	37	46	14	0	0	4	33	49	14
University of Central Texas	Killeen	B,M	691	30																		
University of Dallas	Irving	B,M,D	1,096	70	0	0	1	18	61	20	0	1	5	35	35	24	0	1	7	34	44	14
University of Houston	Houston	B,M,D,P	22,369	825	0	0	15	59	22	4	0	8	36	37	15	4	0	5	30	40	21	4
University of Houston–Clear Lake	Houston	B,M	3,467	380																		
University of Houston–Downtown	Houston	B	8,194	350																		
University of Houston–Victoria	Victoria	B,M	711	100																		
University of Mary Hardin-Baylor	Belton	B,M	1,997	157	0	0	18	53	25	4	0	10	33	39	16	2	0	9	41	33	16	1
University of North Texas	Denton	B,M,D	18,719	575							0	5	27	44	20	4	0	6	31	40	18	5
University of St. Thomas	Houston	B,M,D,P	1,482	195	0	0	0	34	60	6	0	1	16	43	33	7	0	0	10	50	32	8
The University of Texas at Arlington	Arlington	B,M,D	13,171	600	0	0	12	56	30	2	1	9	34	40	14	2	0	4	32	43	18	3
The University of Texas at Austin	Austin	B,M,D,P	35,701	3,500	0	0	2	31	55	12	0	1	11	41	36	11	0	0	7	34	42	17
The University of Texas at Brownsville	Brownsville	B,M		62																		
The University of Texas at Dallas	Richardson	B,M,D	5,168	360							0	1	16	39	31	13	0	0	8	32	44	16
The University of Texas at El Paso	El Paso	B,M,D	12,852	NR																		
The University of Texas at San Antonio	San Antonio	B,M,D	14,400	800	0	0	18	69	12	1	1	8	45	35	10	1	1	7	44	37	10	1
The University of Texas at Tyler	Tyler	B,M	2,365	107																		
U of Texas Health Science Center at San Antonio	San Antonio	B,M,D,P		1,000																		
U of Texas-Houston Health Science Center	Houston	B,M,D,P	238	NR																		
U of Texas Medical Branch at Galveston	Galveston	B,M,D,P	769	112																		
The University of Texas of the Permian Basin	Odessa	B,M		130																		
The University of Texas–Pan American	Edinburg	A,B,M,D		500																		
U of Texas Southwestern Medical Center at Dallas	Dallas	B,M,D,P		150																		
University of the Incarnate Word	San Antonio	B,M	2,606	200							2	13	47	30	7	1	1	20	46	27	5	1
Wayland Baptist University	Plainview	A,B,M	3,463	253	0	1	31	40	25	3	1	9	38	33	15	4	0	14	40	28	15	3
West Texas A&M University	Canyon	B,M	5,458	800	0	0	12	58	26	4	0	0	38	46	14	2	0	0	37	45	15	3
Wiley College	Marshall	A,B		30																		

Action Career Training
273 CR 287
Merkel, Texas 79536
915-695-1594

American Trades Institute
6627 Maple Avenue
Dallas, Texas 75235
214-352-2222

Business Skills Training Center
325 Pearl Street
Denton, Texas 76201
940-383-2626

Capitol City Careers
4630 Westgate Boulevard
Austin, Texas 78745
512-892-4270

Conlee College of Cosmetology
402 Quinlan
Kerrville, Texas 78028
210-896-2380

Executive Secretarial School
4849 Greenville Avenue, Suite 200
Dallas, Texas 75206-4125
214-369-9009

Houston Training School
704 Shotwell Street
Houston, Texas 77020
713-675-4300

International Aviation and Travel Academy
5757 Alpha Road
Dallas, Texas 75240
977-387-0553

International Aviation and Travel Academy
4846 South Collins Street
Arlington, Texas 76018
817-784-7000

International Travel Institute
2400 Augusta, Suite 180
Houston, Texas 77057-4911
713-785-4268

Joe G. Davis School of Vocational Nursing–Huntsville Memorial Hospital
3000 Interstate Highway 45
P.O. Box 4001
Huntsville, Texas 77340
409-291-3411

Larry's Barber and Hairstyling College
6614 South R.L. Thorton Freeway
Dallas, Texas 75232-3672
214-372-4871

Le Chef College of Hospitality Careers
6020 Dillard Circle
Austin, Texas 78752
512-323-2511

Lincoln Technical Institute
2501 East Arkansas Lane
Grand Prairie, Texas 75051-9990
214-660-5701

Lindsey-Cooper Refrigeration School, Inc.
815 South Beltline Road at Shady Grove Road
Irving, Texas 75060
972-790-7404

Memorial Hospital–Memorial City School of Vocational Nursing
920 Frostwood Drive
Houston, Texas 77024-2434
713-932-3799

Microcomputer Technology Institute
7277 Regency Square Boulevard
Houston, Texas 77036
713-974-7181

National Education Center– National Institute of Technology
3622 Fredricksburg Road
San Antonio, Texas 78201-3841
210-733-6000

Ocean Corporation
10840 Rockley Road
Houston, Texas 77099-3416
281-530-0202

San Antonio College of Medical and Dental Assistants
4205 San Pedro Avenue
San Antonio, Texas 78212-1899
210-733-0777

School of Automotive Machinists
1911 Antoine Drive
Houston, Texas 77055-1803
713-683-3817

Southwestern Paralegal Institute
4888 Loop Central Drive, Suite 800
Houston, Texas 77081
713-666-7600

Texas School of Bartenders
3311 Richmond Avenue, Suite 218
Houston, Texas 77098
713-522-4600

Tyler County Hospital–School of Nursing
1100 West Bluff
Woodville, Texas 75979
409-283-8141

Visible Changes University
7075 Southwest Freeway
Houston, Texas 77074
713-778-9100

Williams Barber College
1251 Evans Avenue
Fort Worth, Texas 76104
817-332-0359

What You Need to Know About Distance Learning

What Exactly Is Distance Learning?

Distance learning is the delivery of educational programs to off-site students through the use of technologies such as cable or satellite television, videotapes and audiotapes, fax, computer modem, computer conferencing and videoconferencing, and other means of electronic delivery.

What Does This Mean to You?

It may mean that now you can find the resources of your state's top four-year universities right next door at your local community college.

Or it may mean that you can connect to your professor's e-mail with your home computer modem, exchange messages, and turn in a ten-page "paper" electronically.

Or it may mean that you will use your personal computer to locate library references and information.

Or it may mean that you can walk down the hall at your place of work and spend your lunch hour taking a course with like-minded colleagues seeking career advancement.

Distance learning expands the reach of the classroom by using various technologies to deliver university resources to off-campus sites, transmit college courses into the workplace, and enable students to view class lectures in the comfort of their homes.

Where and How Can I Take Distance Learning Courses?

The proliferation of new, cheaper telecommunications technologies and the demand for broader access to educational resources have prompted the development of diverse educational networks. Most states have established new distance learning systems to advance the delivery of instruction to schools, postsecondary institutions, and state government agencies. Colleges and universities are collaborating with commercial telecommunications entities, including online information services, such as America Online®, and cable and telephone companies, to provide education to far-flung student constituencies. Professions such as law, medicine, and accounting as well as knowledge-based industries are utilizing telecommunications networks for the transmission of customized higher education programs to working professionals, technicians, and managers.

Distance learning offerings may be:

- *Credit courses.* In general, if these credit courses are completed successfully, they may be applied toward a degree.
- *"Noncredit" courses and courses offered for professional certification.* These programs can help you acquire specialized knowledge in a concentrated, time-efficient manner and stay on top of the latest developments in your field. They provide a flexible way for you to prepare for a new career or study for professional licensure and certification. Many of these university programs are created in cooperation with professional and trade associations so that courses are based on real-life workforce needs and the practical skills learned are immediately applicable in the field.

What Does Distance Learning Offer?

Professional Certification

Certificate programs often focus on employment specializations, such as hazardous waste management or electronic publishing, and can be helpful to those seeking to advance or change careers. Also, many states mandate continuing education for professionals such as teachers, nursing home administrators, or accountants. Distance learning offers a convenient way for many individuals to meet professional certification requirements. Health care, engineering, and education are just a few of the many professions that take advantage of distance learning to help their professionals maintain certification.

Many colleges offer a sequence of distance learning courses in a specific field of a profession. For instance, within the engineering profession, certificate programs in *Computer Integrated Manufacturing, Systems Engineering, Test and Evaluation*, and *Waste Management Education and Research Consortium* are offered via distance learning.

Business offerings include distance learning certification in *Information Technology, Total Quality Management*, and *Health Services Management*.

Within the field of education, you'll find distance learning certificate programs in areas such as *Early Reading Instruction* and *Special Education for Learning Handicapped*.

Degree Programs

There are opportunities for individuals to earn degrees at a distance at the associate, baccalaureate, and graduate levels. Two-year community college students are now able to earn baccalaureate degrees—without relocating—by transferring to distance learning programs offered by four-year universities. Corporations are forming partnerships with universities to bring college courses to worksites and encourage employees to continue their education. Distance learning is especially popular among people who want to earn their degree part-time while continuing to work full-time. Although on-campus residencies are sometimes required for certain distance learning degree programs, they generally can be completed while employees are on short-term leave or vacation.

Continuing Education Units (CEUs)

If you choose to take a course on a noncredit basis, you may be able to earn Continuing Education Units (CEUs). The CEU system is a nationally recognized system to provide a standardized measure for accumulating, transferring, and recognizing participation in continuing education programs. One CEU is defined as 10 contact hours of participation in an organized continuing education experience under responsible sponsorship, capable direction, and qualified instruction.

How Does Distance Learning Work?

Enrolling in a Course

Enrolling in a distance learning course may simply involve filling out a registration form, making sure that you have access to the equipment needed, and paying the tuition and fees by check, money order, or credit card. In these cases your applications may be accepted without entrance examinations or proof of prior educational experience.

Other courses may involve educational prerequisites and access to equipment not found in all geographic locations. Some institutions offer detailed information about individual courses, such as a course outline, upon request. If you have access to the Internet and simply wish to review course descriptions, you may be able to peruse an institution's course catalogs electronically by accessing the institution's home page on the World Wide Web.

Time Requirements

Some courses allow you to enroll at your convenience and work at your own pace. Others closely adhere to a traditional classroom schedule. Specific policies and time limitations pertaining to withdrawals, refunds, transfers, and renewal periods can be found in the institutional catalog.

Admission to a Degree Program

If you plan to enter a degree program, you should consult the academic advising department of the institution of your choice to learn of entrance requirements and application procedures. You may find it necessary to develop a portfolio of your past experiences and of your accomplishments that may have resulted in college-level learning.

Transferring Credit

If you wish to apply credit for distance learning courses, you should be aware that some institutions may impose certain requirements before they will accept the credit, and some courses or programs may require previous study or experience.

NOTE: If you wish to earn credit for a course and apply it to a degree program, be certain that it meets the requirements of the institution to which you want to transfer the credit, as well as the requirements of your specific program within that institution.

For example, if you want to earn 3 credits from College A's accounting course and apply those credits toward University B's Bachelor of Arts degree, check with University B and its Department of Business before you enroll in the course to ascertain whether the credits will be accepted. Most institutions' catalogs list both the general admission requirements and the prerequisites for individual courses.

Most institutions limit the number and kinds of credits they will accept. You can usually transfer credit earned in a distance learning course from one regionally accredited institution to another. As policies and degree requirements of colleges and universities vary markedly, you should consult the appropriate officials at the institution from which you expect to receive a degree to be sure that the credit is transferable. If you pursue course work at an institution that is not regionally accredited, it may be difficult for you to transfer the credit.

Course Materials

Course materials include a study guide, which is usually provided as part of the initial cost. A course may also require workbooks, procedure manuals, lab kits, videotapes or audiotapes, slides, photographs, or other audiovisual materials, which you must purchase separately. The cost of these items varies from institution to institution. In some cases, you may borrow materials from the institution by paying a deposit that is partially refunded when you return the materials. Audiovisual materials are usually sent with the study guide, and you will be charged as indicated in the institution's catalog. Details about costs for course materials are listed in the institution's catalog or in the study guide.

Cross-Registration

Cross-registration is a cooperative arrangement offered by many colleges and universities for the purpose of increasing the number and types of courses offered at any one institution. This arrangement allows students to cross-register for one or more courses at any participating host institution. While specific cross-registration program requirements may vary, typically a student can cross-register without having to pay the host institution additional tuition.

If your college participates in cross-registration, check with your home institution concerning any additional tuition costs and request a cross-registration form. Check with your adviser and registrar at your home

Did You Know . . . ?

"You should read, read, read. Do your homework, visit the library, check out materials on college and scholarships, and be sure to visit your guidance counselor."

—Barbara Bluestein, Librarian, Princeton High School, Cincinnati, Ohio

institution to make sure the course you plan to take is approved and then contact the host institution for cross-registration instructions. Make sure there is space available in the course you want to take at the host institution, as some host institutions give their own students registration priority.

To participate in cross-registration, you may need to be a full-time student (some programs allow part-time student participation) in good academic and financial standing at your home institution. Check with both colleges well in advance for all of the specific requirements.

Student Snapshot

Elise's right choice

Charlotte Thomas
Career and Education Editor, Peterson's

You can't blame Elise Witman for thinking about choosing a college in Hawaii. She comes from a small town near Buffalo, New York, where, she admits, the winters are

Junior ROTC

Since 1992, national enrollment in Junior ROTC (high school reserve officer training program) has grown from 200,000 to more than 300,000. The number of programs has risen by more than 60 percent, from 1,481 to about 2,400. ROTC teaches high school students about leadership, military organization, physical fitness, and health. About half the students who enroll end up serving in the military. Their ROTC service lets them start two pay grades ahead of other recruits in most branches of the military.

"kind of cold." So right after she took the PSATs and the mail from colleges started flooding in, those luscious postcards from Hawaii and Florida colleges really popped out. But for the time being, they went in the drawer where she kept everything having to do with colleges.

How not to freak out

At the start of her senior year in high school, Elise was beginning what would be for her a relatively hassle-free process of getting into college. For many students at the same point in their lives, this is a period of indecision and uncertainty, if not downright freaking out. Not for Elise, and for that she partly has her father to thank. "He likes to get things done ahead of time," she says. She also credits the relatives who predictably asked in the summer before her senior year, "And what are you going to do when you graduate?"

Elise didn't rely only on the mail she received to come up with a list of final choices. She got videos from her high school

Split-option Enlistment

Split-option enlistment allows students to enlist in the Army National Guard during their junior year in high school. You will attend one weekend drill a month and basic training the summer between your junior and senior year. The summer following graduation, you will attend advanced individual training and return in time to start college in the fall. You must be at least 17 years old to take advantage of Split-option Enlistment. Call your local recruiting office for more information.

counselor's office and sent away for more information from colleges she thought she might like. Her dad helped by searching the Internet for the information she was particularly interested in. She also thumbed through college guidebooks, then bounced ideas off friends. A few of them discussed going to the same college.

Being interested in premed was a biggie when it came to narrowing down her choices. Elise is really interested in science and anything medically related. Perhaps "interested" is an understatement. Elise is in a special high school program that allows her to take some of her classes at a local hospital. "We get to go into operating rooms," she says, which is probably why surgery is her intended focus in medical school.

Elise's wish list
But even though Elise knows what she wants to study, it's not as if there are only a few colleges to choose from. Being premed was a start, but where to look after that? Climate, location, and size entered the picture. "Mostly I looked for premed and a big school, but after that, weather definitely helped," she says.

Nearness to her family got put on her wish list, too. Distance from home was one reason why her parents nixed the idea of Hawaii. Elise agreed with them, realizing she couldn't just hop on a plane and fly 4,000 miles for Thanksgiving. With lots of cousins getting married and grandparents to see, she wanted to be close enough for the occasional long weekend.

This one's it
Elise finally settled on the University of South Carolina. In fact, it's her dream college. It made the top after her campus visit and when she discovered Preston College, a college within a college at the University. Residents are selected to live there, and Elise really likes the setup, which includes a campus mom and dad who live with the students, organized events, weekly dinners, and on-going discussion groups. Because of this living arrangement, she knows that if she's accepted she won't have to endure those awful "first months on campus when I'm homesick, nervous, and why did I ever come here" jitters.

The University of South Carolina also had another attraction—scholarships. She applied for an ROTC Naval scholarship in her junior year and, since the university offers that program, if she gets it, she already will be there. Having slept on a Navy ship during a Girl Scout overnight, she was hooked on life at sea. Plus, with a

clever eye to the future, Elise says, "I know there are limited positions for physicians in the Navy."

Tips from a smooth sailor
Speaking of the Navy, it might seem like Elise encountered few storms in applying to college. It was pretty smooth sailing, but looking back she does have some tips to pass on.

What if you hate to write and can't deal with the dreaded college essay?
Elise lucked out here, too. None of the colleges she applied to required an essay, but she vicariously went through the experience with friends and saw a lot of them crossing off a college because they didn't want to write an essay. "It cut down their choices," she says.

After applying to and being admitted to the University of South Carolina, she had to write a small essay as part of getting into Preston College, which offered the special living arrangement on the campus. But that was fun because one of the questions asked was what animal she would be if she had to choose. With those kinds of questions, it's easy to follow her advice not to write generic answers. She does say, "Paint a [verbal] picture or tell a story of why you love a subject instead of just throwing words at people."

Even if you always wait until the last minute to do anything, don't procrastinate when getting those applications in.

With her dad to get her going, Elise had her applications in by October. Her parents and high school counselors advised her that college admission offices are swamped with paperwork later in the year.

Applying early presented them with plenty of time to look at her application.

That goes for recommendation letters, too. In addition to asking early, Elise provided the people she planned to use as references with a list of activities she is involved in.

The campus visit lowdown
Elise used her campus visits to the max, grilling everybody she met. She asked questions about how easy it is to make friends and get involved in activities. She wanted to know about classes and dorms, volunteering opportunities at local hospitals, tutoring programs, Internet hookups, and on and on. No surprise that she advises students to go on a campus visit prepared with plenty of questions. "Even the silliest things like what is it like when you want to take a shower," she tips. "Some questions might sound funny, but this is your life.

"You'll be there for four years. No question is dumb because all the answers will affect you."

Coming from a suburban hometown, Elise expected to not like the University of South Carolina campus because it's located right in the capital. When she realized that the campus location was near restaurants, parks, and even nearby hospitals where she could volunteer, her fears melted away. "It's always awake," she says of the city.

Choose the college you want, not because your friends will be there

Though Elise chose her college for the right reasons, she saw a good friend make the common mistake of going where her boyfriend plans to attend. She doesn't feel it's particularly smart to base a life decision on someone you've been dating for two months. "Go with the best school for you and where your interests are instead of socially," she reflects.

It sounds like Elise has everything under control, yet, typically looking ahead, she wishes she knew more about what elective courses to take. "There are so many to choose from," she sighs. She knows what's expected for her major, but doesn't know about the hundreds of other possibilities outside of science. "I wish I had more background on which elective courses are good for freshmen, which ones I could handle, and which are not such a workload," she says.

If Elise is as thorough about choosing classes as she was in choosing a college, she'll have no trouble.

Student Snapshot

Early decision

Charlotte Thomas
Career and Education Editor, Peterson's

Want to make a high school counselor or college admissions director shudder? Tell them you want to apply to college early decision but don't know where to apply. To them that's like running fingernails across a blackboard. To Tom Rajala, Director of Admissions at Boston University, such statements are indicative of all the confusion swirling around early decision.

A whole lot of shuddering going on

Chances are if you're applying to colleges, you've heard about early something—early decision, early action, early notification, early admission. Chances are you have an idea about what they mean. Chances are also that what you think is wrong.

Rick Rizoli, Director of College and Academic Counseling at The Rivers School, an independent coeducational day school in Weston, Massachusetts, gets peppered with early decision questions by students and parents all the time. "It's a hot button issue," he says. Some of the confusion exists because the terms sound similar. While there are parallels between them, there are more differences because the specifics of each program vary widely from college to college.

Some simplified definitions

Early admission—High school juniors who have almost all their credits necessary for graduation can attend college for their senior year. This is clearly not for everybody— you must be very bright and very mature.

Early action, early notification—These are very similar. In both, students hear if they've been admitted earlier in the process and so can take action earlier. High school students apply in the fall of their senior year, and the colleges notify them of acceptance generally by January without requiring them to commit financially. Students have until early May to accept or decline an offer of admission.

Early decision—Basically, you commit early to a college that has accepted you by sending in a deposit, and you do not apply to any others. But having said that, there are many variations of early decision. Or, as Geraldine Fryer, an educational consultant for sixteen years, quips, "Tune in to see what version of 'early' colleges will have this year." Early decision is becoming more prevalent and, as it does, institutions add their own twists.

More on early decision

A common denominator is that early decision is a binding agreement between you and the college. If the college accepts you, you pay a deposit within a short period of time and sign an agreement stating you will not apply to other colleges. To keep students from backing out, some colleges mandate that applicants' high school counselors cannot send transcripts to other institutions.

In many ways, early decision is a win-win for both students and colleges. Students can relax and enjoy their senior year of high school without waiting to see if they've been accepted. Colleges know early in the year who is enrolled. But as competition to get into college has increased, students and colleges have started to look for angles, observes Fryer, so that now early decision comes in all flavors. Some colleges have early decision versions one and two. Others have stepped deadlines or rolling deadlines. Some are totally restrictive, others have degrees of binding. Even within one university there might be variations.

Don't think you have to be a member of the Early Decision Club

Competition also creates the situation in which students feel the heat to be accepted at top-notch institutions. Parents are anxious for that bit of inside information that will get their child admitted, while colleges jockey to attract the best applicants. Pressure builds, and in the middle stand high school students feeling as though they have to be members of the Early Decision Club, says Rajala. They think that if they don't show an interest early on, they're not seen as committed. Or they will have a better chance at an Ivy League college if they go early decision. "That's a widely held perception," he says.

Fanning the flames, students and parents read headlines about prestigious universities sewing up 30 to 40 percent of their incoming class with early decision applicants. Panic sets in when they think that they're looking at fewer spots left.

When is early decision the right decision?

For good and bad reasons, early decision is a growing trend, so why not just do it? To that, high school counselors and college admission directors give a resounding "H-h-h-h-old on. Don't rush into it."

Early decision is an excellent idea that comes with a warning. It's not a good idea unless students have done a thorough college search and know without a shred of doubt that this is the college for them. "Don't do early decision unless you've spent time on the campus, in classes and dorms, and you have a true sense of the academic and social climate of that college," advises Fryer. Her concern is that many students are not mature enough to make a decision of that magnitude. High school juniors and seniors are, for the most part, in flux. "Student reactions can change on a dime," observes Fryer. An advocate of early decision, Rizoli feels that students who know where they want to go might as well take advantage of what early decision offers, but again, only if they have meticulously researched their options.

Adding to the admonitions about early decision, Michael R. Heintze, Director of Admissions at Clemson University, notes that the choice of college is probably the first major decision a young person is asked to make. After signing an early decision agreement, students could become interested in a major not offered by the college and be locked into the wrong institution for their field.

Heintze is concerned that often students and parents don't fully understand the ramifications of signing an early decision agreement.

Some abuses of a good idea

"It gets sticky for everyone if students change their minds," says Rajala. This is where some of the abuses of early decision occur. Parents of students who have signed agreements and then want to apply elsewhere get angry at high school counselors, saying they've taken away their rights to choose among colleges. They try to force them to send out transcripts even though their children have committed to one college. To guard against this scenario, Boston University asks parents and students to sign a statement signifying their understanding that early decision is a binding plan. At The Rivers School, Rizoli also has his own form for students and parents to sign acknowledging that they completely realize the nature of an early decision agreement.

The financial reason against early decision

Another common argument against early decision is that if an institution has you locked in, there's no incentive to offer applicants the best financial packages. The consensus seems to be that if you're looking to play the financial game, then don't apply early decision.

But, this issue, too, has many facets. Rizoli argues that the best financial aid offers are usually made to attractive applicants. Generally if a student receives an early decision offer, they fall into that category and so would get "the sweetest" financial aid anyway. "That doesn't mean that there aren't colleges out there using financial incentives to get students to enroll. Take a strong candidate who applies to six or eight schools and gets admitted to them all. Then admission is a nonissue. The question is, how much money will the colleges throw his way. That student can compare financial aid, no question," contends Rizoli.

Questions to ask before you decide to go early decision

- Why are you applying early decision?
- Have you thoroughly researched several colleges and know what your options are?
- Do you know why you're going to college and what you want to accomplish there?
- Have you visited several campuses, spent time in classes, stayed overnight, and talked to professors?
- Do the courses the college offers match your goals?
- Are you absolutely convinced that one college clearly stands out above all others?

Jump INTO SCHOOL

What Schools Look for in Prospective Students

Because requirements differ, students should check with all the colleges that they are interested in attending to find out what the specific requirements are at those schools.

- Academic Record: Admission representatives look at the breadth (how many), diversity (which ones), and difficulty (how challenging) of the courses on your transcript.
- Grades: Consistent performance that shows you have worked to your potential. If your grades are not good initially, colleges look to see that significant improvement has been made. Some colleges have minimum grade point averages they are willing to accept.
- Class Rank: Colleges consider the academic standing of a student in relation to the other members of his/her class. Are you in the top 25 percent of your class? Top half? Ask your counselor for your class rank.
- Standardized Test Scores: Colleges look at test scores in terms of ranges. Highly selective colleges look for ACT scores of at least 27 and SAT I scores above 1220. If your scores aren't high but you did well academically in high school, don't be discouraged. There is no set formula for admission. Even at the most competitive schools, some students' test scores are lower than you would think.
- Out-of-Class Activities: Colleges look for depth of involvement (variety and how long you participated), initiative (leadership), and creativity demonstrated in activities, service, or work.

- Recommendations: Most colleges require a recommendation from your high school guidance counselor. Some ask for references from teachers or other adults.
- College Interview: Required by most colleges with highly selective procedures. For further information, see the College Interview section later in the book.

Admission Procedures

Obtain applications from your high school's guidance department, at college fairs, or by calling or writing to colleges and requesting applications. Admission information can also be gathered from college representatives, catalogs, Web sites, and directories; alumni or students attending the college; and campus visits.

Which admission option is best for you?

Two-year colleges usually have an "open-door" admission policy. High school graduates may enroll as long as space is available. Sometimes vocational/technical schools are somewhat selective, and competition for admission may be fairly intense for programs that are highly specialized.

One of the first questions you will have to answer on an admission application for a four-year institution is which admission option you want. Four-year institutions generally offer the following admission options:

Early admission

A student of superior ability is admitted into college courses and programs before completing high school.

Early decision

A student declares a first-choice college, requests that the college decide on acceptance early (November-January), and agrees to enroll if accepted. Students with a strong high school record who are sure they want to attend a certain school should consider early decision admission.

Early action

Similar to early decision, but if a student is accepted, he/she has until the regular admission deadline to decide whether to attend.

Early evaluation

A student can apply under early evaluation to find out if the chance of acceptance is good, fair, or poor. Applications are due before the regular admission deadline, and the student is given an opinion between January and March.

Regular admission

This is the most common option offered to students. A deadline is set when all applications must be received, and all notifications are sent out at the same time.

Rolling admission

The college accepts students who meet the academic requirements on a first-come, first-served basis until it fills its freshman class. No strict application deadline is specified. Applications are reviewed and decisions are made immediately (usually within two to three weeks). This method is commonly used at large state universities, so students should apply early for the best chance of acceptance.

Open admission

Virtually all high school graduates are admitted, regardless of academic qualifications.

Deferred admission

An accepted student is allowed to postpone enrollment for a year.

What is needed to apply?

Freshman applications can be filed any time after a student has completed the junior year of high school. Colleges strongly recommend that students apply by April (at the latest) of their senior year in order to be considered for acceptance, scholarships, financial aid, and housing. College requirements may vary, so always read and comply with specific requirements. In general, admission officers are interested in the following basic materials:

- A completed and signed application and any required application fee.
- An official copy of your high school transcript, including your class ranking and grade point average. The transcript must include all work completed as of the date the application is submitted. Check with your guidance counselor for questions about these items.
- An official record of your ACT or SAT I scores.
- Other items that may be required include letters of recommendation, an essay, the secondary school report form and midyear school report (sent in by your guidance counselor after you fill out a portion of the form), and any financial aid forms required by the college.

CollegeQuest eApply

In an effort to provide you with more convenient ways to apply, many colleges accept common applications. These make it easier for you to apply to several colleges at once. With CollegeQuest eApply at CollegeQuest.com, you can apply to more than 1,200 colleges using a single application. You can enter all of your basic biographical and academic information into a personal information manager, which stores this data for use on each new application that you open. This reduces the amount of time you have to spend repeatedly entering information, and it also reduces the risk of errors. Once you have completed your applications, you can then print and mail them, or you can submit them electronically through CollegeQuest's secure connection if the college accepts electronic applications. You can visit CollegeQuest at http://www.collegequest.com.

Types of College Academic Calendars

Traditional Semester:	Two equal periods of time during a school year.
Early Semester:	Two equal periods of time during a school year. The first semester is completed before Christmas.
Trimester:	Calendar year divided into three equal periods of time. The third trimester replaces summer school.
Quarter:	Four equal periods of time during a school year.
4-1-4:	Two equal terms of about four months separated by a one-week term.

Application Guidelines

One of the most intimidating steps of applying for admission to college is filling out all the forms. Here is a list of dos and don'ts to help you put your best foot forward on your college applications.

Do

- Read applications and directions carefully.
- Make sure that everything that is supposed to be included is enclosed.
- Fill out your own applications. Type the information yourself to avoid crucial mistakes.
- Start with the simple applications and then progress to the more complex ones.
- Make copies of applications and practice filling one out before you complete the original.
- Type or neatly print your answers, and then proofread the applications several times for accuracy. Also ask someone else to proofread it for you.
- If asked, describe how you can make a contribution to the schools to which you apply.
- Be truthful, and do not exaggerate your accomplishments.
- Keep a copy of all forms you submit to colleges.
- Be thorough and on time.

Don't

- Use correction fluid. If you type your application, use a correctable typewriter or the liftoff strips to correct mistakes.
- Write in script. If you do not have access to a typewriter, print neatly.
- Leave blank spaces. Missing information may cause your application to be sent back or delayed while admission officers wait for complete information.
- Be unclear. If the question calls for a specific answer, don't try to dodge it by being vague.
- Put it off! Do it early.

The College Interview

Not all schools require or offer an interview. However, if you are offered an interview, use this one-on-one time to evaluate the college in detail and to sell yourself to the admission officer. The following list of questions can help you collect the information you may need to know.

Academic questions

- How many students apply? How many are accepted?
- What are the average GPA and average ACT or SAT I score(s) for those accepted?
- How many students in last year's freshman class returned for the sophomore year?
- What is the school's procedure for credit for Advanced Placement high school courses?
- As a freshman, will I be taught by professors or teaching assistants?
- How many students are there per teacher?
- When is it necessary to declare a major?
- Is it possible to have a double major or to declare a major and a minor?
- What are the requirements?
- How does the advising system work?
- Does this college offer overseas study, cooperative programs, or academic honors programs?
- What is the likelihood, due to overcrowding, of getting closed out of the courses I need?
- What technology is used in the classroom?
- How well equipped are the libraries and laboratories?
- Are there internships available?
- How effective is the job placement service of the school?

If you have already chosen a major:
- What is the average class size in my area of interest?
- Have any professors in my area of interest recently won any honors or awards?
- What teaching methods are used in my area of interest (lecture, group discussion, fieldwork)?
- How many students graduate in four years in my area of interest?
- What are the special requirements for graduation in my area of interest?

Social questions

- What is the student body like? Age? Sex? Race? Geographic origin?
- What percentage of students live in dormitories? Off-campus housing?
- What percentage of students go home for the weekend?
- What are some of the regulations that apply to living in a dormitory?
- What are the security precautions taken on campus and in the dorms?
- Is the surrounding community safe?
- Are there problems with drug and alcohol abuse on campus?
- Are there dorms available that are free of any use of drugs and alcohol?
- Do faculty members and students mix on an informal basis?
- How important are the arts to student life?
- What facilities are available for cultural events?
- How important are sports to student life?
- What facilities are available for sporting events?

- What percentage of the student body belongs to a sorority/fraternity?
- What is the relationship between those who belong to the Greek system and those who don't?
- Are students involved in the decision-making process at the college? Do they sit on major committees?
- What other activities can students get involved in?

Financial questions

- What percentage of students receive financial aid based on need?
- What percentage of students receive scholarships based on academic ability?
- What percentage of a typical financial aid offer is in the form of a loan?
- If my family demonstrates financial need on the FAFSA (and FAF, if applicable), what percent of the established need is generally awarded?
- How much did the college increase the cost of room, board, tuition, and fees from last year?
- Do opportunities for financial aid, scholarships, or work-study increase each year?

Admission questions

- When is the application deadline?
- When does the school notify you of the admission decision?
- If there is a deposit required, is it refundable?

Writing the College Essay

College essays show the way you think and how you write. They also reveal additional information about you that is not in your other application material. Not all colleges require essays, and those that do often have a preferred topic. Make sure you write about the topic that is specified.

Some examples of essay topics include:

Tell us about yourself

Describe your personality and a special accomplishment. Illustrate the unique aspects of who you are, what you do, and what you want out of life. Share a travel experience that made an impact on you, or write about something you have learned from your parents.

Tell us about an academic or extracurricular interest or idea

Show how a book, experience, quotation, or idea reflects or shaped your outlook and aspirations.

Tell us why you want to come to our college

Explain why your goals and interests match the programs and offerings of that particular school. This question requires some research about the school. Be specific.

Show us an imaginative side of your personality

This question requires some originality but is a great opportunity to show off your skills as a writer. Start writing down your thoughts and impressions well before the essay is due. Think about how you have changed over the years so that if and when it comes time to write about yourself, you will have plenty of information. Write about something that means a lot to you, and support your thoughts with reasons and examples. Then explain why you care about your topic.

The essay should not be a summary of your high school career. Describe yourself as others see you, and use a natural, conversational style. Use an experience to set the scene in which you will illustrate something about yourself. For example, you might tell how having a disabled relative helped you to appreciate life's simple pleasures. Or you may use your athletic experiences to tell how you learned the value of teamwork. The essay is your chance to tell something positive or enriching about yourself, so highlight an experience that will make the reader interested in you.

Outline in the essay what you have to offer the college. Explain why you want to attend the institution and how your abilities and goals match the strengths and offerings at the university. Write, rewrite, and edit. Do not try to dash off an essay in one sitting. The essay will improve with time and thought. Proofread and concentrate on spelling, punctuation, and content. Have someone else take a look at your essay. Make copies and save them after mailing the original.

Admission officers look for the person inside the essay. They seek students with a breadth of knowledge and experiences, someone with depth and perspective. Inner strength and commitment are admired, too. Not everyone is a winner all the time. The essay is a tool you can use to develop your competitive edge. In other words, your essay should explain why you should be admitted over other applicants.

As a final word, write the essay from the heart. It should have life and not be contrived or one-dimensional. Avoid "telling them what they want to hear" and, instead, be yourself.

Peterson's © 1999

Sample Letter to College Requesting General Information

If neither you nor your guidance counselor has an application for a college that you are interested in, write a brief letter to the admission office of the college to request an application or use the Instant Inquiry feature on petersons.com.

Date

Your Street Address
City, State, Zip

Office of Admission
Name of College
Street Address
City, State, Zip

To Whom It May Concern:

My name is _____, and I am a (freshman, sophomore, junior, senior) at (name of your school). I will graduate in (month) (year).

Please send me the following information about your college: a general information brochure, program descriptions, an admission application, financial aid information, and any other information that might be helpful. I am considering _____ as my major field of study (optional, if you know your major).

I am interested in visiting your campus, taking a campus tour, and meeting with an Admission Counselor and Financial Aid Officer. I would also like to meet with an adviser or professor in the (major) department, if possible (optional, if you know your major). I will contact you in a week to set up a time that is convenient.

If you would like to contact me directly, I can be reached at (your phone number with area code). Thank you.

Sincerely,

(Signature)
Name

Auditions and Portfolios

The following tips will help you showcase your talents and skills when preparing for an audition or portfolio review.

Music auditions

Freshmen who wish to pursue a degree in music, whether it is vocal or instrumental, typically must audition. If you are a singer, prepare at least two pieces in contrasting styles. One should be in a foreign language, if possible. Selections should be chosen from operatic, show music, or art song repertories and should be memorized. If you are an instrumentalist or pianist, be prepared to play scales and arpeggios, at least one étude or technical study, and a solo work. Audition pieces need not be memorized. Sight-reading may be requested.

When performing music that is sight-read, it is recommended that the student take time to look over the piece and make certain of the key signature and time signature before proceeding with the audition. Additional advice includes bringing a familiar accompanist to an audition, remaining confident, practicing breathing exercises, and taking private music and music theory lessons.

"My advice is to ask for help from teachers, try to acquire audition information up front, and know more than is required for the audition,"

Student Resume

Just as a potential employee sends in a resume, it helps admission counselors see who you are "at a glance" if you send along a student resume with your admission application. Modify this resume to highlight your strengths and experiences. Keep the resume to one page if possible.

Name
Street Address
City, State, Zip
Phone
E-mail, if applicable

High School	Name Address City, State, Zip
Graduation Date	Month, Year
Current GPA	3.5
Current Class Rank	Top 25 percent
Test Scores	SAT I May 1998 V—6000; M—540 ACT April 1998 Composite-22 English-22; Math-21; Reading-22; Science Reasoning-24
Academic Honors	National Honor Society, April 1998 Honor Roll, 1995–98
Athletics	Soccer, October 1996–present Most Valuable Player–1997
Activities	Student Government, September 1996-present Secretary, 1997–98 Volunteer, spring 1996–present Children's Hospital, Philadelphia, PA 5 hours per week
Part-Time Work	Sales Clerk, May 1996–present Philadelphia Zoo gift shop Cashier/Sales, July 1995–May 1996 Petsmart
Interests	Sports, reading, animals
Major Goals	To major in biology or zoology (optional, if you know your major)

---

says one student. "It is also a good idea to select your audition time and date early."

"Try to perform your solo in front of as many people as you can as many times as possible," says another student. "You may also want to try to get involved in a high school performance."

Programs differ, so students are encouraged to call the college and ask for audition information. In general, music departments are seeking students who demonstrate technical competence and performance achievement.

Tips from a college music professor:

- Work with a private or high school choir, orchestra, or band teacher to select solo materials. Selections from your state music contest list are recommended.
- Attend concerts of varying styles of music.
- Build a music library of jazz, non-Western, and classical music.
- Attend music camps and all-state programs.
- Talk to adults involved in the industry (professionals).
- Talk to a music professor about your interests.
- Take a music theory/history course.
- Get involved in community youth ensembles.
- Gain as much performance experience outside of high school as possible.

Peterson's © 1999

Admission to music programs varies in degree of competitiveness, so it is recommended that you audition at a minimum of three colleges and a maximum of five to maximize your opportunity. The degree of competitiveness varies also by instrument, especially if a renowned musician teaches a certain instrument. At many colleges, a second audition is available if you feel you did not audition to your potential. Ideally, you will be accepted into the music program of your choice, but it does occasionally happen that a student is accepted academically but not to the music program. You must then make the decision to either pursue a music program at another college or consider another major at that college.

Dance auditions

At many four-year colleges, an open class is held the day before auditions. A performance piece that combines improvisation, ballet, modern, and rhythm is taught and then students are expected to perform the piece at auditions. Professors look for coordination, technique, rhythm, degree of movement, and body structure. The dance faculty members also assess your ability to learn and your potential to complete the curriculum. Dance programs vary, so check with the college of your choice for specific information.

Art portfolio

A portfolio is simply a collection of your best pieces of artwork. The pieces you select to put in your portfolio should demonstrate your interest and aptitude for a serious education in the arts. A well-developed portfolio can assist you in gaining acceptance into a prestigious art college, as well as increase your chances of being awarded a scholarship in national portfolio competitions. The pieces you select should show diversity in technique and variety in subject matter. The work may be executed in any medium and in either black-and-white or color. Your portfolio can include classroom assignments as well as independent projects. You can also include your sketchbook.

Specialized art colleges request that you submit an average of ten pieces of art, but remember—quality is more important than quantity. The admission office staff will review your artwork and transcripts to assess your skill and potential for success in the visual arts field. There is no simple formula for success other than hard work. In addition, there is no such thing as a "perfect portfolio," nor any specific style or direction to achieve one.

Portfolio tips

- Try to make your portfolio as clean and organized as possible.

- It is important to protect your work, but make sure the package you select is easy to handle and does not interfere with the viewing of the artwork.
- Drawings that have been rolled up are difficult for the jurors to handle and view. You may shrink-wrap the pieces, but it is not required.
- Avoid loose sheets of paper between pieces.
- If you choose to mount or mat your work (not required), use only neutral gray tones, black, or white.
- Never include framed pieces or three-dimensional work.
- Use spray fixative on pieces that could smudge.
- A slide portfolio should be presented in a standard 8½ × 11 plastic slide sleeve, which can be purchased at any photo or camera supply store.
- Be sure paintings are completely dry before you place them in your portfolio.
- Label each piece with your name, address, and high school.

Theater auditions

Most liberal arts colleges do not require that students audition to be accepted into the theater department, unless the college offers a Bachelor of Fine Arts (B.F.A.) degree in theater.

Students generally should apply to the college of their choice prior to scheduling an audition. A full day on campus is also advised so that you may talk with theater faculty and students, attend classes, meet with your admission counselor, and tour the facilities.

Although each college and university has different requirements, generally those students who audition for a B.F.A. acting program should prepare two contrasting monologues taken from plays of your choice. The total length of both pieces should not exceed 5 minutes, and it is advised that you take a theater resume and photo to the audition.

Musical theater requirements generally consist of one up-tempo musical selection and one ballad, as well as one monologue from a play or musical of your choice. The total of all your pieces should not exceed 5 minutes. Music for the accompanist, a resume of your theater experience, and a photo are also required.

Audition suggestions

- Choose material suitable to your age.
- If you choose your monologue from a book of monologues, you should read the entire play and be familiar with the context of your selection.
- Select a monologue that allows you to speak directly to another person; you should play only one character.
- Your selection must be memorized.
- Avoid using "characterization" or "style," as they tend to trap you rather than tapping deeper into inner resources.

Should You Specialize?

If you're not absolutely sure you want to paint or play music for a living, it's probably more advantageous to attend a liberal arts university with a respected music, art, or engineering department. Nadine Bourgeois, Assistant Dean and Director of Admissions at Parsons School of Design in New York City, observes that specialty schools accelerate the process of developing talent, as students are quickly immersed into the very heart of their skills. Such a focused environment is not the place for the undecided student.

Passion is a key element to look for if you think you want to attend a specialized school or conservatory. Allison Ball, Dean of Enrollment Services at the New England Conservatory of Music in Boston, knows students are right for her institution when they demonstrate that they are all music all day and can't imagine a future without it. Then she knows they have the kind of commitment and inner drive characteristic of conservatory students.

Campus Visits

Is it a good match?

The best time to get used to the college environment is during the spring and summer of your junior year or the fall of your senior year. Be sure to visit during the regular school year to see the campus in full swing. Open houses are a good idea and provide you with opportunities to talk to students, faculty, and administrators. Write or call in advance to take student-conducted campus tours. If possible, stay overnight in a dorm to see what living at college is really like.

Bring your transcript so that you are prepared to interview with admission officers. Take this opportunity to ask questions about financial aid and other services that are available to students. You can get a good "snapshot" of campus life by reading a copy of the student newspaper. The final goal of the campus visit is to study the school's personality and decide if it matches yours. Your parents should be involved with the campus visits so that you can share your impressions.

Tips for campus visits

- Read campus literature prior to the visit.
- Ask for directions and allow ample travel time.
- Make a list of questions before the visit.
- Dress in neat, clean casual clothes and shoes.
- Ask to meet one-on-one with a current student.
- Ask to meet personally with a professor in your area of interest.
- Ask to meet a coach or athlete in your area of interest.
- Offer a firm handshake.
- Use good posture.
- Listen and take notes.
- Speak clearly and maintain eye contact with people you meet.
- Don't interrupt.
- Be honest, direct, and polite.
- Be aware of factual information so that you can ask questions of comparison and evaluation.
- Be prepared to answer questions about yourself. Practice a mock interview with someone.
- Don't be shy about explaining your background and why you are interested in the school.
- Ask questions about the background and experiences of the people you meet.
- Convey your interest in getting involved in campus life.
- Be positive and energetic.
- Don't feel as though you have to talk the whole time or carry the conversation yourself.
- Relax and enjoy yourself.
- Thank those you meet and send thank-you notes when appropriate.

Greek Life

At the National Interfraternity Council in Indianapolis, four predominant qualities are stressed when speaking about fraternities and sororities: scholarship, friendship, leadership, and service. High school students who already have experience in these four areas have a jump on Greek life. What's more important, however, is that students who decide to pledge a fraternity or sorority gain additional opportunities in these four areas. For ease of reading the rest of this section, the word fraternity will be used to apply to sororities as well.

Scholarship

A fraternity experience assists you in making the academic transition from high school to college. Although the classes taken in high school are challenging, even more is expected of college students. While there are no overall academic requirements for entering a fraternity, each fraternity may require certain academic standards for their

Campus Visit Checklist

Excellent = 4
Good = 3
Fair = 2
Poor = 1

	College 1	College 2	College 3	College 4
Arts facilities				
Athletic facilities				
Audiovisual center				
Bookstore				
Campus media				
Classrooms/lecture halls				
Computer labs				
Dining hall				
Dorms				
Fraternity/sorority houses				
Religious facilities				
Student union				
Surrounding community				
TOTAL				

members. Many hold mandatory study times, and the Interfraternity Council requires all fraternity members to carry a minimum grade point average of 2.0. A network system among members exists in which older members can assist younger students. Old class notes and exams are usually kept on file for study purposes, and personal tutors are often available. Members of a fraternity have a natural vested interest in seeing that other members succeed academically.

Friendship

Social life is an important component of Greek life. Social functions offer an excellent opportunity for freshmen to become better acquainted with others in the chapter. Whether it is a Halloween party or a formal dance, there are numerous chances for members to develop poise and confidence. By participating in these many functions,

College Comparison Worksheet

Fill in your top five selection criteria and any others that may be of importance to you. Once you narrow your search of colleges to five, fill in the colleges across the top row. Using a scale of 1 to 5, where 1 is poor and 5 is excellent, rate each college by your criteria. Total each column to see which college rates the highest based upon your criteria.

Selection Criteria	College 1	College 2	College 3	College 4
1.				
2.				
3.				
4.				
5.				
Other Criteria				
6.				
7.				
8.				
9.				
10.				
TOTAL				

Final Selection

Now that you have evaluated the characteristics that are most important to you and have made some decisions based on that information, make sure that you apply to more than one college and to ones with a range of admissions possibilities. In other words, don't put all your eggs in one basket.

	College 1	College 2	College 3	College 4
Sure thing				
Likely admission				
Stretch, but possible				

students enrich friendships and build memories guaranteed to last a lifetime. Remember, social functions aren't only parties; they can include such activities as intramural sports and Homecoming.

Leadership

Because fraternities are self-governing organizations, leadership opportunities abound. Students are given hands-on experience in leading committees, managing budgets, and interacting with faculty and administrators. Most houses have as many as ten or more officers, along with an array of committee members. For instance, a fraternity treasurer gains invaluable experience by working with a budget that may exceed $200,000. There are also numerous officer positions available on the Interfraternity Council.

In today's world, employers are looking for well-rounded individuals with leadership skills. By becoming actively involved in leadership roles while still in high school as well as after joining a fraternity, students gain valuable experience that is essential for a successful career. Interestingly, although Greeks represent less than 10 percent of the undergraduate student population, they hold the majority of leadership positions on campus.

Chris Baker, former Interfraternity Council President at the Ohio State University, stressed that while individual fraternities vary in what they are looking for in individuals, they are all looking for people to become involved. "It's about making leaders out of individuals," he noted.

Service

According to the National Interfraternity Council, fraternities are increasingly becoming involved in various philanthropies and hands-on service projects. Helping less fortunate people has become a major focus of Greek life. This can vary from work with Easter Seals, blood drives, and food pantry collections to community upkeep, such as picking up trash, painting houses, or cleaning up area parks. Greeks also get involved in projects with organizations such as Habitat for Humanity, the American Heart Association, and Children's Miracle Network, to name a few. By being involved in philanthropic projects, students not only raise money for worthwhile causes, but they also gain a deeper insight into themselves and their responsibility to the community.

Tips for pledging a fraternity

Mollie Monahan, who served as president of her school's chapter of Sigma Kappa, offered these tips to high school students who are considering pledging a fraternity.

- Fraternities like to accept individuals with a strong commitment to academics. "The better your grades, the better are your chances." A student who has been actively involved in the community as well as at high school has an added advantage.
- A major misconception of Greek life is that it revolves around wild parties and alcohol. Students should not mention either of these elements when seeking membership in a fraternity. "It's a turnoff," said Monahan. "That's not what we're about."

For more information about fraternities and sororities on the campus of your choice, contact the Office of Greek Affairs at that campus location. You'll be embarking on the adventure of a lifetime.

Understanding the Language

There are lots of terms in education that may be confusing to students and parents. In this section, we'll define some of these terms and tell you why they are important to understand.

What is an articulation agreement?

Articulation agreements facilitate the transfer of students and credits among state-assisted institutions of higher education by establishing transfer procedures and equitable treatment of all students in the system.

One type of articulation agreement links two or more colleges so that students can continue to make progress toward their degree, even if they must attend different schools at different times. For example, most of Ohio's community colleges have agreements with its universities that permit graduates of college parallel programs to transfer with junior standing.

A second type of articulation agreement links secondary (high school) and postsecondary institutions to allow students to gain college credit for relevant vocational courses. This type of agreement saves students time and tuition in the pursuit of higher learning.

Because articulation agreements vary from school to school and from program to program, it is recommended that students check with their home institution and the institution they are interested in attending in order to fully understand the options available to them and each institution's specific requirements.

Transferring

Why transfer?

- You completed two years of a bachelor's program at a two-year college, and you're ready to transfer to complete your degree.
- The college you currently attend is not a good match for you.
- Another college will allow you to pursue a program of study that is not available at the first institution.
- You want to make a geographic change.
- You were not originally accepted to your first-choice college, and you feel your circumstances are different now.

How it's done

- If you know you're going to transfer, plan ahead by taking courses you know will transfer.
- Transfer admission is similar to the freshman admission process, except you fill out a transfer admission application.
- If applying again to a college where you were originally denied admission, do not use the same essays or letters of recommendation.
- Explain your desire to transfer and ways in which the new college will suit you better than the college where you are currently enrolled.
- Don't speak poorly of your current college. Use your experiences as stepping stones to your goal.
- Take the opportunity to interview with college admissions personnel.
- Abide by the same deadlines as all other applicants. To apply for admission to a four-year college, apply by October or November of your college sophomore year or earlier.

How likely is it that I will be accepted?

- State universities generally have more openings for transfer students than highly selective private colleges.
- Students most likely to be admitted as transfers are those who have been the most successful in their college experience to date.
- Your chances for admission are better if you are a freshman or sophomore or have completed an associate degree recognized as a "college parallel" program.
- There are a relatively small number of spaces available for admission on a transfer basis, because availability is often based on the number of students who transferred out or who did not succeed academically.

Things to remember

- Transferring credits from one institution to another is not an automatic process. One must strictly comply with the policies of each institution. Advance planning is strongly recommended.
- Check to see if your school and/or program has an articulation agreement with the school you'd like to attend. Many colleges and universities have such agreements, which makes transferring easy.
- Four-year institutions may vary greatly in the kind and amount of transfer credit they will accept from two-year or other four-year colleges.
- Course work taken at a vocational school is not generally accepted at four-year colleges.
- Difficulties may arise in converting quarter-hour credits into semester-hour credits or in transferring courses with grades of C or lower.

What admissions directors look for in transfer students

- High school and college transcripts.
- SAT or ACT scores, but there is no need to take these tests again.
- A college curriculum that corresponds to the college to which you'd like to transfer.
- Students with energy and commitment who have the ability to communicate this to others.
- Consistent academic record. Usually the cutoff is a 3.0 or B average.
- Difficulty of college courses taken.
- Wait list students who have sustained or improved their performance since applying the first time.
- Completion of a rigorous two-year program.
- Articulation/transfer agreement affiliation.

Transfer agreements vary, so students are advised to seek more detailed information regarding transfer from their adviser and from the college or university to which they plan to transfer.

Accreditation and Affiliation

What is accreditation?

Accreditation is recognition of a college or university by a regional or national accrediting organization. This indicates that the institution has met its objectives and is maintaining prescribed educational standards. Colleges may be accredited by one of six regional associations of schools and colleges and any one of many national specialized accrediting bodies.

Specialized accreditation of individual programs is granted by national professional organizations. This is intended to ensure that specific programs meet or exceed minimum requirements established by the professional organization. States may require that students in some professions graduate from an accredited program as one qualification for licensure.

Does accreditation guarantee quality?

Accreditation is somewhat like a "pass/fail" grade. It does not differentiate colleges and universities that excel from those that meet minimum requirements. Accreditation applies to all programs within an institution, but it does not mean that all programs are of equal quality within an institution. Accreditation does not guarantee transfer recognition by other colleges. Transfer decisions are made by individual institutions.

Affiliation

Not-for-profit colleges are classified into one of the following categories: state-assisted, private/independent, or private/church-supported. The institution's affiliation does not guarantee the quality or nature of the institution, and it may or may not have an effect on the religious life of students.

State-assisted colleges and universities and private/independent colleges do not have requirements related to the religious activity of their students. The influence of religion varies among private/church-supported colleges. At some, religious services or study are encouraged or required; at others, religious affiliation is less apparent.

Student Snapshot
The Big Switch
Charlotte Thomas
Career and Education Editor, Peterson's

In the best of worlds you compile a list of colleges, find the most compatible one, and are accepted. You have a great time, graduate, and head off to a budding career.

Let's talk reality

Halfway through your first semester of college you come to the distressing conclusion that you can't stand being there—for whatever reason. The courses don't match your interests. The campus is out in the boonies and you don't ever want to see another cow. The selection of extracurricular activities doesn't cut it. You hate the dorm wallpaper (well, scratch that one).

Or . . .

You have methodically planned to go to a community college for two years and move to a four-year college to complete your degree. Transferring takes you nearer to your goal.

Or . . .

You thought you wanted to major in art, but by the end of the first semester you find yourself more interested in English lit. Things get confusing, so you drop out of college to sort out your thoughts and now you want to drop back in, hoping to rescue some of those credits.

Or . . .

You didn't do that well in high school—some major socializing got in the way of studying. But you've wised up, have gotten serious about your future, and two years of community college has brightened your prospects of transferring to a four-year institution.

Any one of these fit?

Circumstances shift, people change, and, realistically speaking, it's not all that uncommon to transfer. Lots of people do. Actually, the most common transfers are students who move from a two-year college to a four-year university or the person who opts for a career change midstream.

The reasons why students transfer run the gamut, as do the institution policies that govern them. "There are a zillion reasons why college students decide they don't want to be at an institution," says Dr. Rose Rothmeier, Director of Student Services and Counseling at Austin College in Sherman, Texas. She's got a particular interest in the challenges facing transfers and as a counseling psychologist has probably heard about every transfer situation there is. In fact, she recently began a pilot program to mentor incoming transfer students, matching them their first semester with settled transfers already at Austin College. This project was a success and indicated a real need for efforts to reduce the problems that transfers run into now that it's known there's a lot more to transferring than changing scenery.

Indeed there is, observes Rothmeier, who then asks the killer questions, "Are you walking toward a goal or running away? Will a new institution move you closer to where you want to be academically and socially?" Her questions spotlight the need to be an intentional transfer.

College Application Checklist

Keep track of the application process by inserting a check mark or the completion date in the appropriate column and row.

	College 1	College 2	College 3	College 4
Campus visit				
Campus interview				
Letters of recommendation				
NAME:				
Date requested				
Follow-up				
NAME:				
Date requested				
Follow-up				
NAME:				
Date requested				
Follow-up				
Counselor recommendation form to counselor				
Secondary school report form to counselor				
Test scores requested				
Transcripts sent				
Application completed				
Essay completed				
All signatures collected				
Financial aid forms enclosed				
Application fee enclosed				
Postage affixed/copies made/ return address on envelope				
Letters of acceptance/denial/wait list received				
Colleges notified of intent				
Tuition deposit sent				
Housing and other forms submitted to chosen college				
Orientation scheduled				

Visit: www.petersons.com

That means you have mapped out a plan based on information about yourself, your current college, and the one you want to attend.

When doubts come

Pauline Bartolone had to face those tough questions. The rural upstate New York college she initially chose seemed to fit her criteria—small class size, less expensive. Halfway into her first semester, Bartolone started having doubts but pushed them aside. It's hard to admit you've made a mistake of that magnitude, plus the thought of transferring was too complicated.

The fact that everyone on campus looked and thought alike was a fact she couldn't ignore. She wanted diversity in people and classroom discussions. She resolved the situation by transferring to College at the New School University Eugene Lang smack dab in the middle of Manhattan and found the diverse student population and social activism she was looking for.

Bartolone is not alone. Incoming students often tell Vikki Weinhaus, Associate Director of Admissions at American University in Washington, D.C., that the reason they've transferred there is because they were unhappy with their former college environment and/or major.

Think before you leap

Whatever the reasons, transferring involves more than switching academic gears. Adjusting to a new academic environment is difficult even under the best circumstances. For that reason, Bartolone, speaking from personal experience, warns others considering transferring to thoroughly evaluate why they want to leave one college for another. She admits she began at the wrong school because she hadn't given much thought to what she wanted before choosing to go there.

People can choose a college for arbitrary reasons, agrees Rothmeier. For that reason, admissions departments try to ensure a good match between the student and campus before matriculation. But sometimes students don't realize they've made a mistake until it's too late.

Out of the frying pan

Transferring might be the solution. However, moving from your present situation might land you in another uncomfortable one. Bartolone cautions students to extensively research the possibilities at the new campus before making the move. "Stay with students, talk to admissions, try to learn as much as you can about the school," she strongly advises.

Chapter 6 • Jump into School 107

Aside from losing credits, time, and money, transferring brings up the problem of adjusting to a new situation. This affects just about all transfer students—from those who made a mistake in choosing a college to those who planned to go to a two-year college and then transferred to a four-year campus.

What to watch out for

Differences in student populations

Students at two-year colleges usually are commuters and thus find a traditional academic environment startlingly different. Says Rothmeier, "If you transfer to a four-year college, you'll find that things happen at all times of the day or night. For instance, meetings can take place Sunday night at 10 p.m. Lives revolve around the campus."

Different teaching methods

The first year at a four-year institution sets the tone for the rest of the undergraduate years. Transfers miss out on learning the fundamentals of their major the way everyone else in the class was taught. Everything, from how professors present material to how tests are given to computer systems, is different. Even grade values can change. It might be harder to attain a 4.0 at a new school. "It's an across-the-board change," says Rothmeier.

Different expectations

Community college transfers are suddenly taking upper-level courses at the four-year college, with faculty expectations that they can perform as well as the juniors who have been there since year one. Warns Rothmeier, "Professors could make references to material and you won't know what they're talking about."

Different faculty-student interaction

At some institutions, college students are not used to interacting with faculty and being an active participant in the learning process. At Austin College, professors do more than just give lectures—they act as resources. "Students who haven't had this kind of experience are hesitant and cautious to relate with faculty and don't realize this kind of interaction is an important part of their education," explains Rothmeier.

Dealing with transfer shock

Stress is an inherent part of the transfer process no matter where you've come from and where you're going. "You're considered a new student, but you're not really a new student," observes Weinhaus. Freshmen get the benefit of an extensive orientation. Transfers have many of the same adjustment problems that freshmen have, but to ask them to sit in an orientation class would be insulting, notes Weinhaus.

Freshmen have an entire semester to fit in and make mistakes. Transfers don't have that luxury. "Just because you're a junior, doesn't mean you don't need help," offers Rothmeier.

What makes a happy transfer?

Be prepared to still question your decision to transfer. Transfers tend to be very goal directed. They've made a mistake and now they're anxious to right it and are alarmed when they find they still have doubts. Rothmeier says don't be. This is the time to question the decisions you're making about your life. "It doesn't have to be catastrophic to think you might want to experience something else," she advises. Don't cram too many classes into your first semester on the new campus. "You're setting yourself up for mental breakdown," says Bartolone. She took 16 credits and was maxed out. Another reason not to overload on credits is to have more time for campus life, which is an important step in smoothing out the bumpy adjustment process.

Don't be a hermit

Transfers tend to be very academically focused, but in their fervor to crank out the grades, they can become reclusive, points out Rothmeier. Weinhaus concurs, adding that many colleges that accept a lot of transfers usually have receptions and gatherings for them. Get out and meet people. Join clubs. Participate in campus activities.

Take out a loan rather than working to pay for college

Transfers from community colleges often worked part time and did well academically at their prior institutions. When they transfer to another institution, Rothmeier counsels them to "get a loan at least for the first semester. Now is not the time to divide loyalty between study and a job," she says.

Be patient about finding your niche

It can be discouraging at first to see other students in established relationships. Bartolone says she is still weeding out the friends she wants to cultivate. She advises not to listen to the little voice that says everyone else has friends but me, because relationships take time. "It's tough to be wedging your way in between people who are already settled," observes Bartolone. On the other hand, she says it was exciting to be able to start over.

CHAPTER 7

Dollars AND CENTS

Financial Aid Facts

Finding the money you need to go to a two- or four-year institution or vocational or trade school is a challenge, but you can do it if you plan ahead and know where to look. Financial aid is available to help meet both direct educational costs (tuition, fees, books) and personal living expenses (food, housing, transportation).

Times have changed to favor the student in the financial aid process. Because the pool of potential traditional college students has diminished, colleges and universities are competing among themselves to attract good students. In fact, some colleges and universities no longer use financial aid primarily as a method to help students fund their college education but rather as a marketing and recruitment tool. This puts students and families at an advantage, one that should be recognized and used for bargaining power.

It used to be that colleges and universities offered "need-based" and "merit-based" financial aid to needy and/or academically exceptional students. Now some offer what might be called "incentive" or "discount" aid to encourage students to choose them over another college. This aid, which is not necessarily based on need or merit, is aimed at students who meet the standards of the college but who wouldn't necessarily qualify for traditional kinds of aid.

If you qualify, don't let the "sticker price" of the college or program scare you away, because you may get enough outside money to pay for the education you want. Do not rule out a private institution until you have received the financial aid package from the school. Private colleges, in order to attract students from all income levels, offer significant amounts of financial aid. Public-supported institutions tend to offer less financial aid because the lower tuition acts as a form of assistance. In addition, students attending school in their home state often have more aid possibilities than if they attend an out-of-state college.

Students and families should be assertive in negotiating financial aid packages. It used to be that there was no room for such negotiation, but in today's environment it is wise to be a comparison shopper. Families should wait until they've received all their financial offers and then talk to their first-choice college to see if the college can match the better offers from other colleges.

To be eligible to receive federal/state financial aid, you must maintain satisfactory academic progress toward a degree or certificate. This criterion is established by each college or university. You'll also need a valid Social Security number, and all male students must register for selective service on their 18th birthday.

Once you apply for federal aid, your application will be processed in approximately four weeks (one week if applying electronically). You'll then receive a Student Aid Report (SAR) in the mail, which will report the information from your application and your Expected Family Contribution (EFC—the number used in determining your eligibility for federal student aid). Each school you listed on the application will also receive your application information.

You must reapply for federal aid every year. Also, if you change schools, your aid doesn't necessarily go with you. Check with your new school to find out what steps you must take to continue receiving aid.

Once you've decided which schools you want to apply to, talk personally to the financial aid officers of those schools! There is no substitute for getting information from the source when it comes to understanding your financial aid options. That personal contact can mean the difference in substantial amounts of financial aid to which you might have access.

Types of Financial Aid

Be sure you understand the differences between types of financial aid so you are fully prepared to apply for each. One or more of these financial resources may make it possible to pursue the education you want.

Grants

Grants are given for athletics (Division I only), academics, demographics, special talent potential, and/or need. Repayment is not required.

Scholarships

Scholarships, also called "merit aid," are awarded for academic excellence. Repayment is not required.

Loans

Student loans, which have lower interest rates, may be college-sponsored or federally sponsored or may be available through commercial financial institutions. Loans must be repaid, generally after you have graduated or left school.

College Work-Study

College work-study is a federally sponsored program that enables colleges to hire students for employment. If eligible, students work a limited number of hours throughout the school year. Many private colleges offer forms of "self-help employment" aid as their own supplement to the diminishing supply of federally funded work-study.

Applying for Financial Aid

Applying for financial aid is a process that can be made easier by taking it step-by-step.

- Complete the Free Application for Student Aid (FAFSA). All students are required to complete the FAFSA to be considered for federal financial aid. Pick up the FAFSA from your high school guidance counselor or college financial aid office.
- The FAFSA is due any time after January 1 of the year you will be attending school. Submit the form as soon as possible but never before the first of the year. If you need to estimate income tax information, it is easily amended later in the year.

College Cost Comparison

Chart your course to see which college or university best fits your financial resources.

	College 1	College 2	College 3	College 4
Expenses				
Tuition and fees	$	$	$	$
Books and supplies	$	$	$	$
Room and board	$	$	$	$
Transportation	$	$	$	$
Miscellaneous	$	$	$	$
TOTAL	$	$	$	$
Funds Available				
Student and parent contributions	$	$	$	$
Grants	$	$	$	$
Scholarships	$	$	$	$
Work-study	$	$	$	$
Loans	$	$	$	$
TOTAL	$	$	$	$
Funding gap	$	$	$	$

- Apply for any state grants.
- Many four-year private colleges, as well as some public universities, require the PROFILE in addition to the FAFSA. The PROFILE is a need analysis report, not an aid application. Some institutions have developed their own need analysis report. Check with your college or university to see what is required when you apply. The PROFILE registration is a one-page form available from your guidance counselor or through the College Board.
- Most colleges will have their own financial aid application form that must be completed in order to be eligible for any type of financial aid. There are deadlines for a college's application for financial aid and for the FAFSA/PROFILE applications. These deadlines may or may not be the same, but are usually before March 15. Check these deadlines with your college or university.

Peterson's © 1999

- To be eligible for any type of financial aid, a family must complete the required forms during the student's senior year in high school.
- Conservative borrowing protects your future. Always apply for grants and scholarships before applying for student loans. Grants and scholarships are essentially free money. Loans must be repaid.

Federal Financial Aid Programs

There are a number of sources of financial aid available to students: the federal government, state governments, private lenders, foundations and private agencies, and the institutions themselves. In addition, as discussed earlier, there are four different forms of aid: grants, scholarships, loans, and work-study.

The federal government is the single largest source of financial aid for students. In the 1998–99 academic year, it is estimated that the U.S. Department of Education's student financial aid programs will make more than $47 billion available in loans, grants, and other aid to about 8.1 million students. At the present time there are two federal grant programs, the Federal Pell Grant and the Federal Supplemental Educational Opportunity Grant (FSEOG), and three loan programs, the Federal Perkins Loan, the William D. Ford Federal Direct Loans, and the Federal Family Education Loans (FFEL). The William D. Ford Direct Loan and the FFEL programs essentially differ in the lending source; each makes available two kinds of loans: loans to students—called Direct Stafford Student Loans and FFEL Stafford Student Loans—and PLUS loans to parents-called Direct PLUS loans and Federal PLUS loans. The federal government also has a work program that helps colleges provide jobs for students, Federal Work-Study (FWS), and an income tax credit for paid tuition, called the HOPE Scholarship credits.

The two grant programs, Federal Work-Study and the Federal Perkins Loan, and two "subsidized" loan programs—the Subsidized Direct Stafford Loan and the Subsidized FFEL Stafford Loan—are awarded to students with demonstrated financial need. Interest on the loans is paid by the government during the time the student is in school. For the non-need-based loans, the Unsubsidized Direct Stafford Loan and Unsubsidized FFEL Stafford Loan, interest begins to accrue as soon as the money is received. There is also a parental loan (PLUS) available under either the Direct or the FFEL program.

Federal Direct Lending

Provisions are identical to the Federal Stafford Student Loan programs. However, the primary lending institution is the college or university participating in the Federal Direct Lending Program, as opposed to a bank or other financial institution.

Lender of Last Resort

Program to assist students who have tried to obtain a Federal Stafford student loan and have been denied by two lending institutions. Eligible students must be enrolled at an eligible postsecondary educational institution.

Nursing Student Loan Program

Awarded to nursing students with demonstrated financial need. Up to $2,500 maximum for years one and two; up to $4,000 for years three and four. This loan has a 5 percent interest rate, repayable after completion of studies. Repayment to be completed within ten years. Contact your college financial aid office. Deadline is set by the college.

Federal Pell Grant

The Federal Pell Grant is the largest grant program; almost 4 million students receive awards annually. This grant is intended to be the base or starting point of assistance for lower-income families. Eligibility for a Federal Pell Grant depends on the Expected Family Contribution (EFC). The amount you receive will depend on your EFC, the cost of education at the college or university you attend, and whether you attend full-time or part-time. The highest award depends on how much the program is funded. The maximum for 1998–99 was $3,000.

To give you some idea of the distribution of Federal Pell Grant dollars in 1998–99, the table on page 114 may be helpful. The amounts shown are based on a family size of five, with one in college, no emergency expenses, no contribution from student income or assets, and college costs of at least $3,000 per year.

Federal Supplemental Educational Opportunity Grant (FSEOG)

As its name implies, the Federal Supplemental Educational Opportunity Grant (FSEOG) provides additional need-based federal grant money to supplement the Federal Pell Grant. Each participating college is given funds to award

Financial Aid Glossary

Assets

The amount a family has in savings and investments. This includes savings and checking accounts; a business; a farm or other real estate; and stocks, bonds, and trust funds. Cars are not considered assets, nor are such possessions as stamp collections or jewelry. The net value of the principal home is counted as an asset by some colleges in determining their own awards but is not included in the calculation for eligibility for federal funds.

Citizenship/Eligibility for Aid

To be eligible to receive federally funded college aid, a student must be one of the following:

1. a United States citizen
2. a non-citizen national
3. a permanent resident with an I-151 or I-551 without conditions
4. a participant in a suspension of deportation case pending before Congress
5. a holder of an I-94 showing one of the following designations:

- "Refugee"
- "Asylum Granted"
- "Indefinite Parole" and/or "Humanitarian Parole"
- "Cuban-Haitian Entrant, Status Pending"
- "Conditional Entrant" (valid if issued before April 1, 1980)

Individuals in the U.S. on an F1 or F2 visa only or on a J1 or J2 exchange visa only cannot get federal aid.

Cooperative Education

A program offered by many colleges in which students alternate periods of enrollment with periods of employment, usually paid, and which can lengthen the usual baccalaureate program to five years.

Expected Family Contribution (EFC) or Parental Contribution

A figure determined by a congressionally mandated formula which indicates how much of a family's resources should be considered "available" for college expenses. Factors such as taxable and nontaxable income and the value of family assets are taken into account to determine a family's financial strength. Allowances for maintaining a family and future financial needs are then taken into consideration before determining how much a family should be able to put toward the cost of college.

Independent Student

A student who reports only his or her own income (and that of a spouse, if relevant) when applying for federal financial aid. Students who will be 24 or older by December 31, 1998, will automatically be considered "independent" for 1998-1999. Students who are under 24 will be considered independent if they are:

- married and not claimed as a dependent on their parents' 1998 federal income tax return
- the supporter of a legal dependent other than a spouse
- a veteran of the U.S. Armed Forces
- an orphan or ward of the court
- classified as independent by a college's financial aid administrator because of other unusual circumstances
- a graduate or professional student

Merit-Based Aid

Any form of financial aid awarded on the basis of personal achievement or individual characteristics without reference to financial need.

Subsidized Loan

A loan for which the borrower is not responsible for all of the interest payments. For Subsidized Federal Stafford and/or Direct Loans, the government pays interest to the lender on behalf of the borrower while the student is in college and during approved grace periods.

to especially needy students. The maximum award is $4,000 per year, but the amount a student receives depends on the college's policy, the availability of FSEOG funds, the total cost of education, and the amount of other aid awarded.

Federal Work-Study (FWS)

This program provides jobs for students who need financial aid for their educational expenses. The salary is paid by funds from the federal government and the college (or the employer). You work on an hourly basis in jobs on or off campus and must be paid at least the federal minimum wage. You may earn only up to the amount awarded, which depends on the calculated financial need and the total amount of money available to the college.

Federal Perkins Loan

This loan is a low-interest (5 percent) loan for students with exceptional financial need (students with the lowest Expected Family Contribution). Federal Perkins Loans are made through the college's financial aid office. That is, the college is the lender. Students may borrow a maximum of $3,000 per year for up to five years of undergraduate study. They may take up to ten years to repay the loan, beginning nine months after they graduate, leave school, or drop below half-time status. No interest accrues while they are in school and, under certain conditions (e.g., they teach in low-income areas, work in law enforcement, are full-time nurses or medical technicians, serve as Peace Corps or VISTA volunteers, etc.), some or all of the loan can be canceled within fourteen days after the date that their school sends notice of crediting of the transaction, or by the first day of the payment period, whichever is later, and payments can be deferred under certain conditions such as unemployment.

FFEL Stafford Student Loan

An FFEL Stafford Student Loan may be borrowed from a participating commercial lender such as a bank, credit union, or savings and loan association. The interest rate varies annually (it has gone up to a maximum of 8.25 percent), and the rate for 1998–99 is 7.43 percent. If your child qualifies for a need-based subsidized FFEL Stafford Student Loan, the interest is paid by the federal government while you are enrolled in school. There is also an unsubsidized FFEL Stafford Student Loan not based on need for which you are eligible regardless of your family income.

The maximum amount dependent students may borrow in any one year is $2625 for freshmen, $3,500 for sophomores, and $5,500 for juniors and seniors, with a maximum of $23,000 for the total undergraduate program. The maximum amount independent students can borrow is $6,625 for freshmen (of which no more than $2625 in subsidized Stafford Loans), $7,500 for sophomores (no more than $3,500 in subsidized Stafford Loans), and $10,500 for juniors and seniors (no more than $5,500 in subsidized Stafford Loans). Borrowers must pay a 4 percent fee, which is deducted from the loan proceeds.

To apply for an FFEL Stafford Student Loan, you must first complete a FAFSA to determine eligibility for a subsidized loan then complete a separate loan application that is submitted to a lender. The financial aid office can help in selecting a lender, or you can contact your state department of higher education to find a participating lender. The lender will send a promissory note that your child must sign that agrees to repay the loan. The proceeds of the loan, less the origination fee, will be sent to your school to be either credited to the student account or paid to you directly.

If you qualify for a subsidized Stafford Loan, you do not have to pay interest while in school. For an unsubsidized FFEL Loan, you will be responsible for paying the interest from the time the loan is established. However, some FFEL lenders will permit borrowers to delay making payments and will add the interest to the loan. Once the repayment period starts, borrowers of both subsidized and unsubsidized FFEL Loans will have to pay a combination of interest and principal monthly for up to a ten-year period.

William D. Ford Direct Stafford Loans

The Federal Direct Student Loan is basically the same as the Federal Stafford Student Loan Program. The difference is that the U.S. Department of Education, rather than a bank, is the lender. Not all colleges participate in this program. If your college does not, you can still apply for an FFEL Stafford Student Loan.

Many of the terms of the Direct Stafford Loan are similar to those of the FFEL Stafford Loan. In particular, the interest rate, loan maximums, deferments, and cancellation benefits are the same. However, under the terms of the Direct Stafford Student Loan, students have a choice of repayment plans. They may choose either a standard fixed monthly repayment—at least $50—for up to ten years, an extended repayment plan with lower fixed monthly payments—but still at least $50—for twelve to thirty years at a rate with a higher total amount of interest payment, a graduated monthly repayment plan for twelve to thirty years in which payments grow from 50 percent to 150 percent of the standard plan, and an income contingent repayment plan with monthly payments based on yearly income and family size. Students cannot receive both a Direct Stafford Loan and an FFEL Stafford Loan for the same period of time but may receive both in different enrollment periods.

PLUS Loans

The PLUS loans are for parents of dependent students designed to help families with cash-flow problems. There is no needs test to qualify, and the loans are made by FFEL lenders or directly by the Department of Education. The loan has a variable interest rate that cannot exceed 9 percent (the rate from July 1998 to June 1999 is 7.9 percent). There is no specific yearly limit; parents can borrow up to the cost of their child's education less other financial aid received. Repayment begins sixty days after the money is advanced. A 4 percent fee is subtracted from the proceeds. Parent borrowers must generally have a good credit record to qualify for PLUS loans.

The PLUS loan will be processed under either the Direct or the FFEL system, depending on the type of loan program for which the college has contracted.

HOPE Scholarship Tax Credits

Beginning in 1998, the HOPE Scholarship tax credit helps offset some of the expense for the first two years of college or vocational school. Students or the parents of dependent students can claim an annual income tax credit of up to $1,500—100 percent credit for the first $1,000 of tuition and required fees and a 50 percent credit on the second $1,000. Grants, scholarships, and other tax-free educational assistance must be deducted from the total tuition and fee payments.

This credit can be claimed for two years only for students who are in their first two years of college and who are enrolled on at least a half-time basis in a degree or certificate program for any portion of the year. This credit phases out for families with higher income levels. (See page 126 for more information.)

AmeriCorps

AmeriCorps is a national service program for a limited number of students. Participants work in a public or private nonprofit agency providing service to the community in one of four priority areas: education, human services, the environment, and public safety. In exchange, they earn a stipend of between $7,400 and $14,800 per year for living expenses and up to $4725 for up to two years to apply toward college expenses. Students can work either before, during, or after they go to college and can use the funds to either pay current educational expenses or repay federal student loans. We suggest speaking to the college financial aid office for more details about this program and any other new initiatives available to students.

ROTC Scholarships (Army, Air Force, Navy, Marines)

The Armed Forces may offer up to a four-year scholarship that pays full college tuition plus a monthly allowance.

Table Used to Estimate Federal Pell Grants for 1998–99

Adjusted Gross Income	Family Assets							
	$50,000	$55,000	$60,000	$65,000	$70,000	$75,000	$80,000	$85,000
$ 5000	$ 3,000	$ 3,000	$ 3,000	$ 3,000	$ 3,000	$ 3,000	$ 3,000	$ 3,000
$10,000	3000	3000	3000	3000	3000	3000	3000	2700
$15,000	3000	2700	2700	2700	2700	2700	2700	2600
$20,000	2500	2400	2300	2200	2100	1900	1800	1700
$25,000	1700	1600	1500	1300	1200	1000	900	800
$30,000	800	700	700	400	400	0	0	0
$35,000	400	400	400	400	0	0	0	0

Federal Financial Aid Programs

Name of Program	Type of Program	Maximum Award Per Year
Federal Pell Grant	Need-based grant	$3,000
Federal Supplemental Educational Opportunity Grant (FSEOG)	Need-based grant	$4,000
Federal Work-Study	Need-based part-time job	no maximum
Federal Perkins Loan	Need-based loan	$3,000
FFEL Stafford Loan/Direct Stafford Loan (Subsidized)	Need-based student loan	$2625 (first year)
FFEL Stafford Loan/Direct Stafford Loan (Unsubsidized)	Non-need-based student loan	$2625 (first year, dependent student)
PLUS Loans	Non-need-based parent loan	Up to the cost of education

Note: Both Direct and FFEL Stafford Loans have higher maximums after the freshman year.

Very competitive. Based upon GPA, class rank, ACT or SAT scores, and physical qualifications. Apply as soon as possible before December 1 of the senior year. Contact the headquarters of the armed forces for more information: ARMY, 800-USA-ROTC; Air Force, 800-423-USAF; Navy, 800-USA-NAVY; Marines, 800-MARINES.

Scholarships from Federal Agencies

Federal agencies such as the CIA, NASA, Department of Agriculture, and Office of Naval Research offer an annual stipend as well as a scholarship. In return, the student must work for the agency for a certain number of years or repay all the financial support. See your counselor for more information.

Visit: www.petersons.com

Projected College Expenses

Listed below are the projected average costs for four years of tuition, room, board, and fees at a typical public university, assuming an annual 7 percent tuition inflation and 6 percent room and board inflation. Because the cost of higher education is expected to increase, families are encouraged to begin planning and saving early.

2000	$42,000
2005	$58,000
2010	$79,000
2013	$102,000

Source: Ohio Tuition Trust Authority.

Robert C. Byrd Honors Scholarship

Must demonstrate outstanding academic achievement and excellence in high school as indicated by class rank, high school grades, test scores, and leadership activities. Award amounts of $1,500 are renewable for four years. Contact your high school counselor for application information. Deadline: March 14.

National Science Scholars Program (NSSP)

Must be a graduating high school senior with a minimum 3.5 GPA and an ACT score of at least 25 or SAT score of at least 1100 and demonstrate excellence and achievement in the physical, life, or computer sciences; mathematics; or engineering. Scholarships are as much as $5,000 per year or the student's cost of attendance, whichever is less, for up to five years of study. Awards are made to two students from each congressional district. Contact your high school counselor or NSSP coordinators at your state Department of Education for application information. Deadline: October 21.

Financial Aid Fact

More than 80 percent of all aid awarded comes from federal and state programs. Another 19 percent comes from institutional and other sources of aid.

National, Statewide, and Local Scholarships

Requirements for the financial resources listed below are approximate and may vary. Check with your guidance counselor for the most up-to-date information as to the availability of these resources and the requirements to qualify.

National Scholarships

Amoco Foundation Scholarships

Awards to students majoring in geology, geophysics, and petroleum engineering. An unspecified number of $3,400 awards over a four-year period. Eligibility requirements: graduating senior, "B" grade point average, entrance in career related to above fields. Deadlines vary from school to school.

Coca-Cola Scholars Program

Awards to seniors planning to attend an accredited college/university. Based on academics, school and community activities, and motivation to serve and succeed in all endeavors. Contact Coca-Cola Scholars Foundation, Inc., at 800-306-2653 for an application. Deadline Oct. 31.

Financial Need Equation

Need is the difference between what it costs to attend a particular college and what your family and you are expected to pay toward those costs.

Total College Cost Per Year
— Parent Contribution
(Based on Federal Methodology*)

— Student Contribution
(Students are expected to pay a minimum of $700 to $900. Additional dollars are dependent upon employment income and savings under Federal Methodology guidelines.)

= Financial Need

---

* The expected family and student contributions toward college are calculated using a set of federal formulas. However, some colleges use their own "institutional methodology" rather than the "federal methodology" for calculating need. And some colleges use both! It is important for families to inquire about that issue, and make sure the college is using the most "lenient" and "generous" calculation for the interests of the family.

Source: The Student Guide, U.S. Department of Education, Federal Student Aid Information Center.

Applying for Scholarships

Start early

Your freshman year is not too early to plan for scholarships academically, choose extracurricular activities that will highlight your strengths, and get involved in your church and community—all things that are important to those who make scholarship decisions.

Search for scholarships

A couple of hours a week in the public library will help you learn about hundreds of scholarships and assess those for which you might qualify.

Apply, apply, apply

One student applied for nearly 60 scholarships and was fortunate enough to win seven. "Imagine if I'd applied for five and only gotten one," she says.

Plan ahead

It takes time to get transcripts and letters of recommendation. Letters from people who know you well are more effective than letters from prestigious names who know you only vaguely.

Be organized

In the homes of scholarship winners you can often find a file box where all relevant information is stored. This method allows you to review deadlines and requirements every so often. Computerizing the information, if possible, allows you to change and update information quickly.

Follow directions

Make sure you don't disqualify yourself by filling the forms out incorrectly, missing the deadline, or failing to supply important information. Type your applications, if possible, and have someone proofread them.

A Checklist for Seniors

Applying for financial aid can become confusing if you don't record what you've done and when. Use this chart to track important information. Remember to keep copies of all applications and related information.

	College 1	College 2	College 3	College 4
College Applications				
Application deadline				
Date sent				
Official transcript sent				
Letters of recommendation sent				
SAT/ACT scores sent				
Acceptance received				
Individual College Financial Aid and Scholarship Applications				
Application deadline				
Date sent				
Acceptance received				
Free Application for Federal Student Aid (FAFSA), Financial Aid Form (FAF), and/or PROFILE				
Form required				
Date sent				
School's priority deadline				

	College 1	College 2	College 3	College 4
FAFSA Acknowledgment				
Date received				
Correct (Y/N)				
Date changes made, if needed				
Date changes were submitted				
Student Aid Report				
Date received				
Correct (Y/N)				
Date changes made, if needed				
Date changes were submitted				
Date sent to colleges				
Financial Award Letters				
Date received				
Accepted (Y/N)				

Source: The Dayton-Montgomery County Scholarship Program.

Duracell/National Science Teachers Association Scholarship Competition

Open to all students in grades 9 through 12. Student must design and build a device powered by Duracell batteries. Call 703-243-7100 for more information. Deadline: Jan. 12.

Elks National Scholarship

More than 1 million dollars in awards to "most valuable students" nationwide. Must be in upper 5 percent of class and have an "A" average. Awards based upon scholarship, leadership, and financial need. Call 614-476-2226 for application. Deadline: Jan. 16.

Intel Foundation, Manufacturing Institute and National Association of Manufacturers Robert N. Noyce Scholarship

High school senior, with a minimum 3.0 GPA, planning to enroll at an accredited two- or four-year postsecondary institution the fall following graduation and major in engineering, computer science, industrial design or technology, diagnostic/scientific equipment design, or information sciences and systems. Essay required. Call 800-537-4180. Deadline: Oct. 31.

Mensa Education and Research Foundation

Awards based on essay. $200–$1,000. Geared toward students scoring higher than 98 percent on standardized IQ tests. Contact local Mensa chapter. Deadline: Feb. 28.

National Foundation for Advancement in the Arts/Arts Recognition & Talent Search (NFAA/ARTS)

Awards based on talent in dance, music, theater, visual arts, writing, voice, jazz, or photography. Call 800-970-2787. Early application is June 1 of junior year. Last application deadline is October 1 of senior year.

National Merit Scholarship Program

Based on the PSAT test taken in the junior year. Also investigate the National Honor Society Scholarship.

National Society of Professional Engineers

Must be a U.S. citizen with 3.0 GPA during sophomore and junior years. SAT: 600 math, 500 verbal. ACT: 29 math, 25 English.

Norelco Tripleheader Scholarship Awards

Must be a senior student-athlete, having excelled in athletics, academics, and service. Write P.O. Box 385, Milford, MA 01757 for application. Deadline: Feb. 18.

Little-Known Scholarships

Chick Evans Caddie Scholarship

Offers full tuition to high school seniors who have worked two years as caddies at a Western Golf Association member club, demonstrate need, have outstanding character, and rank in the top 25 percent of their class.

Durango Boots Scholarship

Awarded to two-year or four-year college students studying agriculture and who are members of Future Farmers of America.

Harlan M. Smith "Builders of a Better World" Scholarship

Granted to students whose goals have potential to most closely contribute to the World Federalist Association's vision for a better world.

Prudential Spirit of Community Award

Nationwide program to honor exemplary, self-initiated community service by middle and high school students. Each school may nominate its top volunteer. Contact the National Association of Secondary School Principals or call 703-860-0200. Deadline: Nov. 6.

Servisar All-American Vocational Student

Must be enrolled in a state-approved vocational education program during the current school year. Selection based on success in vocational classes, project and work experiences, academic success, character and leadership, and school/community activities or other activities. Write P.O. Box 1221, Butler, PA 16003-1221. Deadline: Nov. 15.

Tylenol

Award based 40 percent on leadership in school and community, 50 percent on grade point average, and 10 percent on clear statement of goals. Call 800-676-8437 between November 1, 1999, and January 5, 2000, for an application.

Statewide Scholarships

General Scholarship Programs for Nursing Students

Several awards for Texas residents enrolled at least half-time in a nursing program leading to License of Vocational Nursing bachelor's or master's degree at a Texas institution. ADN and B.S.N. students must not be licensed to practice as a licensed RN. One-time award of up to $2,000.

Academic/Career Areas: Nursing.

Award: Scholarship for use in freshman, sophomore, junior, senior, or graduate years; not renewable. Award amount: up to $2,000.

Eligibility Requirements: Applicant must be enrolled at a two-year or four-year institution, a resident of Texas, and studying in Texas. Restricted to U.S. citizens.

Application Requirements: Application, financial need analysis, test scores, transcript.

Application Deadline: July 15.

Contact: Tanya Montez, Program Technician, Texas Higher Education Coordinating Board, PO Box 12788, Austin, TX 78711-2788. Phone: 512-427-6457.

Scholarship Program for Licensed Vocational Nurses Becoming Professional Nurses—Texas

Scholarships available to Texas residents enrolled at least half-time in a nursing program leading to an associate, bachelor, or graduate degree in Texas. Must already be a licensed vocational nurse. Deadline varies. Renewable award of up to $2,500.

Academic/Career Areas: Nursing.

Award: Scholarship for use in freshman, sophomore, junior, senior, or graduate years; renewable. Award amount: up to $2,500.

Eligibility Requirements: Applicant must be enrolled at a two-year or four-year institution, a resident of Texas, studying in Texas, and have employment experience in career field. Restricted to U.S. citizens.

Application Requirements: Application, financial need analysis, test scores, transcript.

Contact: Tanya Montez, Program Technician, Texas Higher Education Coordinating Board, PO Box 12788, Austin, TX 78711-2788. Phone: 512-427-6457.

Scholarship Program for Rural Bachelor of Science in Nursing or Graduate Nursing Students—Texas

Scholarships for Texas residents who are at least half-time undergraduate or graduate students. Must be enrolled in a nursing program leading to a B.S.N. or graduate degree at a Texas institution. Must be from a rural county in Texas. Deadline varies. One-time awards of up to $2,500 each.

Academic/Career Areas: Nursing.

Award: Scholarship for use in freshman, sophomore, junior, senior, or graduate years; not renewable. Award amount: up to $2,500.

Eligibility Requirements: Applicant must be enrolled at a four-year institution, a resident of Texas, and studying in Texas. Restricted to U.S. citizens.

Application Requirements: Application, financial need analysis, test scores, transcript.

Contact: Tanya Montez, Program Technician, Texas Higher Education Coordinating Board, PO Box 12788, Austin, TX 78711-2788. Phone: 512-427-6457.

Scholarship Programs for Rural Professional or Vocational Nursing Students—Texas

Scholarships for Texas residents of rural counties. Must be enrolled in a nursing program at an institution in a nonmetropolitan county of Texas. Maximum awards: $1,500 for LVN/ADN students; $2,500 for B.S.N./graduate students. Deadline varies. One-time award.

Academic/Career Areas: Nursing.

Award: Scholarship for use in freshman, sophomore, junior, senior, or graduate years; not renewable. Award amount: $1,500–$2,500.

Eligibility Requirements: Applicant must be enrolled at a two-year or four-year institution, a resident of Texas, and studying in Texas. Restricted to U.S. citizens.

Application Requirements: Application, financial need analysis, test scores, transcript.

Contact: Tanya Montez, Program Technician, Texas Higher Education Coordinating Board, PO Box 12788, Austin, TX 78711-2788. Phone: 512-427-6457.

State Scholarship Programs in Professional or Vocational Nursing—Texas

State scholarships for Texas residents enrolled in a nursing degree/licensure program. Maximum awards are $1,500 for licensed vocational nurse, $2,000 for associate degree in nursing, and $3,000 for Bachelor of Science in Nursing or graduate degree. Deadline varies.

Academic/Career Areas: Nursing.

Award: Scholarship for use in freshman, sophomore, junior, senior, or graduate years; not renewable. Award amount: up to $3,000.

Eligibility Requirements: Applicant must be enrolled at a two-year or four-year institution, a resident of Texas, and studying in Texas. Restricted to U.S. citizens.

Application Requirements: Application, financial need analysis, test scores, transcript.

Contact: Tanya Montez, Program Technician, Texas Higher Education Coordinating Board, PO Box 12788, Austin, TX 78711-2788. Phone: 512-427-6457.

State Tuition Exemption Program: Veterans and Dependents—Texas

Renewable awards for veterans or their dependents who have been honorably discharged or killed in the line of duty. Must be Texas resident at time of service. Must have exhausted federal education benefits.

Award: Scholarship for use in any year; renewable.

Eligibility Requirements: Applicant must be a resident of Texas and studying in Texas. Restricted to U.S. citizens.

Military Service: General.

Application Requirements: Application.

Application Deadline: Continuous.

Contact: Texas Higher Education Coordinating Board, PO Box 12788, Austin, TX 78711-2788.

Student Incentive Grant—Texas

Available to residents and nonresidents attending public colleges or universities in Texas. Must be enrolled at least half-time and show financial need. Deadlines vary by institution. Award is renewable.

Award: Grant for use in any year; not renewable. Award amount: up to $1,250.

Eligibility Requirements: Applicant must be studying in Texas. Restricted to U.S. citizens.

Application Requirements: Application, financial need analysis.

Application Deadline: Continuous.

Contact: Texas Higher Education Coordinating Board, PO Box 12788, Austin, TX 78711-2788.

Students from Other Nations of the American Hemisphere—Texas

Renewable aid for students residing in Texas who are citizens of another country of the Americas. Must attend public college in Texas. Student is exempt from tuition.

Award: Scholarship for use in any year; not renewable.

Eligibility Requirements: Applicant must be Canadian or Latin American/Caribbean, enrolled at a two-year or four-year institution, and studying in Texas. Available to non-U.S. citizens.

Application Requirements: Application, test scores, transcript.

Application Deadline: Continuous.

Contact: Gustavo DeLeon, Asst. Director of Grants, Texas Higher Education Coordinating Board, PO Box 12788, Austin, TX 78711-2788. Phone: 512-427-6331. Fax: 512-427-6420.

Texas College Access Loans

Loans available to Texas residents. Submit financial need analysis with application. Promissory notes must be cosigned and creditworthiness of cosigners is checked. Applications received on a continuous basis. Must attend Texas institution.

Award: Loan for use in any year; not renewable. Award amount: up to $7,500.

Eligibility Requirements: Applicant must be a resident of Texas and studying in Texas. Restricted to U.S. citizens.

Application Requirements: Application, financial need analysis.

Application Deadline: Continuous.

Contact: Texas Higher Education Coordinating Board, PO Box 12788, Austin, TX 78711-2788.

Texas Outstanding Rural Scholar Recognition and Forgiveness Loan Program

Scholarship/loan for Texas residents to pursue a health-related career in rural Texas. Need nomination by a sponsoring rural community. Sponsor applies for student. Must work one year for sponsoring community per award received. For use at Texas postsecondary institutions. Deadlines are the third Fridays in September, January, and May. Renewable award based on merit. College applicants must have minimum 3.0 GPA. High school applicants must be in upper quarter of class.

Academic/Career Areas: Dental Health/Services; Health Administration; Health and Medical Sciences; Health Information Management/Technology; Nursing; Therapy/Rehabilitation.

Award: Scholarship, loan for use in any year; renewable. Award amount: $500–$33,000.

Eligibility Requirements: Applicant must be a resident of Texas and studying in Texas.

Application Requirements: Application, essay, references, test scores, transcript.

Contact: Ms. Carol Peters, Program Administrator, Texas Center for Rural Health Initiatives, 211 East 7th, Suite 915, PO Box 1708, Austin, TX 78767-1708. Phone: 512-479-8891. Fax: 512-479-8898.

Texas Public Educational Grant

Renewable aid for students currently enrolled in a public college or university in Texas. Based on need. Amount of award is determined by the financial aid office of each school. Texas residence not necessary. Deadlines vary.

Award: Scholarship for use in any year; not renewable.

Eligibility Requirements: Applicant must be studying in Texas. Available to non-U.S. citizens.

Application Requirements: Application, financial need analysis.

Contact: Texas Higher Education Coordinating Board, PO Box 12788, Austin, TX 78711-2788.

Texas State Tuition Exemption Program: Highest Ranking High School Graduate

Award available to Texas residents who are the top-ranked seniors of their high school. Must attend a public college or university within Texas. Recipient is exempt from certain charges for first two semesters. Deadlines vary.

Award: Scholarship for use in freshman year; not renewable.

Eligibility Requirements: Applicant must be a high school student, enrolled at a two-year or four-year institution, a resident of Texas, and studying in Texas.

Application Requirements: Transcript.

Contact: Texas Higher Education Coordinating Board, PO Box 12788, Austin, TX 78711-2788.

Tuition and Fee Exemption for Blind or Deaf Students

Aids certain blind or deaf students by exempting them from payment of tuition and fees at public colleges or universities in Texas. Must be a resident of Texas. Deadlines vary. Renewable. Must submit certificate of deafness or blindness.

Award: Scholarship for use in any year; renewable.

Eligibility Requirements: Applicant must be a resident of Texas and studying in Texas. Applicant must be hearing impaired or visually impaired. Restricted to U.S. citizens.

Application Requirements: Application.

Contact: Texas Higher Education Coordinating Board, PO Box 12788, Austin, TX 78711-2788.

Tuition and Fee Exemption for Children of Disabled Firemen and Peace Officers—Texas

Renewable award for children of firemen, game wardens, peace officers, or custodial employees of the Department of Corrections disabled or deceased while serving in Texas. Must attend a Texas institution. Must apply before 21st birthday.

Award: Scholarship for use in any year; renewable.

Eligibility Requirements: Applicant must be enrolled at a two-year or four-year institution, a resident of Texas, studying in Texas, and have employment experience in fire service or police/firefighting. Restricted to U.S. citizens.

Application Requirements: Application.

Application Deadline: Continuous.

Contact: Texas Higher Education Coordinating Board, PO Box 12788, Austin, TX 78711-2788.

Tuition and Fee Exemption for Children of Prisoners of War or Persons Missing in Action—Texas

Assists children of prisoners of war or veterans classified as missing in action. Must be a Texas resident and attend a public college or university within Texas. Submit proof of service. Award is exemption from tuition and fees. Must be under 21 years of age. Renewable.

Award: Scholarship for use in any year; renewable.

Eligibility Requirements: Applicant must be age 20 or under, enrolled at a two-year or four-year institution, a resident of Texas, and studying in Texas. Restricted to U.S. citizens.

Military Service: General.

Application Requirements: Application.

Application Deadline: Continuous.

Contact: Texas Higher Education Coordinating Board, PO Box 12788, Austin, TX 78711-2788.

Tuition and Fee Exemption for Firemen Enrolled in Fire Science Courses—Texas

Assists firemen enrolled in fire science courses as part of a fire science curriculum. Award is exemption from tuition and laboratory fees at publicly supported Texas colleges. State residence not required. One-time award.

Academic/Career Areas: Applied Sciences; Physical Sciences and Math; Trade/Technical Specialties.

Award: Scholarship for use in freshman, sophomore, junior, or senior year; not renewable.

Eligibility Requirements: Applicant must be enrolled at a two-year or four-year institution, studying in Texas, and have employment experience in fire service or police/firefighting. Restricted to U.S. citizens.

Application Requirements: Application.

Application Deadline: Continuous.

Contact: Texas Higher Education Coordinating Board, PO Box 12788, Austin, TX 78711-2788.

Tuition Equalization Grant (TEG)—Texas

For Texas residents enrolled at least half-time at an independent college or university within the state. Based on financial need. Deadlines vary by institution. Award is renewable. Must not be in religion program or receiving athletic scholarship.

Award: Grant for use in any year; not renewable. Award amount: up to $2,640.

Eligibility Requirements: Applicant must be enrolled at a two-year or four-year institution, a resident of Texas, and studying in Texas. Restricted to U.S. citizens.

Application Requirements: Application, financial need analysis.

Contact: Texas Higher Education Coordinating Board, PO Box 12788, Austin, TX 78711-2788.

Local Scholarships

It is not possible within the scope of this book to list all of the sources of local scholarship dollars. The following are excellent resources for seeking local financial assistance:

- Your guidance counselor
- A high school teacher or coach
- Your PTA
- The local librarian
- College admissions office
- Your parents' alma mater
- Your employer
- Your parents' employer
- Professional and social organizations

Scholarship Scams

What They Are and What to Watch Out For

Several hundred thousand students seek and find scholarships every year. Most students' families require some outside help to pay for tuition costs. Although most of this outside help, in the form of grants, scholarships, low-interest loans, and work-study programs, comes either from the federal government or from the colleges themselves, scholarships from private sources are an extremely important component of this network. An award from a private source can tilt the scales with respect to a student's ability to attend a specific college during a particular year. Unfortunately for prospective scholarship seekers, the private aid sector is virtually without patterns or rules. It has, over many years, developed as a haphazard conglomeration of individual programs, each with its own award criteria, timetables, application procedures, and decision-making processes. Considerable effort is required to understand and effectively benefit from private scholarships. Books like *Peterson's Scholarships, Grants & Prizes* were developed to facilitate the task of grabbing the applicable prize from this complex tangle of scholarships.

Regrettably, the combination of a sharp urgency to locate money, limited time, and this complex and bewildering system has created opportunities for fraud. Although a preponderance of scholarship sponsors and most scholarship search services are legitimate, schemes or scams that pose as either legitimate scholarship search services or scholarship sponsors have managed to cheat thousands of students and their parents.

These fraudulent businesses advertise in campus newspapers, distribute flyers, mail letters and postcards,

provide toll-free phone numbers, and even have sites on the World Wide Web. The most obvious frauds operate as scholarship search services or scholarship clearinghouses. Another quieter segment sets up as a scholarship sponsor, pockets the money from the fees and charges that are paid by thousands of hopeful scholarship seekers, and returns little, if anything, in proportion to the amounts it collects. A few of these frauds inflict great harm by gaining access to individuals' credit or checking accounts with the intent to extort funds.

The Federal Trade Commission (FTC), in Washington, D.C., has undertaken a special combined enforcement effort and education campaign called "Project $cholar-$cam" to confront this type of fraudulent activity. As one phase of its ongoing effort, the FTC last year filed charges against five companies, alleging that they ran fraudulent scholarship search services.

Each of the firms indicted by the FTC operated in a similar way. Typically they sent out a huge mailing (more than 1 million postcards each year for some of them) to college and high school students, which claimed that the company had either a scholarship or a scholarship list for the students. Four of the five defendants provided toll-free numbers. When recipients called, they were told by high-pressure telemarketers that the company was a source of unclaimed scholarships and that for fees ranging from $10 to $299 the callers would get back at least $1,000 in scholarship money or the fee would be refunded. Customers who paid, if they received anything at all, were mailed a list of sources of financial aid that were no better than, and were in many cases inferior to, what can be found in *Peterson's Scholarships, Grants & Prizes* or any of the other major scholarship guides available in bookstores or libraries. In all cases, the recipients had to apply on their own for the scholarships. Many of the programs were contests, loans, or work-study programs rather than gift aid. Some were no longer in existence or had expired deadlines or eligibility requirements that the students could not meet. Customers seeking refunds had to demonstrate that they had applied in writing to each source on the list and received a rejection letter from each of them. Frequently, even when customers could provide this almost-impossible-to-obtain proof, refunds were not made. In the worst cases, the companies asked for consumers' checking account or credit card numbers and took funds without authorization.

The FTC warns students and their parents to be wary of fraudulent search services that promise to do all the work for you. "Bogus scholarship search services are just a variation on the 'you have won' prize-promotion scam, targeted to a particular audience—students and their parents who are anxious about paying for college," said Jodie Bernstein, Director of the FTC's Bureau of Consumer Protection. "They guarantee students and their families free scholarship money . . . all they have to do to claim it is pay an up-front fee."

There are legitimate scholarship search services. However, a scholarship search service cannot truthfully guarantee that a student will receive a scholarship, and students almost always will fare as well or better by doing their own homework using a reliable scholarship information source, such as *Peterson's Scholarships, Grants & Prizes*, than by wasting money and time with a search service that promises a scholarship.

The FTC warns scholarship seekers to be alert for these six warning signs of a scam:

1. "This scholarship is guaranteed or your money back." No service can guarantee that it will get you a grant or scholarship. Refund guarantees often have impossible conditions attached. Review a service's refund policies in writing before you pay a fee. Typically, fraudulent scholarship search services require that applicants show rejection letters from all of the sponsors on the list they provide. If a sponsor no longer exists, or if it has a rolling application deadline, letters of rejection are almost impossible to obtain.

2. "The scholarship service will do all the work." Unfortunately, nobody else can fill out the personal information forms, write the essays, and supply the references that many scholarships may require.

3. "The scholarship will cost some money." Be wary of any charges related to scholarship information services or individual scholarship applications, especially in significant amounts. Some legitimate scholarship sponsors charge fees to defray their processing expenses. True scholarship sponsors, however, should give out money, not make it from application fees. Before you send money to apply for a scholarship, investigate the sponsor.

4. "You can't get this information anywhere else." In addition to Peterson's, scholarship directories from other publishers are available in any large bookstore, public library, or high school guidance office.

5. "You are a finalist—in a contest you never entered," or "You have been selected by a national foundation to receive a scholarship." Most legitimate scholarship programs almost never seek out particular applicants. Most scholarship sponsors will only contact you in response to an inquiry. Most lack the budget and mandate to do anything more than this. Should you

Q. Are a student's chances of being admitted to a college reduced if the student applies for financial aid?

A. Generally not. Most colleges have a policy of "need-blind" admissions, which means that a student's financial need is not taken into account in the admission decision. However, there are a few colleges that do consider ability to pay before deciding whether or not to admit a student. There are a few more that look at ability to pay of those whom they placed on a waiting list to get in or those students who applied late. Some colleges will mention this in their literature, others may not. In making decisions about the college application and financing process, however, families should apply for financial aid if the student needs the aid to attend college.

think that there is any real possibility that you may have been selected to receive a scholarship, before you send any money investigate first to be sure that the sponsor or program is legitimate.

6. "The scholarship service needs your credit card or checking account number in advance." Never provide your credit card or bank account number on the telephone to the representative of an organization that you do not know. Get information in writing first. An unscrupulous operation does not need your signature on a check. It will scheme to set up situations that will allow it to drain a victim's account with unauthorized withdrawals.

In addition to the FTC's six signs, here are some other points to keep in mind when considering a scholarship program:

- Fraudulent scholarship operations often use official-sounding names containing such words as federal, national, administration, division, federation, and foundation. Their names often are a slight variant of the name of a legitimate government or private organization. Do not be fooled by a name that seems reputable or official, an official-looking seal, or a Washington address.

- If you win a scholarship, you will receive written official notification by mail, not by telephone. If the sponsor calls to inform you, it will follow up with a letter in the mail. If a request for money is made by phone, the operation is very probably fraudulent.

- Be wary if an organization's address is a box number or a residential address. If a bona fide scholarship program uses a post office box number, it usually will include a street address and telephone number on its stationery.

- Beware of telephone numbers with a 900 area code. These may charge you a fee of several dollars a minute for a call that could be a long recording that provides only a list of addresses or names.

- A dishonest operation may put pressure on an applicant by saying that awards are on a "first-come, first-serve" basis. Some scholarship programs will give preference to the earlier qualified applications. However, if you are told, especially on the telephone, that you must respond quickly, but you will not hear about the results for several months, there may be a problem.

- Be wary of endorsements. Fraudulent operations will claim endorsements by groups with names similar to well-known private or government organizations. The Better Business Bureau (BBB) and government agencies do not endorse businesses.

If an organization requires you to pay money for a scholarship and you have never heard of it before and cannot verify that it is a legitimate operation, the best advice is not to pay anything. If you have already paid money to such an organization and find reason to doubt its legitimacy, call your bank to stop payment on your check, if possible, or call your credit card company and tell it that you think you were the victim of a consumer fraud.

To find out how to recognize, report, and stop a scholarship scam, contact the Federal Trade Commission at P.O. Box 996, Washington, D.C. 20580. On the Web go to http://www.ftc.gov or call the National Fraud Information Center at 800-876-7060 (toll-free). The Better Business Bureau maintains files of businesses about which it has received complaints. You should call both your local BBB office and the BBB office in the area of the organization in question; each local BBB has different records. Call 703-276-0100 or 703-525-8277 to get the telephone number of your local BBB, or look at http://www.bbb.org for a directory of local BBBs and download-able BBB complaint forms. The national address is National Advertising Division of the Council of Better Business Bureaus, 845 Third Avenue, New York, NY 10022.

There are many wonderful scholarships available to qualified students who spend their time and effort to locate and apply for them. Use caution in using scholarship search services and, when you must pay money, practice careful judgment in considering a scholarship program's sponsor. Take full advantage of the many real opportunities that have been opened to college students by the many organizations, foundations, and businesses that have organized to help you with the burden of college expenses.

Families' Guide to the 1997 Tax Cuts for Education

Many new tax benefits for adults who want to return to school and for parents who are sending or planning to send their children to college are available due to the balanced budget signed into law in August, 1997. These tax cuts effectively make the first two years of college universally available, and they will give many more working Americans the financial means to go back to school if they want to choose a new career or upgrade

College Funds Available

Use this chart to estimate your family's resources that will be available for college expenses. Check your progress at the end of your sophomore and junior years to see if your plans for seeking financial aid need to be revised.

	Estimated amount available	Actual amount: 11th grade	Actual amount: 12th grade
Your Resources			
Savings and other assets	$	$	$
Summer earnings	$	$	$
Part-time work during school year	$	$	$
Miscellaneous	$	$	$
Parents' Resources			
From their current income	$	$	$
From college savings	$	$	$
Miscellaneous (insurance, annuities, stocks, trusts, home equity, property assets)	$	$	$
TOTAL	$	$	$

Source: American College

their skills. When fully phased in, 12.9 million students are expected to benefit—5.8 million under the "HOPE Scholarship" tax credit, and 7.1 million under the Lifetime Learning tax credit.

Up to a $1,500 HOPE Scholarship tax credit for students starting college

The HOPE Scholarship tax credit helps make the first two years of college or vocational school universally available. Students will receive a 100% tax credit for the first $1,000 of tuition and required fees and a 50% credit on the second $1,000. This credit is available for tuition and required fees less grants, scholarships, and other tax-free educational assistance and will be available for payments made after December 31, 1997, for college enrollment after that date. A high school senior going into his or her freshman year of college in September 1998, for example, could be eligible for as much as a $1,500 HOPE tax credit.

This credit is phased out for joint filers who have between $80,000 and $100,000 of adjusted gross income and for single filers who have between $40,000 and $50,000 of adjusted gross income. The credit can be claimed in two years for students who are in their first two years of college or vocational school and who are enrolled on at least a half-time basis in a degree or certificate program for any portion of the year. The taxpayer can claim a credit for his own tuition expense or for the expenses of his or her spouse or dependent children.

A married couple, with an adjusted gross income of $60,000, has two children in college at least half-time, one at a community college with a tuition of $2,000 and the other a sophomore at a private college with tuition of $11,000. Using the HOPE Scholarship tax credit, this couple would have their taxes cut by as much as $3,000.

The Lifetime Learning tax credit

This tax credit is targeted to adults who want to go back to school, change careers, or take a course or two to upgrade their skills; to college juniors and seniors; and to graduate and professional degree students. A family will receive a 20 percent tax credit for the first $5,000 of tuition and required fees paid each year through 2002, and for the first $10,000 thereafter. Just like the "HOPE Scholarship" tax credit, the Lifetime Learning tax credit is available for tuition and required fees less grants, scholarships, and other tax-free educational assistance; families may claim the credit for amounts paid on or after July 1, 1998 for college or vocational school enrollment beginning on or after July 1, 1998. The maximum credit is determined on a per-taxpayer (family) basis, regardless of the number of post-secondary students in the family, and is phased out at the same income levels as the "HOPE Scholarship" tax credit. Families will be able to claim the Lifetime Learning tax credit for some members of their family and the "HOPE Scholarship" tax credit for others who qualify in the same year. For example:

A homemaker, whose family has an adjusted gross income of $70,000, wants to attend a graduate teacher training program at a public university ($3,500 tuition) after being out of college for 20 years. Using the Lifetime Learning credit, her family's income taxes would be cut by as much as $700.

A married couple has an adjusted gross income of $32,000. The husband, who is working as an automobile mechanic, decides to go back to a local technical college to take some computer classes in the hope of getting a better job. He will pay tuition of $1,200. Using the Lifetime Learning credit, this family would have their taxes cut by as much as $240.

Financial Aid Directory

You can use these numbers for direct access to federal and state agencies and processing services. However, your guidance counselor may have the answers or information you need.

Federal Agencies

Federal Student Aid Information Center

P.O. Box 84
Washington, DC 20044-0084
800-4-Fed-Aid

Provides duplicate student aid reports and aid applications to students. Also answers questions on student aid, mails Department of Education publications, makes corrections to applications, and verifies college federal aid participation.

United Student Aid Funds (USAF)

P.O. Box 6180
Indianapolis, IN 46206-6180
800-824-7044

Provides aid application forms and information on loan amounts. Also provides information on guarantee dates and assists students in filling out application forms.

Internal Revenue Service

Duplicate Income Tax Returns
P.O. Box 145500
Cincinnati, OH 45250-5500
800-829-1040

Provides answers to tax questions, especially those in relation to financial aid and the tax structure.

Veterans Benefits Regional Office (VBRO)

Federal Building
1240 E. 9th Street
Cleveland, OH 44199
800-827-1000

Provides dependent education assistance for children of disabled veterans. College-bound students should call the VBRO to determine whether or not they qualify for assistance, what the benefits are, and if a parent's disability qualifies them for benefits.

Processing Services

ACT Student Need
Analysis Service
P.O. Box 168
Iowa City, IA 52243-0168
319-337-1200

Provides financial aid, test registration, and test score information. Also provides ACT assessment services to students.

ACT Financial Aid Need Estimator (FANE)

P.O. Box 4029
Iowa City, IA 52243-4029
319-337-1615

Mails financial tabloids to students, provides information on filling out financial aid forms, and estimates financial aid amounts. Also mails financial need estimator forms so students can estimate contributions.

College Scholarship Service

(PROFILE)
P.O. Box 6350
Princeton, NJ 08541-6350
800-239-5888

Provides free applications and registration forms for federal student aid. Helps students fill out applications.

Financial Aid on the Web

There are a number of good financial aid resources on the World Wide Web. It is quick and simple to access general financial aid information, links to relevant Web sites, loan information, employment and career information, advice, scholarship search services, interactive worksheets, forms and free expected family contribution (EFC) calculators.

Also visit the Web sites of individual colleges to find more school-specific financial aid information.

General Information

FinAid: The Financial Aid Information Page
http://www.finaid.org

This incredibly rich site is the best overall resource for student financial aid information on the World Wide Web. Sponsored by the National Association of Student Financial Aid Administrators, it includes a comprehensive alphabetical index of all financial aid resources on the Web.

Student Financial Assistance Information, Department of Education.
http://www.ed.gov/

This page takes you to some of the major publications on student aid, including the latest edition of the Student Guide.

College Board Online
http://www.collegeboard.org

In addition to several financial aid interactive calculators and access to FUND FINDER (the College Board's database of more than 3,000 sources of scholarships, internships, contests and loans) this site provides a wealth of information, such as a glossary of financial aid terms, a bibliography of financial aid books, and financial planning and borrowing tips and tools for students and parents.

Scholarship Search Services/ Searchable Databases

ExPAN Scholarship Search
http://www.collegeboard.org/fundfinder/html/ssrchtop.html

A free Web version of the College Board's FUND FINDER scholarship database.

SRN Express
http://www.srnexpress.com/execsrch.htm

A free Web version of the Scholarship Resource Network (SRN) database. Focuses on portable, private-sector, non-need-based aid. The award listings here contain more detailed information than most scholarship databases and scholarship listing books.

Sallie Mae's Online Scholarship Service
http://www.salliemae.com

Offers free access to the College Aid Sources for Higher Education (CASHE) database. Contains listing of numerous private sector awards from more than 3,600 sponsors.

Did you know . . .?

The University of Texas at Austin hosted a competition for graduate students at seven U.S. business schools. One event judged how far participants could throw a briefcase full of documents.

Founded in 1845, Baylor University, a private institution with Baptist roots, is the oldest institution of higher education in the state of Texas to remain in continuous operation since it opened.

Forty-nine percent of Texas high-school seniors took the SAT in 1998. Their average score was 995.

The average tuition and fees at a public four-year institution in Texas were $2,022 in 1998.

Proportion of Texas students who speak a language other than English at home: 25.4 percent.

Degrees Awarded in Texas in 1998

Associate	25,800
Bachelor's	70,048
Master's	22,740
Doctorate	2,727
Professional	4,775

GET a JUMP!

...on more information

The institutions and companies who have provided these cards would like to tell you more about their programs.

Please fill out the information on the reverse side and mail these cards today.

BUSINESS REPLY MAIL
FIRST-CLASS MAIL   PERMIT NO. 3071   AMES, IOWA
POSTAGE WILL BE PAID BY ADDRESSEE

No postage necessary if mailed in the United States

IOWA STATE UNIVERSITY

OFFICE OF ADMISSIONS
ALUMNI HALL
AMES, IOWA 50010-9967

BUSINESS REPLY MAIL
FIRST CLASS MAIL   PERMIT N 23486 MIAMI, FL
POSTAGE WILL BE PAID BY ADDRESSEE

NO POSTAGE NECESSARY IF MAILED IN THE UNITED STATES

Florida National College
11373 W. Flagler St.
Miami, FL 33174-9947

OUR LADY OF THE LAKE
UNIVERSITY

NO POSTAGE NECESSARY IF MAILED IN THE UNITED STATES

BUSINESS REPLY MAIL
FIRST-CLASS PERMIT NO. 2056 SAN ANTONIO, TX

POSTAGE WILL BE PAID BY ADDRESSEE

OUR LADY OF THE LAKE UNIVERSITY
ADMISSIONS & ADVISEMENT CENTER
411 S.W. 24TH STREET
SAN ANTONIO TX 78207-9968

To receive information from the school or company on the reverse side,
please complete and mail.

Name Mr./Ms_____
(first, middle initial, last)

Street_____

City_____

State_____ Zip_____

Telephone (_____) _____

E-mail Address_____
(if available)

I expect to graduate from_____
(high school name)

in_____
(city, state, zip)   month/year

Get A Jump 1999

To receive information from the school or company on the reverse side,
please complete and mail.

Name Mr./Ms_____
(first, middle initial, last)

Street_____

City_____

State_____ Zip_____

Telephone (_____) _____

E-mail Address_____
(if available)

I expect to graduate from_____
(high school name)

in_____
(city, state, zip)   month/year

Get A Jump 1999

To receive information from the school or company on the reverse side,
please complete and mail.

Name Mr./Ms_____
(first, middle initial, last)

Street_____

City_____

State_____ Zip_____

Telephone (_____) _____

E-mail Address_____
(if available)

I expect to graduate from_____
(high school name)

in_____
(city, state, zip)   month/year

1-670-384-2   Get A Jump 1999

GET a JUMP!

...on more information

The institutions and companies who have provided the cards would like to tell you more about their programs.

Please fill out the information on the reverse side and mail these cards today.

Financing Higher Education Through the U.S. Armed Forces

The U.S. military provides a number of options to help students and their parents get financial aid.

The Montgomery G.I. Bill

Available to enlistees in all branches of the service, the G.I. bill pays up to $14,998 toward education costs at any accredited two-year or four-year college or vocational school, either during active duty or up to ten years after discharge. There are two options under the bill:

- Active duty—If you serve on active duty, you will allocate $1,200 of your pay ($100 a month for twelve months) to your education fund. Then, under the G.I. bill, the military contributes up to $14,998.
- Reserve Duty—If you join a Reserve unit you can receive up to $7,124 to offset your education costs.

The College Fund

Once enrolled in the G.I. bill program, qualified candidates in the U.S. Army, Navy, or Marine Corps can earn an additional $15,425 in education assistance (a total of $30,000) from the College Fund after discharge.

Reserve Officers' Training Corps (ROTC)

The ROTC offers college scholarships that pay most of the recipient's tuition and other expenses and includes a monthly allowance of $150. The Army, for example, provides an ROTC scholarship of up to $48,000, depending upon the tuition of the school, plus a living allowance of $150 per month for the academic year. After graduation, most trainees enter the service as officers and complete a four-year tour of duty. The application deadline is December 1.

Tuition Assistance

All branches of the military pay up to 75 percent of tuition for full-time, active-duty enlistees who take courses at community colleges or by correspondence during their tours of duty. Details vary by service.

The Community College of the Air Force

Members of the Air Force, Air National Guard, or Air Force Reserves can convert their technical training and military experience into academic credit, earning an associate degree, an occupational instructor's certificate, or a trade school certificate. Participants receive an official transcript from this fully accredited program.

Educational Loan-Repayment Program

The Armed Services can help repay government-insured and other approved loans. One third of the loan will be repaid for each year served on active duty.

Other forms of tuition assistance

Each branch of the military offers its own education incentives. To find out more, check with a local recruiting office.

Financial Aid Reading List

Most bookstores and libraries have resources to help you find financial aid information. Listed below are several books that may help you in your search.

The A's and B's: Your Guide to Academic Scholarships. Deborah Klosky, ed. Octameron Associates, P.O. Box 3437, Alexandria, VA 22302.

Applying for Financial Aid: A Guide for Students and Parents. American College Testing Program, P.O. Box 168, Iowa City, IA 52243. Free.

Borrowing for College. Educational Testing Service, Publications Order Service, CN 6736, Princeton, NJ 08541. Free.

Chronicle Student Aid Annual. Chronicle Guidance Pub. Inc., Aurora Street Extension, P.O. Box 1190, Moravia, NY 13118-1190.

The College Blue Book—Scholarships, Fellowships, Grants and Loans. New York: McMillan Publishing Co., 1991.

The College Cost Book. College Board Publications, Box 886, New York, NY 10101.

College Grants from Uncle Sam: Am I Eligible and How Much? Anna T. Leider. Alexandria, Va.: Octameron Associates, 1989.

Directory of Financial Aid for Minorities, 1991–92. Gail A. Schlachter. Redwood City, Calif.: Reference Service Press, 1988.

Directory of Financial Aid for Women, 1991–92. Gail A. Schlachter. San Carlos, Calif.: Reference Service Press, 1989.

Don't Miss Out: The Ambitious Student's Guide to Financial Aid, 1992–1993. Robert Leider. Octameron Associates, P.O. Box 3437, Alexandria, VA 22302.

Earn & Learn: Cooperative Education Opportunities with the Federal Government. Octameron Associates, P.O. Box 3437, Alexandria, VA 22302.

Educational Financial Aids—AAUW Guide to Aid Fellowships, Scholarships & Internships for Higher Education. AAUS Sales Office, 2401 Virginia Avenue, NW, Washington, DC 20037.

Family Financial Statement Packet. American College Testing Program, P.O. Box 168, Iowa City, IA 52243. Free.

Financial Aid for the Disabled and Their Families, 1990–1991. Gail A. Schlachter and R. David Weber. Redwood City, Calif.: Reference Service Press, 1988.

Financial Aid Guide for College. Elizabeth W. Suchar. College Entrance Examination Board. Monarch Press.

Financial Aid for Higher Education—A Catalog for Undergraduates. Oreon Keesler. Dubuque, Iowa: Wm. C. Brown Pub., 1984.

Financial Aid for Veterans, Military Personnel and Their Families, 1990–1991. Gail A. Schlachter and R. David Weber. Redwood City, Calif.: Reference Service Press, 1988.

A Foreign Student's Guide to Financial Assistance for Study and Research in the U.S. Joseph Lurio with Jonathan Miller. Garden City, N.Y.: Adelphi University Press.

Foundation Grants to Individuals. The Foundation Center, 888 Seventh Avenue, New York, NY 10019.

Meeting College Costs. The College Scholarship Service, 45 Columbus Circle, New York, NY 10019.

Need a Lift? The American Legion. Indianapolis, 1988.

Peterson's College Money Handbook 1999. Princeton: Peterson's, 1998

The Student Guide: Financial Aid from the U.S. Department of Education—Grants, Loans and Work Study (1991–1992). Washington, D.C.: U.S. Department of Education, 1990. (Available through college financial aid offices.)

Top Dollars for Technical Scholars: A Guide to Engineering, Math, Computer Science, and Science Scholarships. Clark Z. Robinson. Octameron Associates, P.O. Box 3437, Alexandria, VA 22302.

Winning Money for College: The High School Students' Guide to Scholarship Contests. Alan Deutschman. Princeton: Peterson's, 1997.

Sources: The Dayton-Montgomery County Scholarship Program.

CHAPTER 8

Jump into WORK

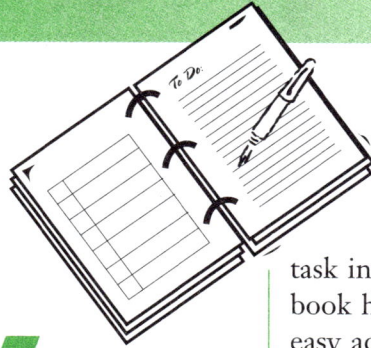

What Employers Expect from Employees

As part of the National City Bank personnel team in Columbus, Ohio, Rose Graham works with Cooperative Business Education (CBE) coordinators in the area who are trying to place high school students in the workplace. When asked what skills she looks for in potential employees, she quickly replies that basic communication skills are at the top of her list. She stresses, "The ability to construct a sentence and put together words cannot be overemphasized." She cites knowledge of the personal computer, with good keyboarding skills, as essential.

In an article published in the Nashville Business Journal, Donna Cobble of Staffing Solutions outlined these basic skills for everyday life in the workplace:

Communication

Being a good communicator not only means having the ability to express oneself with proper use of the English language, it also means being a good listener. If you feel inferior in any of these areas, it's a good idea to sign up for a public speaking class, read books on the subject, and borrow techniques from professional speakers.

Organization

A college professor once said, "Organization is the key to management." We'll take that a step further and say that organization is the key to success in any occupation or facet of life. The ability to plan, prioritize, and complete a task in a timely fashion is a valuable skill. A section of this book has been written on this topic, providing you with easy access to tips for improving your time-management skills.

Problem solving

Companies are looking for creative problem solvers, people who aren't afraid to act on a situation and follow through with their decision. Experience and practice play a major role in your ability to determine the best solution. However, these techniques can be learned by talking with others about how they solve problems as well as observing others in the problem-solving process.

Sensitivity

In addition to being kind and courteous to their fellow workers, employees also need to be sensitive to a coworker's perspective. That might mean putting yourself in the other person's shoes in an effort to better understand that person's feelings. Employers look for individuals who are able to work on a team instead of in favor of their own personal gain.

Judgment

Although closely related to problem solving, good judgment shows up on many different levels of the workplace. It is the ability of a person to assess a situation, weigh the options, consider the risk, and make the necessary decision. Good judgment is built on experience and self-confidence.

Concentration

Concentration is the ability to focus on one thing at a time. Learning to tune out distractions and relate solely to the task at hand is a valuable asset for anyone.

Personal characteristics

After skills and job qualifications have been carefully evaluated, the choice between top candidates may be based on personal characteristics. Here are a few to consider:

- **Willingness to learn.** Be willing to learn how things are done at the company, instead of doing things the way you want to do them.
- **Dependability.** Be on time each and every day, and turn in your work on time.
- **Enthusiasm.** Although not every task you're assigned will be stimulating, continue to show enthusiasm for your work at all times.
- **Acceptance of criticism.** Corrective criticism is necessary for any employee to learn how things should be done. Employees who view criticism as a way to improve themselves will benefit from it.
- **Loyalty.** There is no place for negativity in the workplace. You simply won't be happy working for an employer that you're not loyal to.

Never fail to show pride in your work, the place where you work, and your appearance. By making these traits a part of your personality and daily performance, you will demonstrate that you are a "cut above" other employees with equal or better qualifications.

Resume-Writing Tools and Tips

Because some employers receive dozens of resumes in the mail each week, it's critical that your resume stand out in a crowd. A resume that is too long, cluttered, or disorganized may find its way to the "round file," also known as the trash can. You can avoid this hazard by creating a resume that is easy to read, short, and presentable. Remember that a resume is a summary of who you are, mapping out your experiences, skills, and goals. While writing it, you may discover some talents you weren't aware you had, boosting your confidence for the job search.

Gathering information

Begin by collecting facts about yourself, including where you went to high school, your past and present jobs, activities, interests, and leadership roles. Next to the individual activities, write down what responsibilities you had. For example, something as simple as baby-sitting requires the ability to settle disagreements and supervise others.

Types of resumes

Most experts agree on two predominant types of resumes: chronological and functional. The chronological resume is

- **Cooperation.** Remember that you're being paid to do a job, so cooperate.
- **Honesty.** Dishonesty shows up in many different ways, ranging from stealing time or property to divulging company secrets. Stay honest.
- **Initiative.** Don't always wait to be told exactly what to do. Show some initiative and look around to see what needs to be done next.

Between 1973 and 1994, the proportion of high school graduates going directly to college increased from 47% to 62%.

Source: 1998 Condition of Education Report, US Department of Education

the most traditional, supplying the reader with a chronological listing (from present to past) of your accomplishments. Because the emphasis here is on past employment experience, high school and college students with little or no employment history might want to avoid this type. A functional resume, on the other hand, highlights a person's abilities rather than his or her work history. Entry-level candidates who want to focus on skills rather than credentials should consider using this type.

Parts of a resume

At the very least, your resume should include the following components:

- **Heading.** Centered at the top of the page should be your name, address, phone number, and e-mail address.
- **Objective.** In one sentence, tell the employer what type of work you are looking for.
- **Education.** Beginning with your most recent school or program, include the date (or expected date) of completion, the degree or certificate earned, and the address of the institution. Don't overlook any workshops or seminars, self-study, or on-the-job training you have been involved in. If any courses particularly lend themselves to the type of work you'd be doing on that job, include them. Mention grade point averages and class rank when they are especially impressive.
- **Skills and abilities.** Until you've actually listed these on paper, you can easily overlook many of them. They may be as varied as the ability to work with computers or being captain of the girls' basketball team.
- **Work experience.** If you don't have any, skip it. If you do, begin with your most recent employer and include the date you left the job, your job title, the company name, and the company address. If you are still employed there, simply use "Present" for the date. Include notable accomplishments with each job. High school and college students with little work experience shouldn't be shy about including summer, part-time, and volunteer jobs, such as lifeguarding, baby-sitting, delivering pizzas, or volunteering at the local parks and recreation department.
- **Personal.** Here's your opportunity to include your special talents and interests as well as notable accomplishments or experiences.
- **References.** Most experts agree that it's best to simply state that references are available upon request. However, if you do decide to list names, addresses, and phone numbers, limit yourself to no more than three. Make sure you inform any people whom you have listed that they may be contacted.

Miscellaneous tips

Keep the resume short and simple. Although senior executives may use as many as two or three pages, recent graduates should limit themselves to one page.

- Capitalize headings.
- Keep sentences short; avoid writing in paragraphs.
- Use language that is simple, not flowery or complex.
- Be specific, offering examples when appropriate.
- Emphasize achievements.
- Be honest.
- Don't include information about salary or wages.
- Use high-quality, white, standard-size 8 1/2 x 11" paper.
- Make good use of white space by leaving adequate side and top margins on the paper.
- Make what you write presentable, using good business style and typing it on a computer or word processor.
- Because your resume should be a reflection of your personality, write it yourself.
- Avoid gimmicks such as colored paper, photos, or clip art.
- Make good use of bullets or asterisks, underlining, and bold print.
- Proofread your work and have someone you trust proofread it also.
- Be neat and accurate.
- Never send a resume without a cover letter.

The cover letter

Because every resume should be accompanied by a cover letter, the letter will ultimately be the first thing a potential employer reads. When you include a cover letter, you're showing the employer that you care enough to take the time to address him or her personally and that you are genuinely interested in the job.

Always call the company and verify the name and title of the person you are addressing the letter to. Although you will want to keep your letter short, introduce yourself and begin with a statement that will catch the reader's attention. Indicate the position you are applying for and mention if you were referred by someone or if you are simply responding to a newspaper ad. Draw attention to yourself by including something that will arouse the employer's curiosity about your experience and accomplishments. A cover letter should request something, most commonly, an interview. Sign and date your letter. Then follow up with a phone call a few days after you're sure the letter has been received. Persistence pays.

Functional Resume

This is a resume from an actual student, who chose to use the functional resume format.

Ryan Arnold Aspey
3467 River Landings Boulevard
Hilliard, Ohio 43026-7840
614-876-9760
E-mail: r-aspey@onu.edu

OBJECTIVE	Seeking a summer internship in government
EDUCATION	Honors Diploma, June 1999 Hilliard High School, Hilliard, Ohio Cumulative GPS: 3.7/4.0; Rank: 70/465
SKILLS	Computer literate, IBM: MS Works, MS Word, WordPerfect, Netscape; Macintosh: MS Word, Astound Multi-Media
ACTIVITIES/ LEADERSHIP	Varsity Swim Team Water Polo Club National Honor Society U.S. Army Reserve National Scholar/ Athlete

AWARDS	Social Studies Outstanding Senior Award
	Scott Wilcox Outstanding Senior Human
	   Concerns Award
	Spanish Club
	Varsity Swim Club (Capt.; MVP Jr., Sr.;
	   Sportsmanship Award)

EXPERIENCE	Lifeguard, Hilliard Dept. of Recreation & Parks, Hilliard, Ohio; Summers 1996–98 Volunteer, Hilliard Dept. of Recreation & Parks Social Programs, Hilliard, Ohio; 1996–98
INTERESTS	Swimming, weight lifting, sports card collecting
REFERENCES	Available

Job Hunting 101

High school is a time for taking classes and learning, developing relationships with others, becoming involved in extracurricular activities that teach valuable life skills, and generally preparing for college or a job. Wherever you're headed after high school, learn to create a favorable impression. That can mean setting some clear, attainable goals for yourself, putting them down on paper in the form of a resume and cover letter, and convincing interviewers that you are, indeed, the person they are looking for. In short, learn how to sell yourself. A brief course in Job Hunting 101 will help you do just that.

Marketing yourself

There are several approaches you can use to successfully market yourself. Networking, the continual process of contacting friends and relatives, is a method whereby information about job openings can be obtained. Seventy-five percent of the job openings in this country are not advertised, but rather they are filled by hiring friends, relatives, and acquaintances of someone who already works there. From the employer's perspective, there is less risk associated with hiring someone recommended by an employee than by hiring someone unknown. Networking is powerful. Everyone has a primary network of people they know and talk to frequently. Those acquaintances know and talk to networks of their own, thereby creating a secondary network for you and multiplying the number of individuals who know what you're looking for in a job.

Broadcasting is another marketing method in which you gather a list of companies that interest you and then mail them letters asking for job interviews. Although the rate of return on your mailings is small, two thirds of all job hunters use this approach, and half of those who use it find a job. You will increase your response rate by addressing your letter to a particular person, the one who has the power to hire you, and by following up with a phone call a few days after the letter has been received. To obtain the manager's name, simply call the company and ask the receptionist for the person's name, job title, and correct spelling. Good resources for finding potential employers include referrals, community agencies, job fairs, newspaper ads, trade directories, trade journals, state indexes, the local chamber of commerce, and the Yellow Pages.

Job-hunting tips

- Job-hunting is time intensive. Do your homework and take it seriously by using every opportunity available to you.
- Prepare yourself for the fact that there will be far more rejections than acceptances.
- Consider taking a temporary job while you continue the job hunt. It will help pay the bills and boost your morale at the same time.

The World Wide Web

The World Wide Web is the portion of the Internet that has gotten so much attention in the past few years. In fact, the World Wide Web has become so popular that it is generally just called "the Web;" many people incorrectly use "Internet" and "Web" interchangeably.

Well-designed Web pages are easy for computer novices to navigate and can be interesting and fun to explore. More important, for those of us who don't stay up all night learning the latest in programming algorithms, the information that you'll find listed on Web pages is not strictly computer related. If you are looking for a job, you are just as likely to find listings for executive secretary, freelance writer, custodian, or vice president of sales as you are for computer programmer.

- Research the activities of potential employers and show that you have studied them when you're being interviewed.
- Keep careful records of all contacts and follow-up activities.
- Don't ignore any job leads—act on every tip you get.
- Stay positive.

With all these thoughts in mind, you should be ready to begin the process of making people believe in you, and that's a major part of being successful in your job hunt.

The Job Interview

Boost your confidence. You can prevent some of the pre-interview jitters by adequately preparing. Remember that you have nothing to lose and that you, too, are doing the choosing. Just as you are waiting and hoping to be offered a job, you have the option of choosing whether or not to accept an offer. It's all right to feel somewhat anxious, but keep everything in perspective. This is an adventure, and you are in control. Most important, remember to be yourself. With all of this in mind, consider some of the following finer points of the interview process.

Speak up during the interview and furnish the interviewer with the information he or she needs in order to make an informed decision. It is especially impressive if you can remember the names of people you've been introduced to. People like to be called by name, and it shows that you took the initiative to remember them.

Always arrive a few minutes early for the interview, and look your best. The way a person acts and dresses tells the interviewer plenty about that person's attitude and personality. Sloppy dress, chewing gum, and cigarettes have no place at an interview and will probably cut your interview short. Instead, dress professionally and appropriately for the type of job. Avoid heavy make-up, short skirts, jeans, and untidy or flashy clothing of any kind. Although a business suit may be appropriate for certain jobs, a person who is applying for an outdoor position should probably interview in clean, neatly pressed dress slacks and a polo shirt or a skirt and blouse.

Preparing for the interview

The best way to prepare for the interview is to practice. Have a friend or relative play the role of the interviewer and go over some of the most commonly asked questions. Learn as much as you can about the company you're interviewing with—it pays to do your homework. When you show a potential employer that you've taken the time and initiative to learn about his or her company, you're

showing that you care about being a motivated and hardworking employee. Employers fear laziness and minimal effort, looking instead for workers who don't always have to be told what to do and when to do it.

Common interview questions

- Tell me a little bit about yourself.
- What qualifications do you have?
- Why do you want to work for us?
- Tell me about your current (or last) job.
- Why are you leaving that job?
- What did you like most about that job?
- What would you change about that job?
- Do you enjoy school? Why or why not?
- Do you plan to continue your education?
- What do you plan to be doing for work five years from today?
- What is your major strength?
- What is your greatest weakness?
- What motivates you to do a good job?
- Are you at your best when working alone or in a group?
- What are your goals?
- Do you have any questions for me?

Take the time to prepare some answers to these commonly asked questions. For instance, if you haven't set at least one goal for yourself, do it now. Be ready to describe it to the interviewer. Likewise, you should be able to talk about your last job, including what you liked the most and the least. Adapt your answers so they apply to the job you are presently interviewing for. If you are seeking a job as a manager, you might respond by saying you liked the varied responsibilities of your past job. Recall that you enjoyed the unexpected challenges and flexible schedule.

And when describing what you liked least, make sure you respond with some function or area of responsibility that has nothing to do with the functions and responsibilities of the job you hope to get.

When asked about personal strengths and weaknesses, given that the question is two parts, begin with a weakness so you can end on a strong note with your strengths. Again, try to connect your description of a strength or weakness with the requirements for the job. Naturally it wouldn't be wise to reveal a serious weakness about yourself, but you can mention how you have changed your shortcomings. You might say, "I like to get my work done fast, but I consciously try to slow down a little to make sure I'm careful and accurate." When it comes to strengths, don't exaggerate, but don't sell yourself short.

Selling yourself

More than likely, the first question you'll be asked is to tell the interviewer something about yourself. Stick to your work-related experiences. This is your chance to "toot your horn," but don't ramble. You might ask the interviewer specifically what he or she would like to hear about: your educational background or recent experiences and responsibilities in your present or last job. After he or she chooses, stick to the basics; the next move belongs to the interviewer.

Asking questions

You can ask questions, too. In fact, the interview is really two interviews in one. You can ask questions to determine if the job is right for you just as the interviewer will be trying to find out if you'll be successful working for his or her company. When you do ask questions, it shows that you're interested and want to learn more. When the type of question you ask indicates that you've done your homework regarding the job and the company, your interviewer will be impressed. Avoid asking questions about salary or fringe benefits, anything adversarial, or questions that show you have a negative opinion of the company. It's all right to list your questions on a piece of paper; it's the quality of the question that's important, not whether you can remember it.

Follow up

After the interview, follow up with a thank-you note to the interviewer. Not only is it a thoughtful gesture, it triggers the interviewer's memory about you and shows that you have a genuine interest in the job.

During the interview process, remember that not everyone you meet will be attracted to you and what you have to offer. If your first experience doesn't work out, keep trying.

Career Time Line

At each grade level there are specific steps that a student should take regardless of whether or not he or she plans to attend college immediately following high school. In fact, college and career timelines should coincide, according to guidance counselors and career options specialists. The focus today is on "school to work," and although many students plan to attend college or university right after high school, they should have some specific career goals in mind. "We want students to focus more on the relationship between school and work," says Jim Duzan, Career Option Specialist at Whetstone and Columbus Alternative High Schools in Columbus, Ohio. Specifically, students need to think about how much education they need and why they are going to college. "Often students go to college for the sake of going, and they don't stay there," he continues. Duzan recommends that students take college-preparatory courses regardless of whether or not they plan to attend college. They can meet the college requirements and still prepare for work, often giving them a way to pay for their education. In an effort to make sure that you are adequately preparing for both school and work, incorporate these three steps into your career/college timeline:

- Students should take an interest survey or aptitude test as early as the sixth grade. By doing so, they will begin to get a feel for what areas they might be good at and enjoy.
- Beginning in middle school, students should begin to consider what their options are after high school. Keep a notebook of information gathered from field trips, job-shadowing experiences, mentoring programs, and career fairs to help you make sense of the possibilities open to you. This process should continue through high school.
- No later than the tenth grade, but preferably earlier, visit a vocational center to look at the training programs offered. Some public school systems send students to vocational and career program centers for the purpose of career exploration.
- During your junior and senior years, be sure to create a portfolio of practice resumes, writing samples, and listing of work skills. This portfolio, called a Career Passport in some states, should also include your high school transcript and letters of recommendations. It will serve as a valuable reference tool when it comes time for apply for jobs.

Most schools offer job shadowing and internship programs that students can use to explore different vocational

Don't Close the Door

Because of the soaring costs of college tuition, today college is no longer a place to "find yourself." It is a costly investment in your future. The career you choose to pursue may or may not require additional education; your research will determine whether or not it's required or preferred. If you decide not to attend college immediately after high school, however, don't consider it to be a closed door. Taking some time off between high school and college is considered perfectly acceptable by employers. Many students simply need a break after twelve years of schooling. Most experts agree that it's better to be ready and prepared for college; many adults get more out of their classes after they've had a few years to mature.

Source: Street Smart Career Guide: A Step-by-Step Program for Your Career Development.

avenues. Take advantage of these opportunities if you can. Too often, students don't explore the workplace until after they've taken the necessary courses, only to discover it wasn't the career they dreamed of after all.

As the Director of Career Education for Columbus Public Schools, Bill Bigelow sees to it that every eighth grader in the district visits a career center for a walk-through. "It's not for the purpose of recruiting; rather it's for awareness," he says. These same students also visit an institution of higher learning. "The old tracking system of placing kids in either a college-preparatory or a career path is changing," Bigelow explains. "With today's advances in technology, lifelong learning will be a part of everyone's life."

Bigelow recommends that by the tenth and eleventh grades, students start homing in on a specific career path. More employers today are looking for employees who not only have the education but also the work experience that relates to their major. If students are looking for part-time employment, they should consider jobs that pertain to their field of study. "Until you start interacting with people in the field, you don't have a realistic feel of what's involved. It adds to the importance of the learning," says Bigelow.

Whether you decide to attend a two-year community or technical college or a four-year college or university, undertake vocational education, or enter the military, you should plan early. "It's a process of development," explains Bigelow. Duzan agrees. "Today we need to prepare students for it all."

Study . . .

Study . . .

Study . . .

Bibliography

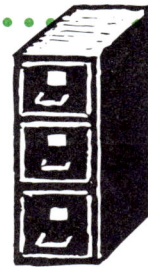

Newspapers

The Columbus Dispatch

Los Angeles Times

The New York Times

USA Today

Periodicals

"1998–1999 Almanac," *The Chronicle of Higher Education*, August 28, 1998.

"The Job Search and Making It," *Hispanic Times Magazine*, March 1996.

"Scholar," Beckley Newspapers, Inc. Beckley, W. Va.: fall 1994.

"Scholar," Beckley Newspapers, Inc. Beckley, W. Va.: spring 1995.

"Six Basic Skills Apply in Workplace, Everyday Life," *Nashville Business Journal*, January 1996.

"Ten Traits of an Effective Leader," *Florist Magazine*, June 1995.

"What Employers Expect From Employees," *OEA Communique*, December 1985.

"You're a What? Forensic Psychophysiologist," *Occupational Outlook Quarterly*, spring 1996.

"You're a What? Medical Illustrator," *Occupational Outlook Quarterly*, winter 1991–92.

"You're a What? Cartographer," *Occupational Outlook Quarterly*, summer 1988.

"You're a What? Herpetologist," *Occupational Outlook Quarterly*, spring 1989.

"You're a What? Music Therapist," *Occupational Outlook Quarterly*, winter 1993–94.

Books

Adams, Jenni. *Stress, A New Positive Approach*. London: David & Charles, 1989.

Bingham, Mindy, and Sandy Stryker. *Career Choices*. Santa Barbara: Academic Innovations, 1990.

Bloch, Deborah P. *How to Have a Winning Job Interview*. Lincolnwood, Ill.: VGM Career Horizons, 1991.

Blonna, Richard. *Coping with Stress in a Changing World*. St. Louis: Mosby, 1996.

Boyer, Ernest L., and Paul Boyer. *Smart Parents Guide to College*. Princeton, N.J.: Peterson's, 1996.

Carter, Carol. *Majoring in the Rest of Your Life*. New York: The Noonday Press, 1990.

Culp, Stephanie. *You Can Find More Time for Yourself Every Day*. Cincinnati, Ohio: Betterway Books, 1994.

Dell, Twyla. *An Honest Day's Work: Motivating Employees to Give Their Best*. Los Altos, Calif.: Crisp Publications, Inc., 1988.

Deutschmann, Alan. *Winning Money for College*. Princeton, N.J.: Peterson's, 1997

Douglass, Merrill E., and Donna N. Merrill. *Manage Your Time, Your Work, Yourself*. New York: American Management Association, 1993.

Eberts, Marjorie, and Margaret Gisler. *How to Prepare for College*. Lincolnwood, Ill.: VGM Career Horizons, 1994.

Graham, Lawrence. *Ten Point Plan for College Acceptance*. New York: Quick Fox, 1981.

Golden, M., L. Kilb, and A. Mayerson. *Explanation of the Contents of the Americans with Disabilities Act of 1990*. Washington, D.C.: Disability Rights Education and Defense Fund, 1992.

Hayden, Thomas C. *Handbook for College Admissions.* Princeton, N.J.: Peterson's, 1995.

Hobbs, Charles R. *Time Power.* New York: Harper & Row, 1987.

Kowadlo, Bonnie F., and Madelyn Schulman. *Working Smart.* Cincinnati: South-Western Publishing Co., 1995.

Kropp, Paul. *Raising a Reader.* New York: Doubleday, 1993.

MacGowan, Sandra, and Sarah McGinty. *Fifty College Admission Directors Speak to Parents.* San Diego: Harcourt Brace Jovanovich, 1988.

Marler, Patty, and Jan Bailey. *Resumes Made Easy.* Lincolnwood, Ill.: VGM Career Horizons, 1995.

Mauro, Bob. *College Athletic Scholarships.* Jefferson, N.C.: McFarland & Company, 1988.

Mayer, Jeffrey J. *Time Management for Dummies.* Foster City, Calif.: IDG Books, 1995.

Miller, Lyle H., and Alma Dell Smith. *The Stress Solution.* New York: Pocket Books, 1993.

O'Brien, Jack. *Kiplinger's Career Starter.* Washington, D.C.: Kiplinger Books, 1993.

O'Brien, Linda. *An Instruction Booklet for the Parents of College Bound Students.* Dayton, Ohio: Woodburn Press, 1996.

Ordovensky, Pat. *USA Today—Getting Into College.* Princeton, N.J.: Peterson's, 1995.

Pedersen, Laura. *Street-Smart Career Guide: A Step-by-Step Program for Your Career Development.* New York: Crown Trade Paperbacks, 1993.

Schmidt, Peggy. *The New 90-Minute Resume.* Princeton, N.J.: Peterson's, 1996.

———. *The 90-Minute Interview Prep Book.* Princeton, N.J.: Peterson's, 1996.

Shanahan, William F. *College Yes or No.* New York: Arco Publishing, 1983.

Shields, Charles J. *The College Guide for Parents.* New York: College Entrance Examination Board, 1986.

———. *How to Help Your Teenager Find the Right Career.* New York: College Board Publications, 1988.

Unger, Harlow. *A Student's Guide to College Admission.* New York: Oxford, 1990.

Wood, Orrin G., Jr. *Your Hidden Assets: The Key to Getting Executive Jobs.* Homewood, Ill.: Dow Jones-Irwin, 1982.

Reference Material

1996 Fact File. Columbus, Ohio: The Association of Independent Colleges and Universities of Ohio, 1996.

America's Best Colleges. Washington, D.C.: *U.S. News & World Report,* 1996.

College Board Guide to 150 Popular College Majors. New York: College Entrance Examination Board, 1992.

College Money Handbook 1999. Princeton, N.J.: Peterson's, 1998.

Colleges for Students with Learning Disabilities and Attention Deficit Disorders. Princeton, N.J.: Peterson's, 1997.

The College Handbook–1996. New York: College Entrance Examination Board, 1995.

Counselor's Guide to Ohio Independent Colleges & Universities. Columbus, Ohio: The Association of Independent Colleges and Universities of Ohio and The Ohio Association of Private College Admission Counselors, 1996.

Culinary Schools 1999. Princeton, N.J.: Peterson's, 1999.

The Dayton-Montgomery County Scholarship Program. The Dayton Postsecondary Education Demonstration Laboratory and The Dayton Foundation. Directory of College Scholarships and Loans. Dayton, Ohio: 1992.

How to Get Into College. Livingston, N.J.: Newsweek, Inc. and Kaplan Educational Centers, 1997.

Insider's Guide to Colleges–1996. New York: St. Martin's Griffin, 1995.

Peterson's College and University Almanac 1999. Princeton, N.J.: Peterson's, 1998.

Peterson's Competitive Colleges 1998–1999. Princeton, N.J.: Peterson's, 1998.

Peterson's Guide to Four-Year Colleges 1999. Princeton, N.J.: Peterson's, 1998.

Peterson's Sports Scholarships and Athletic Programs. Princeton, N.J.: Peterson's, 1997.

Peterson's Vocational Schools 1998. Princeton, N.J.: Peterson's, 1997.

Scholarships, Grants & Prizes 1999. Princeton, N.J.: Peterson's, 1998.

Study Abroad 1999. Princeton, N.J.: Peterson's, 1998.

Summer Jobs for Students 1999. Princeton, N.J.: Peterson's, 1998.

Summer Opportunities for Kids and Teenagers 1999. Princeton, N.J.: Peterson's, 1998.

Summer Study Abroad 1999. Princeton, N.J.: Peterson's, 1998.

United States Department of Labor. *Occupational Outlook Handbook.* Lincolnwood, Ill.: 1996.

Brochures/Literature

"1992 Current Population Report," U.S. Bureau of Census.

"1994 Investing in Futures," Ohio Department of Education, Columbus, Ohio.

"1996 Institute Announcement-The Ohio Summer Institutes for Gifted and Talented Students," Ohio Department of Education, Division of Special Education, Worthington, Ohio.

"ACT College Planning Guide," American College Testing, Iowa City, Iowa.

"ADA Handbook," Equal Employment Opportunity Commission and U.S. Department of Justice, Washington, D.C. (EEOC-BK 19), October 1991.

"ASVAB Student & Parent Guide," Department of Defense, North Chicago, Ill.

"Adult Vocational Education," Ohio Department of Education, Division of Vocational and Career Education, Columbus, Ohio.

"The Americans with Disabilities Act," Heath Resource Center, American Council on Education, Washington, D.C.

"Answering the Challenge," Ohio Department of Education, Division of Vocational and Career Education, Columbus, Ohio.

"Associate Degree Preferred," Ohio Association of Two-Year College Admission Officers, Piqua, Ohio.

"Audition and Portfolio Information," Otterbein College, Westerville, Ohio.

"Bulletin for the SAT Programs," College Board SAT Program, Princeton, N.J.

"A Call to College," Newark High School, Newark, Ohio.

"Camp Attracting Prospective Educators," Bowling Green State University, Bowling Green, Ohio.

"Career Skills Checklist," Vocational Instructional Materials Laboratory, The Ohio State University, Columbus, Ohio.

"Changing Lives," Student Loan Funding Corporation, Cincinnati, Ohio.

"Charting Your Future," VIESA Career Guidebook, The American College Testing Services, Iowa City, Iowa.

"College Planning Timeline," I Know I Can, Columbus, Ohio.

"Cool Stuff," Otterbein College, Office of Continuing Studies, Westerville, Ohio.

"The Dayton-Montgomery County Scholarship Program," The Dayton-Montgomery County Scholarship Program, Dayton, Ohio.

"Definition of Disability: Outline," Disability Rights Education and Defense Fund, Washington, D.C., 1992.

"Department of Theatre & Dance," Otterbein College, Westerville, Ohio.

"Discover Card Tribute Award Program," American Association of School Administrators, Arlington, Va.

"Education in America: Historic Forces and Current Counterforces," Cleveland Commission on Higher Education, Cleveland, Ohio.

"The Employee Handbook of New Work Habits For a Radically Changing World," Pritchett & Associates, Dallas, Texas.

"Equity Exchange Fall 1995," College of Human Ecology, The Ohio State University, Columbus, Ohio.

"Fifteenth Annual OWJL '96," OWJL Program, Ohio Wesleyan University, Delaware, Ohio.

"Fraternity Friends Forever," National Interfraternity Council, Indianapolis, Indiana.

"Futures for the Class of '97," Scholastic, Inc., New York, New York.

"General Educational Development (GED) Test," State GED Office, Ohio Department of Education, Columbus, Ohio.

"Get Set for College," American College Testing, Iowa City, Iowa.

"Get the Answers to Your Questions at the College Information Center," Cincinnati Youth Collaborative, Cincinnati, Ohio.

"Going to College?" The College Board, Princeton, N.J.

"A Guide to Higher Education in Greater Cincinnati," Greater Cincinnati Consortium of Colleges and Universities, Cincinnati State Technical and Community College, Cincinnati, Ohio.

"A Guide to the College Admission Process," National Association of College Admission Counselors, Alexandria, Va.

"Guide for Parents," National Association of College Admission Counselors, Alexandria, Va.

"Happiness is Having a Job," Hilliard High School Business Education Department, Hilliard, Ohio.

"I Know I Can," I Know I Can, c/o Columbus City School District, Columbus, Ohio.

"Interactive for Gifted and Talented Students in Grades 6–8," Higher Education Council of Columbus, The Ohio State University, Columbus, Ohio.

"The Key to Experiencing Any of 14 Campus One Colleges," Cleveland Commission On Higher Education, Cleveland, Ohio.

"Kids in College," Columbus State Community College, Columbus, Ohio.

"Making Sure You Are Eligible to Participate in College Sports," NCAA Initial-Eligibility Clearinghouse, Iowa City, Iowa.

"Midwest Talent Search," Northwestern University, Center for Talent Development, Evanston, Ill.

"Midwestern SAT Program," The College Board, Princeton, N.J.

"Music at Otterbein," Otterbein College, Westerville, Ohio.

"Need Something to Do This Summer?" The Dayton-Montgomery County Scholarship Program, Dayton, Ohio.

"Occupational Trends," The Ohio Bureau of Employment Services, Columbus, Ohio.

"Ohio Career Information System," Ohio Department of Education, Columbus, Ohio.

"Ohio Job Outlook," Ohio Bureau of Employment Services, Columbus, Ohio.

"Ohio's Career Development Blueprint, Individual Career Plan, High School," Ohio Department of Education, Division of Vocational and Career Education, Career Planning, Transition and Intervention, Columbus, Ohio.

"Ohio's Statewide Testing Program: Rules for Proficiency Testing," Ohio Department of Education, Columbus, Ohio.

"The ONGEA Needs You," The Ohio National Guard Enlisted Association, Groveport, Ohio.

"Outstanding Fiction for the College Bound," American Library Association, Chicago, Ill.

"Parent and Student Guide," Dayton-Montgomery County Scholarship Program, Dayton, Ohio.

"A Parent's Guide to Fraternities," National Interfraternity Conference, Indianapolis, Indiana.

"Planning for College," Columbus Public Schools Guidance Services, Columbus, Ohio.

"Portfolio Development," The Columbus College of Art & Design, Columbus, Ohio.

"Post-Secondary Enrollment Options Programs," Higher Education Council of Columbus, Columbus, Ohio.

"Preparing For College Success," Otterbein College, Westerville, Ohio.

"Preparing For the ACT Assessment," ACT Registration Department, Iowa City, Iowa.

"Preparing Your Child For College," A Resource Book For Parents, 1996–97 edition, U.S. Department of Education.

"Programs and Services for Minority Students at Ohio State," The Ohio State University, Office of Minority Affairs, Columbus, Ohio.

"School-to-Work Opportunities," National School-to-Work Opportunities Office, Washington, D.C.

"School-to-Work Update," Ohio Department of Education, Division of Vocational and Adult Education, Columbus, Ohio.

"Section 504," American Council On Education, Washington, D.C.

"Southwestern Ohio Council for Higher Education," SOCHE, Dayton, Ohio.

"The Student Guide," U.S. Department of Education, Washington, D.C.

"Success Kit: A Student's Guide to Academic Success at OSU," The Ohio State University, Columbus, Ohio.

"Summer Scholars-I Know I Can," Columbus City School District, Columbus, Ohio.

"Summertime Favorites," National Endowment for the Humanities, Washington, D.C.

"Support for Talented Students, Inc.," Support for Talented Students, Inc., Columbus, Ohio.

"Taking the SAT/Reasoning Test," The College Board, Princeton, N.J.

"A Technical Manual of the Employment Provisions of the Americans with Disabilities Act: Title I," Equal Employment Opportunity Commission, Washington, D.C., January 1992.

"Tech Prep-What It Takes To Succeed," Ohio Department of Education, Columbus, Ohio.

"Today's College Student," Cleveland Commission On Higher Education, Cleveland, Ohio.

"Toward College In Ohio," The Ohio College Association, Columbus, Ohio.

"Transfer Just Got Easier: The Articulation & Transfer Policy for Ohio's Colleges & Universities," Ohio Board of Regents, Columbus, Ohio.

"The Twenty-First Century Nurse," Alliance for Health Reform, Washington, D.C.

"The Ultimate College Experience–1996 Fall Rush Guide," University of Cincinnati Office of Greek Affairs, Cincinnati, Ohio.

"Visual Arts," Otterbein College, Westerville, Ohio.

"Vocational Equity," Ohio Department of Education Division of Vocational and Career Education, Columbus, Ohio.

"What Work Requires of Schools," The Secretary's Commission on Achieving Necessary Skills, U.S. Department of Labor.

"Women's Panhellenic Greek Community Guide 1996," Ohio University Women's Panhellenic Association, Athens, Ohio.

"You Can Afford College and Grad School," Kaplan Education Centers.

Organizations

ACT Assessment, P.O. Box 414, Iowa City, Iowa 52243-0414 (telephone: 319-337-1270).

Air Force Recruiting Services, Air Force Opportunity Center, P.O. Box 3505, Capitol Heights, Maryland 20791-9988 (telephone: 800-423-USAF).

Amer-I-Can Program, Inc., 1851 Sunset Plaza Drive, Los Angeles, California 90069 (telephone: 310-652-7884).

American Association of Community Colleges, One Dupont Circle, NW, #410, Washington, D.C. 22206-1176.

Association on Higher Education and Disability, P.O. Box 21192, Columbus, Ohio 43221-0192 (telephone: 614-488-4972).

Brighten Your Future, P.O. Box 991, Logan, Ohio 43138 (telephone: 740-385-5058).

Cleveland Scholarship Programs, Inc., 1005 Abbe Road North, Elyria, Ohio 44035 (telephone: 440-366-4870).

COIN Educational Products, 3361 Executive Parkway, Suite 302, Toledo, Ohio 43606-9844.

The College Fund/UNCF, 8260 Willow Oaks Corporate Drive, P.O. Box 10444, Fairfax, Virginia 22031 (telephone: 703-205-3400).

College Scholarship Service, The College Board, P.O. Box 6381, Princeton, New Jersey 08541-6381 (telephone: 609-778-6888).

Columbus Public Schools, Guidance Services, 52 Starling Street, Columbus, Ohio 43215 (telephone: 614-365-5201).

Columbus Urban League Education and Youth Service Department, 788 Mount Vernon Avenue, Columbus, Ohio 43203 (telephone:614-257-6300).

Disabilities Organizational Development Services, 5984 Pinerock Place, Columbus, Ohio 43231-2334 (telephone: 614-895-0238; TTY: 614-895-2541).

Enlisted Association of the National Guard of the United States, P.O. Box 261, Groveport, Ohio 43125 (telephone: 800-642-6642).

Higher Education Council of Columbus, c/o Ohio State University, Mount Hall, Room 204, 1050 Carmack Road, Columbus, Ohio 43210 (telephone: 614-688-4610).

I Know I Can Program, Columbus Public Schools, 270 East State Street, Columbus, Ohio 43215 (telephone: 614-365-5608).

INROADS, 10 South Broadway, Suite 700, St. Louis, Missouri 63102 (telephone: 314-241-7488).

Lake Educational Assistance Foundation, 7519 Mentor Avenue #102, Mentor, Ohio 44060-5410 (telephone: 216-942-5323).

Learning Disabilities Association of Central Ohio, 1422 Taylor Corners Circle, Blacklick, Ohio 43004 (telephone: 614-868-9359).

Lorain County Alliance of Black School Educators, P.O. Box 745, Lorain, Ohio 44052.

NAACP, National Offices, 4802 Mount Hope Drive, Baltimore, Maryland 21215 (telephone: 877-622-2798).

National Association of College Admission Counselors, 1631 Prince Street, Alexandria, Virginia 22314-2818 (telephone: 703-836-2222).

National College Access Network, 204 East Lombard Street, Fourth Floor, Baltimore, Maryland 21202 (telephone: 410-244-7218).

Ohio Tuition Trust Authority, 62 East Broad Street, 4th Floor, Columbus, Ohio 43215 (telephone 800-AFFORD IT).

Peterson's Education Services, 202 Carnegie Center, P.O. Box 2123, Princeton, NJ 08543-2123 (telephone: 800-338-3282).

U.S. Department of Education, Federal Student Aid Information Center, P.O. Box 84, Washington, D.C. 20044 (telephone: 800-4-FEDAID).

Colleges, Universities, Schools, and Businesses

Ashland University
Capital University
Central Ohio Technical College
Columbus College of Art and Design
Columbus State Community College
Grant/Riverside Methodist Hospitals
Groveport Middle School South, Groveport, Ohio
Licking County Joint Vocational School
Ohio Dominican College
The Ohio State University
Ohio University College of Osteopathic Medicine
Otterbein College
Princeton High School, Cincinnati, Ohio

Individuals

Barbara Bluestein, Librarian, Princeton High School, Cincinnati, Ohio.

Bill Bigelow, Director of Career Education, Columbus Public Schools, Columbus, Ohio.

Dan Shay, Counselor, Princeton High School, Cincinnati, Ohio.

Elmer Booth, Guidance Department Head, Blake Senior High School, Tampa, Florida.

Henry Winkler, Guidance Counselor, Overbrook High School, Philadelphia, Pennsylvania.

Jim Duzan, Career Option Specialist, Whetstone and Columbus Alternative High Schools, Columbus, Ohio.

Rose Graham, National City Bank, Personnel Department, Columbus, Ohio.

Jerry Marshall, Career Education Coordinator Supervisor, Knox County Career Center, Mount Vernon, Ohio.